Bob's Story

To Helen
Enjoy

Bob's Story

Memories of Love and War

A Front-line Soldier Remembers World War II
through the Battle of the Bulge

Robert E. P. Moranda
George E. Moranda

Bob

Robert E. P. Moranda

Writers Club Press
San Jose New York Lincoln Shanghai

Bob's Story
Memories of Love and War

Writers Club Press
an imprint of iUniverse.com, Inc.

For information address:
iUniverse.com, Inc.
5220 S 16th, Ste. 200
Lincoln, NE 68512
www.iuniverse.com

ISBN: 0-595-14150-1

Printed in the United States of America

To my family, friends, and all those who served with me during World War II.

CONTENTS

PREFACE

During World War II, I served in combat with the 7th Armored Division in Europe as an Infantry 2d Lieutenant. This is a story of my experiences during that war, especially during the Battle of the Bulge. Why I'm now putting this down in writing creates quite a problem, for memory is not as good a friend as I would like. Names of those with whom I served have faded, unfortunately. But when a couple of my nephews asked me several years ago what I did in the war, I realized that I had kept all of the experiences within myself for these many decades, thinking that no one was interested in hearing about them. I had kept them silent in an attempt to forget most of them. About the same time I watched a documentary about the Ardennes Campaign in which there was no mention of St. Vith, and the viewer got the impression that the whole action revolved around the paratroopers in Bastogne and the famous "Nuts" statement. The 101st Airborne Division and several attached units did a great job there, but there was a lot more to the story of the Battle of the Bulge than that. So between the nephews' question and the film account, I started to write down what I could remember and began corresponding with former comrades in arms, attending reunions, and talking to others who were there with me.

I am disturbed by what I have read recently about the Ardennes Campaign. The Campaign was probably the biggest battle of the war, but there has been a great misunderstanding about what happened there. I saw the war through the eyes of a front line soldier—a guy who was drafted into the U.S. Army having practically no experience with guns or knowledge of military operations other than what I saw in such movies as "All Quiet on the Western Front" and "The Big Parade." I was a happy civilian, married with a young child, had a great family of five brothers and a sister, mother and dad, and, after struggling through a country-wide depression, finally was working in a permanent job that had what appeared to be a future. Perhaps my story will help in furthering the understanding of what so many of us went through during those days and help to improve the perspective about the actions that went on during The Bulge.

Robert E. P. Moranda

ACKNOWLEDGEMENTS

We wish to express our appreciation to the individuals who helped with this story. First, thanks go to my nephews Theodore Waite Moranda and Steven Moranda who pushed and prodded until the story was started. Additionally, those who were there in action with the 7th Armored Division helped read drafts and provided information to fill some of the gaps: Glenn Fackler, Ed Curtin, Maurice Conover, James P. Totoni, Carl Mattocks, and General William A. Knowlton. Colonel and Mrs. Donald P. Boyer assisted greatly and gave us permission to use much of Col. Boyer's material. Several others provided pictures and accounts, such as Mrs. Maurice Conover and her children Bret and Denise. Brother Theodore N. Moranda assisted significantly with advice and encouragement, as did Brother Walter B. "Bill" Moranda and our friend Mary Mackie. And to get this ready for publication we had capable and efficient help from Kathy Watts.

Finally, our thanks go to the men who fought at St. Vith but who never received the credit due to them for thwarting the German offensive at the Battle of the Bulge.

Robert E. P. Moranda
George E. Moranda

INTRODUCTION

Many of those who served in World War II are amazed at how little the younger generations know of that great episode in our country's history, of what sacrifices were made by people from all walks of life who enlisted or were drafted into the military services, or of what it means to them today. We are, at long last, learning more and more from those who participated in that vital struggle because of such popular and successful authors as Professor Stephen Ambrose, who opened a lot of eyes about many things that occurred during that war with his *Citizen Soldiers*. And Bob Moranda's story is an excellent contribution to our understanding, for he was a front-line soldier in one of the biggest and most significant battles of that war: the containment and defeat of Adolf Hitler's plan to split the Allied forces on the Western Front. Hitler's thrust through the Ardennes forest in Belgium has been appropriately named the Battle of the Bulge, although officially and more aptly titled the Ardennes Campaign for it was a major part of the war that contained many, many battles.

When the Battle of the Bulge is mentioned during a conversation today, people less than fifty years of age either know nothing of that critical part of World War II or know only that "the Battered Bastards of Bastogne" performed heroically and that some general defied the German demand to surrender by responding, "Nuts." If St. Vith is mentioned, a blank stare is the response. Many television programs about the Ardennes Campaign never even mention St. Vith, which was the most significant part of the entire campaign in that bitter winter of 1944-45. The small group of soldiers who made a magnificent stand there are never mentioned. That group of soldiers was made up of a hodgepodge mixture of men separated from their units: a small group of engineer troops, several units of the 7th Armored Division's 23rd and 38th Armored Infantry Battalions, portions of its 87th Cavalry Reconnaissance Squadron, and a platoon with six vehicles of the 822d Tank Destroyer Battalion—some approximately 850 men formed into a task force. They were supported by artillery fire from a withdrawing corps unit whose commander had volunteered to do their job of firing artillery rounds—the 275th Field Artillery Battalion of 105mm howitzers. Leadership was provided by a young major who was left with that responsibility after his commanding officer decided he was unable to do the job and departed for a rear echelon. The success of this almost battalion-size group was a major factor in allowing General Eisenhower to shift forces to contain and defeat the German effort.

Even such a competent and popular historian as Stephen Ambrose failed to recognize the heroic stand of these American soldiers of the 7th Armored Division in and around St. Vith. When Ambrose wrote his landmark account titled *Citizen Soldiers*, he evoked a resentful outburst from retired General William "Bill" Knowlton, who was at St. Vith as a lieutenant in the 87th Armored Cavalry Reconnaissance Squadron. General Knowlton told his fellow survivors, "Don't buy this book." And he will undoubtedly have the same recommendation for Ambrose's 1998 book *The Victors: Eisenhower and His Boys; The Men of World War II*, wherein St. Vith is not even mentioned once. Another historian's account, Professor Gerhard L.Weinberg's *A World at Arms*, praised the 81st Airborne for its brilliant defense at St. Vith—a unit that did not even exist.

Why? Why are there such inaccuracies and inadequate interpretations? It may be that Professor Ambrose gave only a slight mention of the 7th Armored Division's performance in the Battle of the Bulge for reasons of space, lack of information, the need to be selective from the mass of material—written and oral—he had gathered, or just plain oversight. Or perhaps he singled out just a few of many separate battle-actions that made up the total scene. His treatment of the part soldiers of both sides played is outstanding and has been needed for a long time. And it will probably open the door for many more accounts by active, front line participants in that struggle, such as the account of Bob Moranda's experiences. Ambrose's *Citizen Soldiers* is a welcome relief from the large number of biographical and personal accounts, many self-serving, by senior officers and officials who played prominent roles in World War II. For, as Ambrose pointed out in an article in *Newsweek* (July 13, 1998), it was "the kids who changed the world." Youngsters called into the service who had thrust upon them "ultimate responsibility... the kids accepted it, endured and prevailed. They were the sons of democracy, and they saved democracy. We owe them a debt we can never repay." However, there is no excuse for the historical revisionism in which Professor Weinberg engaged.

In Bob's story you will meet Maurice Conover, who was in Bob's outfit during the Battle of the Bulge. An article in *The Billings Gazette*, November 7, 1965, titled "From Bastogne to Broadview," told of Pfc. Conover's experiences during the war. Not once was his unit or St. Vith, where he fought and was captured, mentioned. The article ended: "Twenty-one years ago this Christmas he served with an outfit whose members were immortalized when fellow soldiers named them 'The Battlin' Bastards of Bastogne.'" Conover and his outfit were never in Bastogne. Such errors seem quite commonplace and raise questions about the accuracy of our historians who rely on reportorial coverage in published writings. Perhaps we need more of the participants—like Bob Moranda—telling what they experienced. We can learn much from such men about what went right and what went wrong. And if we don't learn from them, mistakes will recur and retard the U. S. Army's ability to improve its efficiency.

Do such inaccurate accounts happen? Too often! Today's newspapers have errors of fact, warped interpretations, and false or fictional writing by inexperienced or self-seeking reporters. Yet these are the accounts that historians in future years will use in their research and writings. As for this critical battle during World War II and the impressions now in the minds of readers, perhaps a parallel might be found concerning the Battle of Gettysburg during our Civil War. Mention it and Pickett's Charge comes to the forefront in the knowledge of most people. Who knows about Generals Armistead, Pettigrew, and Trimble and their forces that played a much larger and more devastating role during that battle, or of Generals Meade and Hancock and a number of their subordinates who receive little praise or credit? We know of Pickett's Charge but little of Hancock's Defense. Professor Carol Reardon, in "Pickett's Charge in History and Memory" (*The Washington Post Magazine*), points out that the dominant Richmond press celebrated with great fanfare the brave, albeit foolhardy, charge made by Pickett's all-Virginian force. The news of Pickett's Charge was then picked up by the Northern chroniclers who amplified the spin. Trimble's and Pettigrew's brigades consisted of soldiers from North Carolina, Tennessee, Alabama, and Mississippi, with only a few Virginians, and suffered much greater losses. Additionally, the Virginians ignored their Southern compatriots from other states and even went so far as to accuse them of cowardice and blame them for the losses suffered by Pickett as well as for the Confederate defeat.

True history is the accurate accounting of what events actually occurred. But historians usually base their writings on hearsay—reports of others, sometimes non-participants, of the events. This account is from Bob's memory and from the men who were there on the ground—they do not tell flowery or embellished stories, just what they remember.

The first-hand stories by the bloodied participants in the World War II struggles are important to our understanding of its history. Hopefully the true and accurate recounting of those stories, even after so many years have passed, will lead us to the truth. Those soldiers are passing from us at a steady rate. Bob is in his mid-eighties now, still with a keen mind and his great sense of humor. His memory of events is clear, but, like so many of his compatriots, he has forgotten names and minor incidents. After all, many of those men have spent decades trying to forget much of what they went through in order to put it behind them. Some have never been successful doing so, and Christmas comes every year to remind them what they were doing during those days more than fifty years ago.

When Bob asked me to look over his writings about his experiences during World War II, I was delighted, for his family had wanted him to do it for many, many years. Of the seven of our parents' children who served in the several Services during that war, Bob was the only one whose duties involved actual front-line combat service. For decades after the war he avoided the subject whenever it came up, and we didn't press him. As an example, I was stationed for duty in the Pentagon when the Office of the Chief of Military History published the volume of its World War II series entitled *U.S. Army in World War II, European Theater of Operations, The Ardennes Battle of the Bulge*, by Hugh M. Cole. I purchased a copy and arranged to meet with General Bruce Clarke, then retired and living in Arlington, Virginia, who kindly inscribed the book to Bob, and I sent it to him. General Clarke commanded the first units of the 7th Armored Division that were ordered to the scene of the German breakthrough that became the Bulge. A couple of years later, when visiting Bob, I noticed the volume on his bookshelf and asked what he thought of it. His reply was that he hadn't read it and probably wouldn't, but he did appreciate my getting General

Clarke to acknowledge his service. That was more than twenty years after the Bulge! And it wasn't until many years later that he responded to his grandchildren and nephews by recounting some of his experiences, and then began to get in touch with several of his comrades in arms. It has been just in the last couple of years that he started to put his memories down on paper.

In order for me to do the job, I was forced to get into the various accounts written about the Ardennes Campaign, and my interest increased with each article and book I read about it. The "Bulge" was a campaign critical to the success of the Allies against the German war machine and for the demise of Hitler and the Nazis. I thought Bob's story should be told within the events of history as they occurred. For that reason explanatory notes are interwoven throughout Bob's Story, italicized and inserted in appropriate places to give the reader a better understanding of the historical events surrounding his story. For those who are not familiar with the U. S. Army structure during World War II, nor of some of the military nomenclature and acronyms, you will find explanatory notes in the Glossary. And at the end you will find a commentary presenting my opinions and discussion of the events which, hopefully, will provide a better perspective of the Ardennes Campaign and a better appreciation of the role of the 7th Armored Division.

George E. Moranda
Colonel, U. S. Army, Retired

The Home Front

HUENEME

[Probably no other man had such a large and powerful impact on most of the world during the period of the 1930s and 1940s as Adolf Hitler. With his rise to power in 1933 and his marshaling a country and military forces to conquer by ruse, wile, threats, and pressure the neighboring countries of Austria and Czechoslovakia (1938-39), he triggered the war we know as World War II. When he invaded Poland on September 1, 1939, Europe was immediately divided into two opposing forces in an open conflict that eventually drew in the United States. He ruthlessly exploited and controlled his German subjects and those of his allies. His deeds affected the lives of almost everyone living in the world during that period.]

Tolstoy wrote of War and Peace. Not me! This is a story of War and Love—of a young man and a beautiful girl. It begins at the first meeting of the two, which happened at the local assembly point of the kids of our small town of Hueneme (Port was added to the name shortly after the harbor there was completed in 1939). The local tennis court was located at the Woman's Improvement Club—one old cement court which the whole town had to share. I was playing doubles, and I just happened to look up and see two young, pretty girls standing outside of the fence. They were just watching the action on the tennis court. I knew that I had to meet the older girl, so I yelled to one of the other boys who was standing around waiting to play and asked him to take my place. When that change was made, I walked outside the court and approached the two girls and introduced myself.

"Hi, I'm Bob."

The two girls smiled and introduced themselves. The oldest said, "I am Amelia and this is my sister Rozeel Swain. We just moved here from the San Fernando Valley and live nearby— next to the Glen Dewar's, if you know where that is."

I did know where that was, and after we talked for some time, they excused themselves and left. I continued playing tennis for some time. But I was smitten—and my mind was not on the game. I knew that I had to find out more about Amelia.

The next day it just happened to be a drizzly day. I walked over to the house near the Glen Dewar's and knocked on the door. Amelia opened the door and invited me in. Her mother was doing some work in the kitchen. After some chit chat with her mother and the girls and clucking at a cute little girl, the youngest child Shirley, I asked Amelia and Rozeel if they would like to go for a walk in the rain. Both said yes, so, after they put on some outer clothes, we departed and walked for some time. During the walk I discovered that Amelia was going steady and was serious about another young man in our town. Well that knocked me for a loop but I still enjoyed the walk and the talk. The younger sister and I had an instant rapport and the three of us had a good time.

After the walk I returned home. I felt that my quest was over. The girl of my dreams was already spoken for, and at that time I was without a job so any further pursuit was out of the question. But I had really been impressed with the girls. Rozeel was small—her nickname was "Tiny"—and young, but I was taken with her forwardness and knew that the two of us were going to be good friends forever. As for Amelia, I really wished that she was available but at that time it just wasn't to be. The way she talked and smiled, her beauty was something that would stay with me forever. I know that I could never describe her as she really was but only as I saw her. A cameo face below a beautiful head of hair that would glint when the light shined through it. When she walked, her carriage was straight and with an air of stateliness.

After a couple of years doing odd jobs such as cutting sugar at the sugar factory in Oxnard, picking lemons, and swinging a sledge hammer for the railroad and the Santa Rosa Farms, I survived but never had enough money to do much. The highest pay during that time varied from twenty-seven cents per hour to higher paying jobs of forty cents per hour working at the sugar factory. The Depression was still in effect and there just were not many jobs I could find. The most steady job I had in those days was the time I spent working for Mr. J. E. Dewar in his grocery store. After a few months working there I could see that soon the Dewar's were going to have their son Glen take over the business, so I left. The pay was eighteen dollars a week. The Dewars took the lion's share of the first months of my pay to apply to our family grocery bill that had soared during the sickness of my Dad.

Photo taken about 1938 of Moranda family.
Left to right with year of birth: George (1918), Paul (1920), Theodore
(Ted) (1921), Walter (Bill) (1915), Maye (1910), Robert (Bob)
(1913), Dad (Lawrence) (1884), Earle (1908), Mother (Nona) (1889)

I'll not dwell on all the good and the bad about the different jobs except to say that I was surviving. I certainly was not happy about lacking a good job with a future, but during those days people were living day by day, doing anything to survive. I even went on a mining expedition with a couple of friends, Norman Nichols and Bud Valentine. Norm had gone to the University of Colorado and had become a mining engineer. He had found a mine in the desert near Death Valley that he could work on as a partner with the owner, a prospector with the name of Carl Mingle. Norm came to town and got the two of us to go with him on the venture. To participate, I was required to put up two hundred dollars into a fund for the operation. Mom came up with the money, just so I could have a chance to go into the venture, by borrowing on her life insurance policy. The mine was in the Mojave Desert near Randsburg. Everything went pretty well until the mine caved in on me. I scratched and fought my way out from under a pile of rock that was covering me. I was hauled out and driven home in the back of a pickup. I felt every bounce on the trip until we finally got home, where I was taken to the doctor's office and bound up with tape and turned loose. I never went back. I knew then I was not a miner, and the danger was too great. But I will say the experience was something I'll never forget.

In 1937 a friend of mine, John Moore, asked me if I would help him, his brother Hobart ("Buck"), and their father in their restaurant, the Yellow Jacket Café, on Oxnard Boulevard in Oxnard, which was five miles from home in Hueneme. I asked what I would do and he said I would be the combination dish washer and counter man. As I was not working at the time, I agreed. A week after I started work, the night cook didn't show up for the 2:00 a.m. shift. Buck, the second shift cook, asked me if I could handle the shift from 2:00 a.m. until John could get there in the morning. I said I would try. He showed me the recipe for the hot cake batter and how to fry eggs, so I covered the shift. I must admit that I liked the job, and after a short time I became quite proficient at it.

So I had a job. I worked the graveyard shift from 2:00 a.m. until 10:00 a.m. every day. I didn't have a day off for quite a while and really didn't want one as I was making 50 cents per hour and got my meals, too. Hell, I was rolling in dough! I got so rich that I went down to A. J. Dingman's Ford agency and bought a used 1931 Model A Roadster. It cost me almost $200, and I soon named it the "Blue Goose." What a great car! Everyone loved it. Brothers George, Ted, and Paul borrowed it on occasion, so the car didn't rest much, but it was always ready for a romp around the town. All it wanted was to be loved and to receive an occasional pat and a compliment such as, "Good car."

Each day after work I went home and slept until about 7:00 p.m., then got up and went to Oxnard and either played softball for one of the local teams or visited various people. The previous year, after working at the sugar factory, I had gone back to Salt Lake City with my brother Earle so that he could visit with his then girlfriend, Donna Rudd. He had met her at our next door neighbors, the John Trehers; she was the niece of Mrs. Treher. I went along with Earle to share the driving and the expenses, and I was going to get reacquainted with some friends I had met in Spanish Fork, Utah, a couple of years before when I had gone back there with Gerald "Shorty" Lykins to work with his grandparents. I had become quite chummy with a couple of boys and a girl there and thought it to be a good opportunity to see them again. When we got to Spanish Fork they were not able to entertain me so I went on with Earle. I wondered why the two boys couldn't accept me when I came to visit, but a year is a long time and things do change. The same thing happened with the young lady. She was somewhat glad to see me but there was no way that she could put me up at her house so my plans went sour. There was nothing else to do but go on with Earle and hope Donna could find a bed for two instead of one. She did.

At the Rudd's home I met Donna's sister Flora. She was a beautiful girl but was going steady and about to marry a fellow she had been going with for some time. When Flora came home from her date and I was sitting in the living room reading and playing the piano, we became acquainted. Every night when she came home we would sit and talk. When Earle and I left she asked me to write which I did. And for some reason my words impressed her, and soon she came out to see me on her way to San Francisco where she was going to live and work for a relative. She stayed for a week or so. Mom really liked her as did the rest of the family. So when she left we continued to write and mom wrote to her, too. But the idea of my marrying on my salary of four dollars a day was out of the question. On one of my few weekends off, Tom Murphy and I drove to San Francisco to visit with her. I noted something wrong because she didn't invite me to her house.

When Tom and I drove home from San Francisco, we went through the heaviest fog I had ever encountered. Going through one town I had my head out of the window following the white line. Suddenly a red light came on, and I was pulled over by a police car. He asked how fast I was going, and I told him slow because of the fog. He asked for my driver's license, and somehow I couldn't find my wallet. Because I had just purchased the Ford I couldn't show him a bill of sale. The police hauled us into the jail as they thought we had stolen the car. I was about ready to call home when Tom brought out his wallet, and the policeman noted that Tom was a member of the Elks Lodge. That was enough for him. He dismissed us with a ticket and told me to send proof that I owned the car when I got home. I forgot about the damned thing until one day as I was sitting in Dad's Justice of the Peace Office, I looked in my wallet and there was the citation. I asked Dad what I should do, and he said he would write a letter explaining everything. He instructed me to include a twenty dollar bill in the letter to pay for the fine, which he estimated would be enough, and to indicate that if the fine was more to please advise him and the money would be sent post haste. I never heard from them again.

In about two months I got a letter from Flora asking me to quit writing as she had met a new friend and was soon going to marry. She remained a friend of my mother's for the rest of mother's life. She was a great girl, pretty and intelligent, but it just wasn't to be for the two of us.

The place to be on a Saturday night in our county was a dance hall, the Green Mill, in Ventura. On one of the Saturdays, I went to the dance hoping to pick up a date. Most of the time the boys went stag and met the girls inside the hall. The ladies weren't charged for admittance. As I was dancing I looked along the side of the dance hall, and I saw Amelia Swain sitting alone. After the tune ended, I walked over to her and we started to talk. I asked her if she would dance with me, and she stated that she didn't know how, that she had come to the dance with a couple of her friends just to watch. What I had seen on my first encounter with her was still there. She was beautiful! We talked quite a bit, and I asked if she would go home with me. She said no as she had come with friends, and they expected her to ride home with them. I remember how great it was to talk to her, but I thought she was still not too sold on me, although she seemed to radiate warmth. I could listen to her talk with enjoyment. Yes, I was "smitten."

A couple of weeks later I drove into Oxnard early in the evening, and after visiting with the gang at the Yellow Jacket Cafe, I decided I would take in a movie. I walked to the theater and there in the booth selling the tickets was Amelia. She smiled and we exchanged a few words and I went in and sat in the back. In about an hour Amelia came to where I was sitting and asked if she could sit beside me. Man, oh man, you never saw anyone move so fast getting up to allow her to get to the seat beside me. We didn't say much during the movie but it was a comfortable feeling just being beside her.

When the show was over we walked out together, and I asked if I could take her home in the Ford. She said she only lived a few blocks away. I then said, "I'll walk you home." We talked all the way to her house. I found out that she and her old boyfriend had broken up quite some time ago. We talked about everything people usually talk about when first meeting. When we walked up to the front door of her house I said to her, "Miss Swain, I am going to marry you." She didn't say no, nor did she say yes. She just smiled.

That encounter changed my way of living and entertaining. Nightly, I worked until 10:00 a.m. and then drove home and slept until about eight in the evening. At 10:00 p.m. I drove into town, stopped by the theater, picked up Amelia, and we would go some place—to Ventura or Santa Barbara—or stay for the second show at the movie. But we would do something. On one of the days when we were together at the Swain house, Amelia Habib was there. Amelia Habib said to my Amelia, "Remember when we called you 'Amolia' in Spanish class?" When I heard that I exclaimed, "That's it! From now on I am going to call you 'Molly.'" And the name stuck. The only ones who continued to call her Amelia were her mother and father and my mother.

For the first year we went together, her mother, Isabelle, and I became really good friends but her father remained aloof. I guess as I was there so much he finally got used to seeing me and finally accepted me. But Isabelle, as everyone called her, was a joy. She was a devout Christian Scientist, as was Molly. Together they would read the lesson daily and go to the church on religious days. Molly was a better Christian than anyone I had ever met. She really believed. She had never been to a doctor, though at times she had a very hard time breathing due to a form of asthma. But medication was taboo to her and her mother. It concerned me, but I had little or no knowledge of Mary Baker Eddy and her teachings. However, after watching the healings I became more and more interested and finally accepted that if a person really believed, it was the only way he could live. I remember so well the two of them singing the hymns of the church. Their favorite song was, "Shepherd Show me, How Go O'er the Hill Side Steep, How to Gather, How to Sow, How to Feed Thy Sheep." Molly sang in her pleasant voice and Isabelle sang in her rolling contralto, complete with a slight waver.

One of the things that I really loved about our relationship was talking to Molly. I don't know how else to describe the chatter except cute. Her phrasing and interests were continually making me chuckle. When she and her mother talked while I was around, they often would not finish their conversation. All of a sudden the topic would change. As I was interested in what they were talking about, I would ask what the rest of the story was. Their answer was always the same, "Oh, she already knew the rest of the story." And that was it. No more embellishing on a subject when the answer was known.

Isabelle loved to hear funny stories. Daily she would walk down a couple of blocks to the grocery store owned by the Fulton brothers. There they would exchange stories. One day I had heard the story of the man who was entering the hospital. As he was walking down one of the halls, suddenly one of the doors flew open and a man in his hospital gown started to run down the hall. Running right behind him was a nurse, and in her hand was a pair of surgical scissors. Behind the nurse the doctor appeared to find out what the commotion was all about, sized up the situation, and called to the nurse, "Nurse, nurse! I told you to slip off his spectacles." Isabelle really enjoyed the story and said she would tell that to the boys at the market tomorrow. The next day when I stopped in at the Swains', Isabelle came to me and asked how the story went again. She said she had told the story to the boys and they didn't laugh. I asked her to retell the story so I could know what she had said. She told everything well until she came to the punch line, which was, "And the doctor came right behind the nurse yelling, 'Nurse, you misunderstood me. I said to take off his glasses!'"

The father, Henry Roe Swain, was a small man physically but strong when it came to being in control of his family. He didn't say much but by his actions and inactions a person knew immediately how it affected him. Everyone called him Roe and that is what he wanted. He hated the name of Henry. One day I asked if I could call him "Hank". He didn't answer so that's what I called him from then on. In fact almost everyone started calling him that and he enjoyed the name more and more.

When I was working at the Yellow Jacket Café, I would stop by the Swain house to see Molly. If she wanted the car, she would take me home and come get me just before she had to go to work at the theater. The old Blue Goose was a great car; it would go and go and go without much maintenance or gasoline. Sometimes we would do something during the day, and then I would get some sleep in the evening. I saw Molly almost every day. We became very close, and it was apparent that we were an item. But to get married on four dollars a day was impossible. Even so, it surely didn't stop our relationship. We were in love and were willing to wait. We started to save for the day. We weren't able to save much, but every bit of change I received on a purchase that was in silver I gave to Molly. She saved it first in small jars and then in much larger containers. When Molly told her friends that we were saving for our marriage, the word got around and most of the cashiers in town made sure that I got a lot of change. If, after having a coke or something, I had to pay with a five dollar bill, the change would all be in silver. Oh sure, they would say, "I am sorry, I don't happen to have any ones."

One Saturday night I came into Oxnard early and, as the stores were still open, I went into the A. E. Little's Jewelry Store. I worked out an arrangement with Mr. Little that allowed me to pick out the ring I wanted and to pay for it so much a week. So, with the ring in my pocket, I walked to the theater where Molly was selling tickets and said to her, "Hi Molly, will you marry me?" And with that I shoved the ring through the opening of the kiosk. She opened the box and with a smile that I will never forget, she said, "Yes, I love you." She then continued, "But I won't put the ring on until you ask my father and get his blessing." That I agreed to.

On the next day, Sunday, after I got off work, I drove to the Swain house. Hank was out mowing the front lawn. I said hello to him, then sat on the porch step, and talked to him as he worked. I could see he really didn't want to talk to me as he knew what I was there for. I just waited. The thought of his losing his daughter was something he really did not want to face. But I waited until he finished. When he walked close to where I was sitting, I stood up and approached him and said, "Hank, you know that I love your daughter very much and we would like to get married one day soon. We would like your blessing." He looked at me, and with tears in his eyes he replied very sincerely, "I knew it would soon happen and I am glad that it will."

I looked up at the front door and there stood Molly, Isabelle, Shirley, and Rozeel listening to the conversation. They had been standing in the doorway all the time I was waiting to talk to him. They were all happy and came out and gave the two of us a couple of hugs and kisses. It was then I formally placed the ring on Molly's finger and again there were hugs and kisses.

The town soon knew about the engagement. We did not set a date, as we knew I had to have a better job before we could take the big step. We continued to see each other almost every day, but I could never get her to go to a dance with me—which I liked to do. Even so, our courtship was wonderful. We were in love and everyone could see it. We went everywhere together in the 1931 Ford. Because it was a roadster and some of the nights were cold, I purchased a long type overcoat from Al Rodaway at the Wineman's Men's Store. It was part of the costume. a hat, a coat, and the Blue Goose—the open roadster. Molly's father used to kid me about the overcoat because when I came in to pick up Molly I wouldn't take the coat off. He asked why I wore the coat, but I am sure if he rode around in the Blue Goose he too would have dressed warmly. We were married a few months later, and after the marriage Molly decided we should have an enclosed sedan. I teased her that she couldn't stand the cold after the marriage. She would smile and say, "You no longer have to wear an overcoat to keep us warm."

OXNA RD

It was not long after our announced engagement I was offered a job as the truck driver for the Railway Express. I worked for Bob Barriclaw, who was the Railway Express agent. I worked for him as an agent and not for the Express Company. Had the job been for the main company, I would have stayed with them for my working career as I did enjoy the job. My salary was about a $100 a month.

Later I was approached by a friend, Archie Petre, with another opportunity. The year before I had been playing baseball for the Hueneme team, and we had a pretty good team. I had a good batting average and did hit the occasional long ball. Archie was the manager of the Shell Oil team, though he worked for Standard Stations, Inc., at the station located at 3rd and Oxnard Boulevard. He asked me, "How would you like to work for Standard? If you will play for me and the Shell Oil team I think I can get you my job. I am leaving Standard to take over one of their stations in Camarillo." It didn't take me long to say yes. Archie set up a time for me to see Bill Haydock, the station manager, for an approval. Bill and I hit it off right away, and he arranged for me to go to Pasadena to see about my going to work for them.

I drove to the office of Standard Stations, Incorporated (it is now Chevron Oil). I was first interviewed by Mr. H. S. Nottingham, and after being okayed by him, I was led into the office of Mr. P. J. Sullivan. I guess I passed but not without his telling me I was getting a great break because I was the first man hired who didn't have at least two years of college. Then he told me that I would have to drive to Pasadena and go through a week of training at their school before I could work for the company (we laugh about such a deal now as service station personnel would certainly not be one of the greatest starting jobs). He also informed me that even if I were to make it through the school I would be on probation for at least a month while working at my first assignment. I understand that in today's world it is hard to appreciate why it was so difficult to get a job of any type then. But to be able to work for a leading company then was a great break.

I made it through the school. The main man would come down and watch us as we waited on customers to see if we were treating the customers well. Mr. Sullivan graduated us with a promise he would be watching our progress with interest. I then purchased my uniforms and went back home. I had been away from Molly for a week and soon we were together, talking and planning our lives together. We knew if I could get over the probation period we could soon marry.

I remember the type of uniforms we had to wear—three white and two brown. When you waited on the customers in the front at the gas pumps you were to wear the white, and when you were assigned to the lubrication bay the other uniform was to be worn. Both uniforms required black shoes, bow tie, and a belt that had no buckle (as the company didn't want any scratches on the customers' cars when the attendant leaned over). And no outfit was complete without the small whisk broom in the back pocket which you used in every car in the pump block when serving the customers. When a customer wanted the tires checked we asked them to drive to the air and water tower away from the pump block. We also would put in an air chuck in the air hose and blow the dirt out of the car when we had time.

One day a lady drove into the pump block when one of our salesmen was using the air chuck out at the air tower. He was cleaning out a car that had been serviced in the lubrication bay. The lady got out of the car asked for the restroom. The attendant thought she asked for a whisk broom. With that he yelled at the lady, "If you will drive over here I will blow it out for you."

After a month or so at work, Bill Haydock got me promoted to full time. My monthly salary was to be $80 plus commissions, which came to about $30. And I had to buy and have my uniforms laundered. But I was happy—I had a job with a future.

At first the job called for me to work three days in Oxnard and the balance of the week in Ojai. I had to drive about fifty miles a day when working in Ojai, but I did it with pleasure. On those days I would work ten-hour days. That lasted for about three months, and by then we had built up the station business in Oxnard so I had a full shift there. Everything was really going great. Then one day Bill Haydock had an accident and, as there was no one around but me, I had to work long hours opening and closing the station. I did the job. There was no such thing as overtime or extra pay, we just worked.

Shortly after that an auditor came in to check on how we were doing at the station. He asked about the manager, where he was, and how come no one had relieved me for a week or so. I didn't have an answer and let it go. He then noted I had not been paid mileage for the many trips that I had made to Ojai. He asked why not? I said I didn't know I was supposed to be paid for that. He said he couldn't do much about the overtime but he could on the mileage. So I suddenly had an extra few bucks that Molly and I had not planned to have, and we pushed forward the marriage date.

Every night that I had to work I would call Molly at the theater. We had a free phone we could use in the service bay. We answered the phone for the local Standard Oil Co. when they were not in their plant. That number was 320. The pay phone in the station office was our number, 811. Molly's number at the theater was 81. There was no dialing: we had to go through the operator, and we all knew the operators who worked the switch board at the phone company.

One night about nine o'clock I decided to call Molly and tell her I would be along right after work and to wait for me at the theater. So I picked up the free phone, and the operator said, "Number please?"

"811 please."

The phone rang in the office. I said, "Damn," hung up, ran out the service bay and into the office, picked up the phone and answered, "Standard Stations, Moranda speaking." No answer.

I went back to the phone in the service bay, picked up the phone and the operator came on again, "Number please?"

"811 please."

The office phone rang again, and I ran out the service bay and grabbed the receiver and again said into the mouthpiece, "Standard Stations, Moranda speaking." Again a dead phone. I cursed a few times under my breath and went back to the phone in the service bay. This time, when I picked up the receiver and the operator asked, "Number please," I asked the operator, "Hey, Lottie, who in the hell is trying to get me on the phone?"

"You are. I just kept ringing you to see how fast you really were." Lottie knew where I worked, in fact she traded with us at the station and knew the phone setup. Needless to say we had a lot of laughs over my trying to call myself. When I called Molly and told her about what happened, she really had a laugh. And of course the story got around the family and other friends, so we all had a good a good time about it.

When the date was announced to the family, there were many little showers and parties for Molly. Of course my brothers made sure that they gave me a shower with all kinds of dumb presents. They were really excited about the marriage. They all loved Molly. One thing they appreciated about her was how loyal she was to anyone she loved and respected. At ball games, when the brothers were playing, no one could say anything negative about us or she would tear into him and really tell him off.

Soon after we announced the date, our superintendent, R. O. Berryman, drove up from Pasadena to make a contact at the station. Bill Haydock advised him I was going to get married soon. Berryman called me over and asked, "How many hours did you work overtime taking care of the station when Bill was off?" When he heard the amount, he told Bill I was to have a week off with pay to cover the overtime I had worked. So the honeymoon time was paid for.

In planning the wedding, I asked a good friend of mine who traded at the station, Reverend W. Don Brown of the Episcopalian Church, to conduct the ceremony. The ritual was to be performed at the home of the Swains. The biggest problem my family had was to get Brother Paul to shave his beard. It was not my idea he shave, but Mom said, "You shave or you can't go to the wedding!!"

We were married on a bright June day. The front room of the Swains' home was crowded with all of our gathered family. We stood before Reverend Brown—Molly was so beautiful in her wedding dress. As we stood there Molly reached over and squeezed my hand. She was calm and collected, but I was very nervous and almost fainted. Tears filled my eyes as I looked at her.

The ceremony began. Henry responded to Reverend Brown's question, "Who gives this bride away?" in a strong voice: "I do." I was getting a bit queasy and was glad when the Reverend had us kneel on a couple of cushions and prayed over us asking the Lord for His blessing on our marriage. After that he introduced us to our families, "I now present to you Mr. and Mrs. Robert Moranda."

I was still so nervous, but with the usual ribbing from my brothers and the hugs and kisses from the rest of the family, I soon recovered. With all the people in the small room it was quite hot, and I'm sure the rest of the people there also felt it. But it did give the brothers something to kid me about for years after.

After the ceremony and while food was being served, Mother gave me my first and only talk about the birds and the bees. She asked me to come out on the porch so she and Dad could talk to me. So we slipped away from the party and went outside. Mom came up to me and said, very seriously and quietly, "Bob, I want you to remember that Amelia is a girl." (Mom and Mother Swain were the only ones who never used the name Molly as long as they lived.) Dad listened in on the message, and with a smile on his face he shook my hand. As he did so I felt something, which I discovered to be a bill for a large amount. I have always looked back at that little episode with love and respect for my folks, for they wanted me to love and care for my new wife and to be sure that I had enough money for the honeymoon.

When we left on our honeymoon, we fooled all of my "friends" who were laying in wait for me. I don't know what they had planned to do, but I guessed they were going to form a line of cars and escort us out of town. But Brother Bill had suggested that we take his brand new car, so Molly and I sneaked out of the house, got into Bill's car, and drove off. No one spotted us, so we made it!

The boys, I understood, were betting on how far the two of us would get before stopping for the night. Camarillo and Ventura were the best guesses they could come up with, as they thought ten miles was about as far as I could go before consummating our marriage. We drove to Studio City and found a very nice motel and spent a wonderful night getting acquainted. I can still see Molly as she came out of the bathroom dressed in her beautiful gown. She was so pretty and desirable. The next morning when we awakened I looked over at my bride and said to her, "And how are you this morning, Miss Swain." She laughed and corrected me by reminding me that we had waited until marriage before sleeping together, so why should she be called "Miss Swain." She did not forget the incident, as she told both our mothers when we got home from our honeymoon.

As I look back, I must admit I didn't know much about what a groom should do. As I was the first one of our family to get married, I didn't have a big brother to tell me the ins and outs of that part of life. Later I realized I should have arranged for a hotel room and prepared it with finery and flowers. It was part of life's education that I missed. But we were two people really in love, and that made up for all the social graces that I had not learned.

When we returned from our short honeymoon, we moved into our first little home. It was a small house in back of a home on G Street in Oxnard. We moved everything we had in a couple of loads in the Ford. We were there for only a few months. One of the highlights of our stay there was the night the boys—Brothers Paul, George, Ted, and Wannie Woods (who was as close to us as a brother)—came to dinner. We invited them to the first meal Molly had cooked for guests. She bought eight pounds of hamburger with which she made a large meat loaf. The other items were mashed potatoes, all the trimmings, plus dessert. Those guys really enjoyed the food—they ate it all. After a few minutes of visiting following supper, the boys decided they should get on with their life and left. We later asked what they did and learned they went to Rolly's Café and had hamburgers!

The boys would drop in at the house after they had been out on the town. They would knock and come in and it didn't matter that we were in bed. Molly loved them and put up with them. The first thing they would do was to go to the refrigerator to see what they could find to eat. That's when they named me the "Big Bear," because I would try to get rid of them and get some sleep, but Molly always had so much fun talking to them that I didn't have a chance.

We didn't live in that small house for very long, as it was just too small even for the two of us, especially when company came to see us. We had not been married for very long when we had an interesting visit. We had gone to bed and were sound asleep, but were awakened when we heard a disturbance outside of our window. Someone was pounding on the back door. I dragged myself to the door to see what the problem was. There stood the Blackwell's softball team members and their wives. They came bringing food and gifts for the newlyweds. But first we had to earn the rewards, so they loaded us into one of their pickup trucks and drove us to the main street in town. There we got out of the truck, and I had to carry Molly to a wheelbarrow, place her in it, and push her down the main street of Oxnard—she in her negligee and I in my robe. Following the wheelbarrow were the rest of the men and wives in their cars, honking their horns. Even the police came by and, when they saw who it was and what we were celebrating, they joined the ranks and followed with their sirens shrieking. When we finally reached the corner of 5th and Oxnard Boulevard, the parade was over. They all came back to the house, even one police car with two officers—about twenty people in all, and brought in food and gifts and we celebrated. It was then, after the gang left, we decided we had better move to a larger place.

We soon did and moved to a duplex on the corner of F and 5th streets. It only had one bedroom, but the place had a large living room and a huge kitchen. This move was made in a borrowed van. Our first move had been accomplished in the two-door Ford. But by the second move we had accumulated quite a bit more, and it took the full load of a van borrowed from one of my friends. Again the brothers and Wannie would come and knock on the door any time of the night and get us up so they could raid the refrigerator. I would growl, but Molly was always a great hostess and loved the company.

I remember we ran a grocery bill at Ditchfield's. I had said I would never run a grocery bill because of the large ones Mom and Dad had been forced to run up during the time that Dad was down sick. I realized then how difficult it was to pay for something that was no longer around. But we watched the bill very closely and never ran over a two week period. The good part was that Ditchy would deliver the groceries. Ditchy was the catcher and a teammate on the Blackwell's baseball team.

We were so happy. We had a good home with good neighbors, the Atkissons: Fay, Mildred, and baby. And we also were given a dog, a little Scotty. I gave it the name of Trouble, and the dog lived up to its name. Later, after having our child, it bit the baby on the face just below her eye. That was really sad. The baby had played with the dog all the time. This time the dog was eating and the baby came up and tried to pet the dog at the wrong time. We couldn't keep the dog then so I found it a good home, and, with reluctance, we gave it away. Molly and I were alone again but happy to report the baby was OK. The bite did leave a small scar under her eye. I guess I should not have given the dog the name of "Trouble".

Everything seemed to be going the way we wanted. My life was busy and things were going along swimmingly. What went on in the world was of little concern to me. Hell, I was on cloud nine. The war in Europe was of no interest to me. Other than in family discussions, I hardly talked about Hitler and what he was doing, in spite of the attempts by President Roosevelt to try to alert the country to pending problems for us and other countries. My job at the station was going great: Bill Haydock and I had built the station from a "D" to a "B." I got automatic raises and was in line for a promotion.

At that time my father, who had been treated for tuberculosis until it was arrested and was a diabetic, was having a lot of trouble with a wound that would not heal on his right foot. He tried everything but finally he went to the doctor and found out that his toe was going to have to be removed. Dad entered the St. John's Hospital in Oxnard. Our family doctor, Dr. Korts, attempted the operation, and during the procedure Dad's heart stopped After they revived him, the doctor quit the operation and brought him out of the ether. Dr. Korts told my Mom and me about the failed surgery and that Mom should take him to Santa Barbara to the Sansum Clinic for further treatment.

It was at that time that Mr. Sullivan from Pasadena came up and offered me a job as an assistant manager of the training station in Santa

Barbara. I had to turn the promotion down, as I was the blood donor for my Dad. He smiled and said he understood and, further, when I was free for a promotion, to call him at his office in Pasadena.

In a couple of months Dad was operated on at the Sansum Clinic. Dr. Saint was the doctor in charge. All went well this time and soon Dad was able to go home. Under the good care of Mom, he recovered. I must admit he wasn't the best patient for Mom. He was very restless and impatient with himself, and he took it out on her. I am sure at times Mom would have loved to just leave for a time, but the one thing my mother had above all else was her strong sense of duty to the family. She suffered in silence and never said anything to anyone about how miserable she really was.

Soon after that, the district superintendent of Standard Stations came into our station. He greeted us, made the usual inspection of the station, and pointed out some things he would like to have corrected. When he was about ready to leave, I asked him to call Mr. Sullivan and advise him I could now accept the promotion. The superintendent looked at me rather funny and said in so many words that he would not. So I said to him, "Then I will call him. But I asked you to do it while you are here so you won't think I am going behind your back. I was told by Mr. Sullivan that I should call him when I was in a position to accept a promotion." With that the "Super" did go to the phone and called Mr. Sullivan. When he hung up, he came out to me and said, "How would you like to be Station Manager of the Standard Station on State and Islay in Santa Barbara?" What great news!

WAR APPROACHES

[Not to be outdone, soon after the German invasion of Poland in September 1939, Stalin saw an opportunity to extend his country's control. He joined with Germany in taking the eastern part of Poland and then moved Soviet troops into the Baltic states of Lithuania, Latvia, and Estonia. An attempt at the same ruse in Finland failed, so Stalin started the invasion of its northern neighbor. Meanwhile the French and British forces faced the Germans and both sides, for different reasons, stared at each other—the Germans behind the Siegfried Line and the French in their Maginot Line battlements. Hitler, concerned that the Anglo-French Alliance might prevent Swedish iron ore from going into Germany and that they might send aid to Finland through the Scandinavian countries, ordered the invasion of Norway in January,1940.]

Although our local paper, *The Oxnard Courier*, carried little national and international news, we did get some information from *The Los Angeles Times* and from radio, especially Roosevelt's Fireside Chats. There seemed to be little concern about what was going on in the world. Even when the local National Guard unit was called in for Federal service, I never dreamed any of us would be affected. We just continued running through our regular daily routines.

In the fall of 1940, the Selective Service Act was passed by Congress, which called for eligible men to register for the draft. That meant that the Moranda family had six men eligible for duty. None of us had any children, so we all could be called. The oldest, Earle, had applied for a job in Washington, D.C., working for the government as a civil servant. Walter (Bill) was working hauling lemons from the groves to packing houses. George and Paul were attending Fresno State College. And the youngest, Theodore (Ted), was going to Ventura Junior College. Our only sister, Maye, was working at Desmonds, a clothing store in Los Angeles, but after she learned that her brothers might be going off to serve in the military forces, she quit her job and began training to become an Army Nurse.

In April, 1941 George received notice that he was to be drafted. The officials at Fresno State College obtained a deferment for him so he could graduate in June. Things seemed to be getting a little more serious, and people were getting a little more involved. One of the lads who worked for us at the Oxnard station was Charles Porter. He became a pilot in the Air Corps and his mother, who traded at our service station, kept us informed of his progress. It was a real thrill to see him come into the station one day in his uniform with the gold bars of a Second Lieutenant on his shoulders. (Charles was killed very early in the war.)

[Having come to an arrangement with Stalin, Hitler then turned his attention to the west, and in the spring of 1940, the Blitzkrieg through the Low Countries successfully drove the British out through Dunkirk, decimated the French forces, reached Paris, and effectively controlled France both directly and through a puppet government. The German Navy, with marauding surface and undersea vessels, was operating throughout the Atlantic, Mediterranean, and Baltic waters against shipping to prevent supplies and raw material from reaching its enemies' lands. By the end of 1941, Germany had extended its control over most of central Europe, Greece, and North Africa, and was fighting in Yugoslavia and Egypt, and was heavily engaged in Russia, having started that invasion in June. By then Japan had bombed Pearl Harbor, which brought the United States into active war against the German, Italian, and Japanese Axis.]

On December 7, 1941, I was working at the station. It was a Sunday, and I had listened to the Catholic Church's bell ringing. It was a beautiful, clear day. I had opened the station, so I was there alone when one of our regular customers came in to fill his tank. I gave the customary greeting and he responded, "The Japanese have bombed Pearl Harbor." I didn't even know where Pearl Harbor was, and I don't think he did either. I was filling his tank when I noticed a soldier hitchhiking out in front of the station. I called to the soldier and asked him where he was going. He said, "I have to get back to San Francisco to my base." I then asked the customer his destination, which was Santa Barbara, and he agreed to take the man that far. Molly called shortly after that and was upset, and I tried to calm her down but couldn't tell her much because I just didn't know.

After that things really changed for the country. Everyone knew we were all going to be involved in some way. I never knew what my mother thought on that day, but she must have been a really worried one.

I came home one evening after work and was met by Molly at the door dressed in her sexiest outfit, and she announced that she wanted a baby. We had almost decided not to have children because of Molly's health problems. But she was willing, wanted one, and sure enough she became pregnant.

We were transferred to Santa Barbara soon afterwards for a couple of months, and then to a station in Ventura. I had even been offered one in Pasadena, but asked Mr. Sullivan to let me stay closer to our parents for the time being. And I was pleased that I was making progress up the ladder in the company. Besides, I could play ball for our softball team, which I was doing very well hitting with a batting average over .500. Molly was happy too, for she was near her folks, her practitioner, and her doctor during her pregnancy

Molly had a difficult time giving birth to Tomilyn Robin Moranda. The labor was almost a 48-hour ordeal. The doctor knew she was due. Molly knew she was due. I knew she was due. Tomi (as I called her when she became older) didn't think she was due. She was warm and comfortable where she was. So we all waited and waited. I sat in the room with Molly, helped her by timing the contractions, and kept her company. The contractions remained at the same spacing for sixteen hours. I was worried because Molly was not strong, but she was a good patient and ready for the grand experience. She always had high blood pressure, but as a good Christian Scientist she wasn't about to take medication. We had alerted her practitioner, Mrs. Reedy, and Molly had called her a couple of times while we were waiting. But the contractions were coming too slowly. Finally they increased and were severe so the nurse called the doctor and told him she was ready. The nurse, and a dear friend, Sister Alexine, said to me, "Now we take over." I was sent to the waiting room. I paced. I walked the halls. I prayed. I talked to everyone who would listen. Finally at 6:00 p.m., the nurse came and said, "Come in and see your daughter." So the baby was born and I was relieved and happy, for Molly had wanted a girl. She came out loudly, not really wanting to leave that warm cozy place where she had been living for the past nine months. Molly had been given a shot of medication, over her protestations, so she was not alert, but she knew the baby had been born. The birthing system there used what was called "Twilight Sleep," a method developed by local doctors, Drs. Swift and Livingston. It was a popular procedure then for child birthing.

Molly had spent some time writing out different combinations of names. Molly's brother Tommy was in the Navy on a Destroyer somewhere in the Pacific. He had been the family's concern for some time, so she had come up with the name of Tomilyn, and I suppose to make me feel good the middle name was to be Robin. Even today I can close my eyes and still hear Molly singing the baby's name, Tomilyn Robin Moranda, over and over again.

I walked into the delivery room where the baby was on a table and the nurses and doctor were cleaning her. She was beautiful. I watched as they cleaned her, and they placed Molly in a room. Then Sister Alexine said, "You had better go get something to eat and tell the families. Your wife will be out of it for at least two hours." This was the first grandchild on both sides of our families. Our parents and our brothers and sisters had been very interested in Molly's pregnancy, especially my youngest brother Ted who, when around Molly, would ask her if he could listen to the baby or put his hand on her tummy to feel the movement inside. I called Molly's folks and Mother Isabelle answered. I told her the news. I knew that all during the birthing she had been sitting and praying for Molly and the baby. Father Henry was also very pleased. I knew that Isabelle would tell all the rest of the Swain family, so I got in our car, an old Studebaker, and drove to Hueneme where I told Mom and Dad about the birth. As they were eating their supper, I sat down and joined them. They were very happy as were the Swains.

We started to call the rest of the family, but in between calls I had a call from the hospital. It was Sister Alexine who said, "Come back right away. Molly is having a problem." I rushed out, drove the five miles to the St. John's Hospital, and ran up the stairs to Molly's room where I found her crying. Actually she was a bit out of it, being still under the "Twilight Sleep" medication. She cried out to me, "Tell me, Bob, is the baby alive?" I reassured her that the baby was beautiful, healthy, and when last I saw her she was crying and moving her arms and legs. I then asked the nurse to please bring in the baby to reassure Molly. She did and the baby was placed in Molly's arms. What a wonderful sight. A young beautiful mother holding her new born baby. She checked Tomi from head to foot. Now Molly believed. There was instant bonding. Both Molly and the babe relaxed and enjoyed each other. In but a few minutes both were ready for some rest, so the baby was taken to the nursery and Molly went to sleep. With that, I drove home to Ventura and went to bed. Sleep didn't come easily but it finally came. What a couple of days and nights, but it was worth the wait.

Molly was in the hospital for three days. Every day she had visitors. Mom went at the first opportunity she had. Molly loved the role of mother; she loved to show off her daughter. It bothered her that should was unable to nurse Tomi; she really tried but had no success, so Tomi became a "bottle baby." Thankfully she had no problem with the formula. After being released from the hospital, they were taken to her mother's house, where we stayed for a few days. The house was full of love for the new arrival.

Bob and Molly

Molly and Tomi

We were living in Ventura so it was not long after the baby was born that she and Molly came home. The bonding with the baby was so great. Since she was a bit fussy at night, Molly and I would take turns holding her. At night it was my job to quiet the baby so I would place her on my chest and she would quiet down almost at once. I guess it was the beat of my heart that reminded her of the sound or feeling she had when she was in her personal incubator. So for the next six weeks I, too, got to bond with my "Pumpkin." I really don't know of a greater feeling than for a father to hold his newborn baby on his chest while the baby sleeps.

One thing on my mind throughout the birthing was I had not heard from the Draft Board regarding my application for the Volunteer Officers Corps. Just before Molly went into the hospital I had received my notice from the Draft Board I was to report in December. I had read and had investigated that men in my category could volunteer to become officers. To be eligible the men had to volunteer before the Draft Board called them up. As I wasn't 1A, I had thought I would be able to get into the program. So I hurried to the Draft Board in Oxnard and talked to Mrs. Ed Brown, who encouraged me to apply for Volunteer Officer School. If accepted, the men would go into the army, take basic training, and, if they passed that phase, would go directly to the Officers Training School. If a person failed along the way, then the individual would be returned to civilian life. Mrs. Brown, the Draft Board secretary and a personal friend of Molly's, helped me fill out the forms for the V.O.C. in either the Quartermaster Corp or the Transportation Corp. To do this, the Draft Board had to change my draft classification from 3A to 1A. Soon after that I received my notification to report for duty, not into the V.O.C. but into the Army. I went to see the Draft Board, and Mrs Brown told me that when my name came up before the board the President of the Draft Board, "Hap" Maxwell, a personal friend of mine (I thought) said, "I know Bob Moranda personally. Go ahead and draft him. He will become an officer without going to that V.O.C. outfit."

[Stopped near Moscow and Stalingrad during the winter of 1941-42 and in North Africa at el-Alamein, Germany and Italy began to be on the defensive. In the Pacific, American naval and military forces also started to force the Japanese into a defensive posture. And in November, 1942, American and British forces invaded North Africa. The 7th Armored Division was activated at Camp Polk, Louisiana, on March 1st, 1942.]

With that notice, I called my boss at Standard Stations, Inc., Mr. Pat Sullivan, who was sad that I was going to leave, but he told me to call my superintendent, Mr. George O'Brien, and give him my termination notice. I really was sorry that I was leaving. I liked my station at the corner of Meta and California in Ventura. It was my first large service station, and we had built up a good clientele. I loved my little house and really loved my girls. I hated to leave Molly because she was not strong. Her blood pressure was still high, and her asthma was still active. And the beautiful baby! But everyone was sacrificing, so what else was new. By this time every able-bodied man knew that he would soon have to go, so I was not too surprised by the action of the Draft Board.

Molly and I called her parents and asked if Molly and the baby could move back to their home. The answer was an emphatic, "Yes." So we moved back to the house on 4th Street in Oxnard. The house was full with Molly's parents and sister Shirley still at home. But there was plenty of love in the house so we were comfortable. I remember watching Tomi's first bath at the Swain house. Three ladies—Molly, Isabelle, and Molly's best friend, Amelia Habib—all hovering over the baby on the bassinet they had placed on the sink and taking turns trying to bathe that eight pounds of flesh. But Tomi held them at bay, and the ladies were so afraid of so many things happening that never did—"are we hurting her, is the water too hot?"—and so on. There was so much jabbering and fussing, but somehow Tomi survived and probably thought, "I sure hope they get better at this job."

I have always had a deep appreciation for the home folks who rallied around for their children and loved ones during such times of crises, and I've thanked God for the care and help for the families of those who were in the service during the war. So many of us were so fortunate our parents willingly sacrificed for their children and took them in and supported them. The pay in the Army was certainly not enough to keep a family going. The most I could send home was about $30 month for the first few months. As I was promoted, the money was a bit more but really not much more.

The December date for me to report soon came. At 4:00 a.m. on December 7, 1942, the first anniversary of the Pearl Harbor attack, I woke up when the alarm went off. Molly got up also, as did Henry and Mother Swain. It was tough on all of us. I sure didn't want to show tears. I felt I must be strong and show my manliness and not give them cause to break down. I gave our baby a kiss, hugged Isabelle, shook hands with Henry, and then held my darling close, kissed her, told her I loved her, and went out the door. I admit that I had a flow of tears as I walked to A and 5th Streets. There next to the Bank of A. Levy building was an abandoned store, which was our assembly point. The bus that was to carry the draftees to San Pedro was idling in front of the building. Inside the building were the forty draftees with their families, the Draft Board, a reporter from the newspaper, friends, and a few onlookers. Coffee and doughnuts were available and served by Red Cross people. I had a cup of coffee, talked with some people, and met some of the men being called up along with me. I was called to the table where Mrs. Brown and "Hap" Maxwell and others on the Draft Board were standing. Mrs. Brown handed me a list of the draftees and told me I was the acting Corporal and responsible for the group. So when the time came I called out the names on the list and the group entered the bus as their names were called. We all were relieved to get away from the people. They were dear, friendly people but were making it difficult for us to remain dry-eyed.

The ride to San Pedro took about two and a half hours. There wasn't much conversation among the group as most of us were wondering about what would happen, where we would be assigned, what branch of service, whether they would recognize our desires and skills, and about our families. I was worried about my folks too. Dad, a diabetic, had just had his leg removed. There were no males in the family left in Hueneme to drive my folks to needed places. But deep down I knew things would work out.

FORT MACARTHUR

When the bus pulled into Fort MacArthur, the San Pedro Army base, we were met by two acting sergeants. I debarked, gave the roster to one of the acting sergeants, and it was then I made my first discovery—I was a nobody. My first "promotion" to corporal (temporary) had only lasted a little over two hours. They started to yell at us even before we got off the bus. They had only one way to talk and that was with a loud scream. Any kind of error on our part, we were threatened, would be the cause for a court martial. Hell, none of us knew what they were talking about.

We were taken to a nearby barracks and each of us was assigned a bunk—a double-decker for two of us. The other soldier and I flipped a coin and I lost, so the lower bunk was mine. We were then herded to another building to get our supplies which would convert us from being a civilian to being an Army soldier. There we got our clothes issued. They say "issue" but that was a laugh. The real name should be what is "thrown at" you. First we got a duffel bag, into which we put the rest of the stuff as it came at us, after some guy looked at us and yelled out a size and the men behind a counter grabbed items from shelves and threw them at us: shoes (2 pair), fatigues, blouse, pants, socks, mess kit, utensils, underwear (brown), and so on. At the shoe counter they had me put my feet in a foot measurer. When I stepped on it, the soldier yelled out, "11C." I told him I had never worn anything larger than a 9B. That made no difference. He replied, "That's it soldier, you'll grow into them. Next man." After receiving the clothes and stuff, we were taken back to our barracks. There we took off our civvies and put on our uniforms. We were told we could either ship our clothes home or give them to a charity outfit. Before coming I had heard what to expect and had worn old clothes, so I flung mine on the pile for charity. I sure didn't want Molly to have to unpack the old clothes and give her another chance to cry.

We were next marched to another large building. There we were told to take off our shirts and form a long line. We moved along slowly, and the horror stories started about the pending shots. To hear some of them, anyone who got through the series was really a man, that many fainted when they got them. As each man entered the door, he was suddenly attacked, a man on each side hit you in each arm. A couple of guys did faint, but I'll never forget the sadistic look on the faces of the needle pushers. When we were finished we waited outside with all of us rubbing our arms. I think the only one that bothered me was the tetanus shot.

We were then herded into a large hall. We were given a short briefing and then a quick physical, namely a "short arm" inspection. A short arm inspection is nothing more than a medical officer sitting in a chair looking at each man's penis, to check for any venereal disease, as the man walked by. Short arm inspections were done regularly—about once a month—as long as a man was in the Army. (Later in my career one of the men instead of taking his penis out of his pants, stuck one of his fingers through the fly of his shorts. The inspector didn't crack a smile when the man passed. He looked up and said, "Your penis needs a manicure.")

After that sequence, I just sat on my bunk and thought about all that had happened to me during the day so far. I was already homesick, and for the first time it dawned on me that I was not going home that night and for many more to come. About that time and after a few minutes of rest, the "commanding officer" (another corporal) came in and told us that anyone who lived in the area could go home for the night. No one took him up on the offer. Here we were at a camp, ten miles from nowhere, so how could anyone get home and back? Some of us, though, after being dressed in our new uniforms, decided to walk to the Post Exchange. When we got there the stock was depleted except for some dry cookies. So we each bought a box and went back to the barracks.

Night came and we went to bed. Sleep came easy to most of us. I listened to the various noises others were making while sleeping—moaners, gaspers, talkers, whistlers, and so on. Tired as I was, it didn't take me long to fall asleep.

At the end of the day I was Private Moranda, serial number 39548092.

Morning came too soon, awakened in the Army manner with the bugle call Reveille. The routine now started and remained so throughout my career in the Army. Get up, walk to the latrine, and do your ablutions. Every barracks had a latrine equipped with a line of toilets and a line of wash basins—no walls or partitions. You just sat on the throne and the world could see you strain in getting relief. It didn't take long though to get used to the audience as you sat down to play. Then you went back to your bunk where you dressed in your new outfit. The next job was to make your bunk in the military manner—as they said "high and tight, like Saturday night." It took me quite awhile to do the job correctly the first time. One of the men who had been there a day longer than I came by and showed me the correct way to get the blankets on so tight that when the inspector came by and threw a quarter on the top blanket, it would bounce.

When the bugle sounded, we went through the routine and then were called out by the same loud-mouthed corporal. We lined up in formation, did a RIGHT FACE and a FORWARD MARCH, and we were off. About ten yards later we heard the command DOUBLE TIME MARCH. The leading men had never done double time, so they just started to run. The men in the rear were soon really sprinting. By the time we reached where we were going everything was really messed up.

The first two ranks were in formation but the last ranks were scattered to hell and breakfast. We sure didn't look like any Army formation that I had seen in the movies or newsreels. We had arrived at a building with a large room with desks, which we entered and the people in charge started our testing. First the Aptitude Test and then other tests, including an I.Q. type, to see what we were capable of doing and how smart we were. They didn't tell us the results, but I guess I passed. One of the tests was on communications—to determine whether we could understand the difference between a dot and a dash coming in over a wire or radio. I knew the Morse code, as, over the years, Dad used to practice at home using whatever was around—a knife, fork, spoon, or pencil. Dad had, during his early days with the Southern Pacific Railroad, been a telegrapher before he became a station agent. The tests took all morning and a part of the afternoon. Then back to the barracks for what we thought would be a rest. No way! Part of the men were sent out to "police" the area around the camp, and others were given similar busy work duties. Three of us were taken to the mess hall to do KP. I was assigned to vegetables. As I was cleaning them, the Mess Sergeant came and watched me work. He said, "You have done that before. How would you like to join the mess crew?" At that time I was not against the idea, but I was never given the chance. And that was the only time that I worked in an Army mess.

The next day we were herded to a large room with desks and chairs. Behind them sat soldiers conducting interviews. My interviewer was a young man from Oxnard, Corporal Herb Wasserman. His father I knew well, as he was the manager of the Oxnard Savings and Loan, the firm that held the mortgage on my parent's house in Port Hueneme. My first reaction was great—someone will listen and help. It was a bad thought. He asked my background. I told him my occupation of working for Standard Stations, Inc., and one of my main jobs was the maintenance and care of automobiles and trucks. I had also worked for the Railway Express and was aware of waybills and schedules of railroads, which was my reason for my volunteering for the Quartermaster Corp or the Transportation Corp as my choice when I applied for the Volunteer Officer Corp. Wasserman listened. Nothing was done. He listened but that was all he could do. My fate had already been decided before I arrived at the camp. As we went back to the barracks, rumors started about places we would be sent. One rumor we heard even went so far as to say that we would be sent to England directly and be trained there as replacements for the European operations.

So much for the Army classification system. I don't think it would have made any difference whether I was a mensa or a dull ignoramus, or whether I had been a plumber, lawyer, or field hand. The Army apparently needed infantrymen at that time, and the orders came at about 3:00 p.m. the next day. I recalled when Brother George was drafted immediately after graduating from Fresno State College with a degree in political science, he was sent to Camp Leonard Wood for training with the Corps of Engineers! All the people drafted with me had orders for various places but none knew where at the time. We had two hours to be ready to move out, so we packed our duffel bags and sat on them waiting. At five o'clock they called us out and we were marched to a waiting train. It was then I got my first sack lunch—two dry sandwiches, one cheese and the other jam.

TRAINING IN TEXAS

Everything was Top Secret in those days when it came to movement of troops. We all wondered where we were going as we loaded aboard the passenger cars. But no one knew except the officers of our group and the crew of the train. Because of my background of being raised with a railroader father, I knew a lot of rail people, so I looked for an old acquaintance but found none. As we went along, we found out we were going to Texas to a brand new training facility near Fort Worth named Camp Howze. The next day I learned that I had orders assigning me to the 84th Infantry Division, which was just being formed.

We were in Pullman cars, but it wasn't that great. I had to sleep with a total stranger. It seems the Army, to conserve space, assigned three men to a section—two for the lower berth and one in the upper. My bunk mate was a man named Morph from Los Angeles. He was a real nice guy and was honored by being named commander of our car. He didn't know what that job entailed and never did find out. We all figured he would soon become a non-com, but as far as I know he never was more than a private in his whole career. But for the moment he was "King."

We were proud as we were going through towns and people waved at us with friendly hellos. We stood a bit taller and waved as heroes really should. We tried to look like soldiers, but I know the people weren't fooled, they were just being patriotic and friendly. It was a long ride but finally we came to Kansas City where we detrained for a short time. They fed us a hot meal—not good, but we ate it gladly. We weren't allowed to leave the station proper, but I did roam around a bit. There was a group of townspeople in the station serving coffee and doughnuts. It was a labor of love for them and they came out and met every train that passed through. We had some wonderful people in our country.

We were loaded again on the train, this time with a different crew, and headed south through Oklahoma and into Texas. We pulled into a siding near a small town called Gainesville near the Oklahoma border. I overheard someone say Camp Howze—the name of the place we were headed for our training. The Army must have a sadistic General whose only job is to fly over the United States to find enough space in the most unlivable location and report to Washington, D.C., that he has found a spot that has no other use and is a miserable place in which to live. He then recommends that this would be a great place to train our soldiers. And for that he gets another ribbon or medal to wear on his uniform. That had to be true, for Camp Howze fits the description. The weather was terrible, and if you didn't like it, it would change for the worse in a minute.

We debarked in front of the camp and were met at the railroad siding by a group of officers. On a nearby level spot, tables had been set up and the officers interviewed each man. Again I was hopeful. These were officers and non-commissioned officers who were the cadre for the new division. As we approached the tables we were instructed to salute, state our name, rank, and serial number. We were questioned about our civilian backgrounds. I gave them the spiel about my job with Standard Stations—maintenance and care of vehicles. The officer said, "Great, we have need for people like you who know how to service vehicles. We have a great many vehicles of all types in this division. I am sure you will be assigned to a job that the Army can take advantage of your background." I was then assigned to the 333rd Infantry Regiment.

At my next stop, via truck, I was again interviewed by people in the 333rd Infantry Regiment and I repeated my background story. The reply I got again was, "Good, we have a need, we have many trucks and no one knows how to service them. We sure need you."

The next stop, again by truck, was to the 3rd Battalion, 333rd Infantry Regiment, where I was greeted by the new battalion commander. He helped conduct the interview with the same questions. "My name is Colonel Barrett, welcome to the 3rd Battalion. What did you do in civilian life?" Again I told my story and this time I was assured by the Lieutenant Colonel that his outfit really needed men with my training, "Great, we need you in our motor pool." I told myself, maybe this time they listened. I was then marched with a group led by an old soldier, Sergeant Hand. He announced: "I am the First Sergeant of Company M of the 3rd Battalion of the 333rd Infantry Regiment, of the 84th Infantry Division. I will now take you to meet your new Company Commander, Captain DeFriend." He called us to attention and marched us to our new company area. There I was interviewed by Captain DeFriend. "Now Moranda, what did you do in civilian life?" I repeated my background and interests, to which he replied, "Good we need you, we have twenty-four vehicles and no one who knows anything about vehicles and we don't even have a sergeant who is capable of handling a motor pool." I never rode in, much less serviced, one of those vehicles nor did I ever have the opportunity to ride in one of the twenty-four jeeps. And throughout my Army career, I never served in anything involving the servicing of vehicles.

The first few days we really did not do much except police the area and do some physical training. I had plenty of time to write home and tell the folks all about the new world that I was in. It was interesting, but I was homesick and I was not alone as most of the men were in the same predicament. And misery loves company.

We were issued our rifles, mine was #18367, and bedding—which consisted of a mattress cover and two blankets—and other necessities. One new item that we were given was a pair of leggings. These were heavy canvas leg coverings that were something like spats except they went higher up the leg. They were worn over the shoes and had to be laced up, using the hooks on the outside of the leggings. I remember the first time that we were to assemble when we were going to have to wear them and I figured it was easier to lace them on the inside. I looked around at the other men and saw they were as confused as I and none of them knew how to wear them. I took the easiest way and laced them up on the inside. When the first call whistle blew I got up and started to run toward the front door. The hooks caught and I went down on my face. Several others did too. The old First Sergeant got his laugh and then showed us how we were to accomplish their lacing. Honestly, I think that the training cadre knew that some of us would lace them the wrong way and wanted to have a good laugh, for the officers and NCOs were all there to see the falling soldiers.

That problem didn't last very long, for in a couple of weeks each man was issued two new combat boots to replace the shoes and leggings. When we received them it had been raining, so our sergeant told us to put them on and to go outside and stand in a puddle of water and get them thoroughly soaked, then leave them on and let them dry on our feet. That way the boots would be broken in and would never give a person any trouble wearing them. It really worked for me as I never had a blister or any problems with my shoes all the time I wore them.

We were assigned our barracks. This time we had single beds. For the first couple of days we were kept busy policing the area and doing a few exercises. On day two the First Sergeant called us out and said we looked like we were in poor shape and he was going to remedy that. He said, "Now you men will follow me and we will jog until you all fall out from exhaustion. Now here I am an old man going to show you how out of shape you are." He was going to show us up and he did. That man could jog forever. He just kept going and going. One by one the draftees fell out. Soon there were only a couple of us left so he called it off and he wasn't even breathing hard. I lasted but I was really beat.

On the first day with M Company, we were called into our first formation. Our First Sergeant called out our names. Captain Defriend talked about what was expected of us. Sergeant Hand then called out our assignments in the new platoons. I was sent to the .30 caliber Heavy Machine Gun platoon as acting Corporal in a Sergeant's position. Our Platoon Sergeant was Clary Mercer, a tall southern man. Our platoon commander was Lieutenant Babb.

When we were in our new platoon, Lieutenant Babb gave us his message. Our platoon would be the best. No one would ever fall out on a march unless he fell on his chin. No one would ever just say he was so tired he couldn't march. I immediately took a liking to Lieutenant Babb—he was young, good looking, had a dark complexion, curly hair, and stood 6 foot tall with a good build. He was going to be a good man, I thought.

Lieutenant Babb then called, "Moranda."

"Yes sir," I answered loudly.

"Step forward."

That I did, then he asked, "Ever do any drilling or marching?"

"No sir, but when my brother came home on leave from his basic training he called out four of his brothers and gave us a few minutes of drilling. We were armed only with a stick, two brooms, and a yard stick. We weren't very good but we did do the command FALL OUT very well, but did have a few minutes of practicing close order. And I did march in the school band."

He smiled and said: "Come out and see what you can do in drilling the platoon."

I moved to the command position and called the platoon to attention. I did that really in a professional manner. I got the unit to turn by issuing the order RIGHT FACE. Then with the command FORWARD

MARCH we moved along the company street in a fine fashion. Before long I must have given the next command on the wrong foot because things got a bit mixed up. I got them halted. The CO then took over and restored the ranks by giving the proper commands. He dismissed me, but my performance must have put me in his good graces because I was soon made an Acting Sergeant—I never did serve as a private (except at the pay table). I admit I sure didn't know what I was doing, but the men understood me and I always had good relations with them.

I must admit that my being in a sergeant's position was putting someone in charge who didn't know his job or what being a leader of a section of heavy machine guns meant. Hell, the only guns that I had ever fired were an air rifle and once a shotgun. I was lost in that leadership spot for a time, but proved to be a quick learner and the men didn't seem to mind my lack of knowledge. The first few days we didn't do much except get acquainted with our fellow soldiers. Every day a few more came in. As they were assigned, we early birds gave them the dope on what we had been doing and really questioned them about their backgrounds and about where they came from. To keep us busy we were given a lot of make-work jobs. That's when we learned the Army term A & E—ass holes and elbows. When they called for us to go out and do A & E work, we knew it meant we were to walk the area and pick up anything lying around: paper, cigarette butts, and other things. We soon learned to "field strip" our cigarettes—splitting the butts, dropping the remaining tobacco on the ground, and rolling the paper into a small ball before throwing it away.

Our platoon sergeant was part of the cadre that came from Georgia. All the enlisted men of the cadre came from the same Division, and most spoke with a drawl. Many were regular army people. Coming from California, it took some time before I could understand such as: "You peeple, I am goin to make it hoard for you. We are goin to march a couple of moles and then y'all will fol out and some of you will go on gord. Tonight when you go to the winda y'all will see the CO inspecting the area so make shore your raffle is clean and roddy for inspecshun. So make me prod of y'all."

The Platoon Leader's name was Lieutenant Babb, a fine looking officer with good leadership quality about him. In his first speech to us, he stood in front of our platoon and said in a quiet but authoritative manner what he stood for and how we would become the finest machine gun platoon in the Division. No one was ever to fall out on a march—if he did he had better fall on his chin and be out of it because that's the only excuse he would tolerate. In the months that passed, we never lost a man on a march even though we had to carry heavy machine guns with us on most of the marches. But one hot, hot, muggy day when we were on a fifteen mile march, Lt. Babb fell out—fell on his chin. He had followed his own orders.

The Platoon Sergeant, Clary Mercer, was a quiet man. He never asked a man to do something that he hadn't done. He wasn't loud, but he got the job done. He walked with a lope, one short step and his next step long. But, man oh man, he could walk forever. When we came in from an all-day march, he would shower, dress and take off for town, drink a bit, and come back in the early hours of the morning, go to bed, catch a couple hours sleep, and rise at reveille with the rest of us ready for the day, and it never seemed to bother him.

The other two platoon leaders were two 2nd Lieutenants fresh out of officers school. The other machine gun platoon was commanded by 2nd Lieutenant Brown, a big, good-looking young man. He was very quiet, but he was a good officer and seemed a capable, dedicated man who carried himself well. He was steadfast in his ways and his men seemed very happy with him as their boss. The Mortar Platoon Leader was 2nd Lieutenant Zavala. He was full of fun with a great sense of humor, a bit overweight, but carried himself well. The other lieutenants seemed to enjoy picking on him a bit, but the others never got him to change his way of life. His men all seemed to be happy with him too. The Executive Officer for the company was 1st Lieutenant Burns. He stayed with the unit throughout the training period and took over the company when our first commanding officer was promoted to major and was reassigned.

The men in my section were from all parts of the country: Byrd, a man of about thirty from South Carolina, was the gunner of one machine gun; Ashworth, surely an Irishman, was an ammunition bearer; Salee, a young man from Kentucky, was assistant gunner and someone I would have liked to have as a life-long friend; Emiterio, a full blooded Indian and Ashworth's drinking buddy, also an ammo bearer; Oberholster, a young man from Philadelphia, bunked with me when out in the field in tents; and old Bill Marshall, right out of the hills of Arkansas, and quite a character.

Bill always tried to look out for me. I think he was pleased that I placed him in a bunk near the front door and the pot-bellied stove. He took over the chore of making the fire every morning, and those Texas mornings were really cold. He always had a chaw of "tobaccer" in his mouth. At one of the first formations Bill was standing at attention. The Captain stopped and asked Bill, "Marshall, do you have a chew of tobacco in your mouth?"

"Yassuh."

"Do you always have a chew in your mouth?"

"Yassuh."

"Even at night?"

"Yassuh, even when I go to sleep, I go to sleep with a chaw in my mouth."

With that, the CO took his spot in front of the company and made the announcement: "Private Bill Marshall is the only man who can have a chew of tobacco at all times. None of the rest of you will have the same privilege."

Bill had a very limited education. He noticed that I wrote to Molly and the family almost every day. He tried to write a couple of times but it was clear he was having trouble and it was a real chore. After we had been together about a month, he came to me one day and asked if I would write to his folks for him. I agreed and got out some writing paper and asked him what he wanted to say. He replied to just tell them what we do and that I am fine. So I wrote them a long letter in my best penmanship. Bill thanked me and mailed it off to his folks in Mountain View, Arkansas. About a month went by and Bill got a reply to his letter in which the message was, "Dear Bill. Thanx fer the letter that you had rote. That feller can really rite reel good. Don have him rite no more. We had to take it to town to have someone read the letter to usun." So my job as a public stenographer was over—but Bill and I were still friends.

The company spanned the ethnic spectrum. We had northerners, southerners, easterners, and westerners. We had a prince and Jake the Fink, college graduates, and the almost illiterate. We had Italians, Prussians, Mexicans, American Indians, Irishmen, and a group of "Duke mixtures." But there were no Blacks and I wondered why.

We also had in our barracks Rod Munday, a well-known golf pro. I knew that he wouldn't serve long with us, for too many of the officers knew of him. They even gave him time off to play a tournament being held in Texas. He left our company right after we completed basic training.

And then there was Jake the Fink. He advised a couple of his bunk mates he would soon be out of the Army. He claimed he could not use his right arm, and kept his hand in his pocket all the time. If someone forced him to take his hand out, he would let his arm and hand just dangle by his side. When he was told to pick something up, it was quite a show. He was about ready to be discharged when one day, while the rest of the platoon was out, he was left in camp as barracks guard. After we had been gone for a short while, the CO and the 1st Sergeant went into the barracks and found Jake making up his bunk with his bad arm. He was right—he didn't stay long in our outfit.

One of the best guys in our unit was a young man from Utah by the name of Udall. He was groomed to be an officer from the time he came in, and he left right after basic training for Officer Training School and got his commission as an officer. After he graduated he was assigned to a training unit in Texas. While he was giving his first lecture to his troops, a bolt of lightning struck and killed him.

Others in the outfit were Botto from San Francisco, Dave MDvani who claimed to be a Georgian Prince from Russia and that his family was related by marriage to Barbara Hutton the Woolworth heiress, and Esteridge, a sharp young man who had been made an acting non-com. Frank Ledesma was a street smart Mexican lad from Los Angeles. He was small and wiry, unafraid of others, and always had stories to tell of his exploits while growing up in L.A. He became our barber. When the supply sergeant found out he could cut hair he gave him clippers and equipment for haircuts and he kept us shorn.

One day when the company had been on a long march with full field packs, and it was a hot day not very conducive to marching, Ledesma was bitching about the weather and the Army, and claimed he was tired and couldn't finish the march. It was customary in our company that, as we neared camp, we would halt and take a ten minute break, spruce up, and go in looking pretty good. Our Colonel and his staff always were in front of his office to review the troops as they passed. So when Lt. Babb halted us and told us to "Take Ten," we could see the camp hospital about 500 yards away. Frank was really bitching by then, claiming he could never make it the rest of the way. We had our packs on, so Frank sank heavily to the ground. He sat there beefing and moaning and after a couple of minutes he jumped up with his pack still on his back yelling that he had been stung by a scorpion. He took off running toward the hospital and didn't slow down until he charged into it for treatment. Lt. Babb watched the fleeing soldier as he reached the hospital, then turned to us and said, "See, I told you that a person can go farther than he thinks."

Hugh West was my best friend in the 84th Division. He was from Richmond, Virginia. We had been inducted into the Army on the same day. We made Private First Class on the same day, Corporals and Sergeants on the same day, were interviewed for Officer Candidate School and became Second Lieutenants on the same day. When we graduated, we were assigned to different outfits. I missed the guy. Six months later, when I reported to Fort Dix, New Jersey, there sitting in the office waiting to go overseas with me was Hugh West—and we went aboard the same troop transport and spent time together in England, after which we went different ways and never saw each other again. We did exchange Christmas cards for a few years, but how sad that we didn't make a better effort to keep in touch, for we were so close.

While in the service, like most others, I really did look forward to news from home. Molly was very good about writing. Sister Maye was sure to write at least every two weeks. Mom had a lot of letters to write to all her children away from home and she too did a good job. All of us were worried about Dad, so she did keep us posted of the news of the town and family. Mom was the hub of the wheel. To name the spokes of the wheel, Earle was in the Army and stationed in Texas going through basic training, Maye was in nurses training in Los Angeles becoming an Army Nurse, Bill (Walter) was in Hawaii in the Marines, George was a Lieutenant in the Corps of Engineers, Paul was going to school to become a Naval officer, and Theodore was in the Air Transport Command learning to be a radio operator for the C 47s the Army Air Corps delivered all over the world.

Our training had been tough. We went from early morning until late at night. That training molded us into a unit from untrained, raw civilians. I feel that our unit was better trained than any that I came across later in my service. The first six weeks were essentially for the individual, to get each one in shape mentally and physically and to learn his weapon. I can still remember my rifle serial number—I carried it, slept with it, and cleaned it every day but Sunday. It was an

M1. I had never handled a gun before, but my M1 was really a cared-for weapon. I always thought the weapon originally issued to a soldier should stay with him throughout his career, but it wasn't to be. I wasn't fortunate enough to go overseas with a unit, but I learned later that when the division left for the European Theater of Operations the men were all issued new rifles. Before getting the rifles, we were initially taught the .22 calibre. On the short range my grouping of shots on the target was good. Then with the M1 and carbine I made Expert on the regular range. When the CO saw my results, he asked me to "zero in" all the rifles in the company. I did, but at the end of the day my arm was really sore.

Two of my men were the best of buddies: Ashworth, the Irishman, and Emeterio, the American Indian. Every Sunday they would head for the PX and see if they could drink all the beer in the place. At times they did get enough down to get a good buzz on—and I'm sure they must have spiked it. On one of the Sundays I was sitting on my bunk with my writing material, putting together a letter to Molly, when I heard a lot of swearing and noise coming from the front end of our barracks. I looked up and there was Ashworth running as fast as he could and Emeterio yelling as he chased Ashworth: "I'm going to kill you, you dirty Irish bastard." Ashworth ran out of the other end of the barracks. As Emeterio approached my bunk, I saw he was swinging an entrenching tool and looked as though he was going to scalp Ashworth. So I tackled him and took the tool away from him. Both men were drunk. Emeterio calmed down and I got the story. It seemed that they had gotten into a serious argument and were kicked out of the PX. The argument continued as they were coming back to the barracks and along the way Ashworth called Emeterio a drunken S.O.B of an Indian. Emeterio got hold of an entrenching tool and took out after him. Things calmed down, and I had Ashworth assigned to an adjacent barracks. It wasn't long before the two drinking buddies were back at the PX guzzling beer again, but it's a good bet the Irishman never again called the Indian a term of disrespect.

One hot day we were on a fifteen mile march when the cheeks of my "arse" became chaffed from too much rubbing together as I walked. It was almost impossible to continue the march. When it was almost unbearable, I remembered a pair of socks I always carried with me in the arm pits of the sleeves of my jacket. At the first break I took one of the socks and folded it and put it between my cheeks, and that saved the day as I didn't want to fall out. In my next letter home I told of the experience, and that I now knew how women felt wearing kotex. The next letter from Sister Maye told me to wear one for a week and then I'd really get the feeling. I got the message.

In February I received a letter from Molly saying that she had received a large check from Standard Stations, Inc. That really helped as I was unable to send any money to her, except the allowance. It was a fine gesture by my old company. Others in the outfit were also in financial straits.

Another of our field marches, this time for twenty miles, was supposed to be a tactical march. We carried our weapons and full field packs. When we arrived at our objective we halted and dug our foxholes. As we started to pitch our tents, we were attacked by the Aggressor Forces (our troops in enemy uniforms) firing blank cartridges and dummy hand grenades. After much yelling and confusion and pretending to fire our weapons, the problem was called off. We had passed the test, I guessed. We then were fed and slept the night. The next day we returned to camp. When we got to the barracks we flopped on our bunks, as we were tired from the march back. Suddenly the front door opened and in came one of the aggressors still dressed in his enemy uniform. He came in to have some fun with his best buddy. He raised his rifle that was still loaded with a blank cartridge and fired. His friend fell over. We all rushed over to see what had happened. The fallen guy was dead—the blank shell had a wadding in it that kept the powder inside the cartridge. The wadding had pierced his friend's heart. There was a hearing. I testified what I observed, as did others. The judgment was that it was accidental. The GI had not been informed about the wadding and the danger of firing at close range. The lad was transferred to another unit and we never saw him again. I really felt sorry for the guy as well as the victim.

Basic training of six weeks was about to come to an end and we became eligible for weekend passes. I was proud of my unit. We had progressed to a point where the men were feeling they were at their best. They wouldn't back down to any other unit. I guess the maddest that I ever remember getting was the time we had to loan our two machine guns to K Company. They were running a tactical problem and needed machine guns to provide some overhead firing. We really didn't want to loan the guns, and I so advised the Company Commander. He said we had to follow the order. Our guns were absolutely spotless. The men in my outfit cleaned and polished them every day. Well, we loaned the guns to K company. It happened. It rained, and K Company left our guns out in the rain overnight. Hell, it wasn't theirs so why should they worry? They returned the weapons to our supply room and not to us. When my men saw the condition of the weapons, they were ready to have a brawl with K company. I felt the blame belonged to the officers in charge not the men.

It was Friday afternoon and soon the Company Commander and the First Sergeant would be making their weekly inspection. They wanted to see if we could be given weekend passes. We worked on our machine guns all afternoon. The rust had become embedded in the metal and was not coming off. The CO came in, looked at the machine guns, scowled, and said to me, "Your outfit will be confined to camp until your weapons can pass the inspection." I told the CO what had happened, but that is not the way the Army works. So we polished for over an hour. I could see the rust was deeply embedded into the metal, and there was no way were we ever going to get the guns ready for inspection unless we took some different action. I told the First Sergeant what I was going to do. He smiled and said, "You're learning."

So to the supply room I went, obtained a small can of army green paint, went back to the barracks, and within an hour we were again ready for inspection. The captain came in and again looked at the weapons. With a smile on his face, he turned to the First Sergeant and said we passed. He knew what we had done and also knew it was the only way we were going to fix the problem, so it would pass. The sad part is we were never able to get the weapons back to the prime condition they were before we loaned them out.

Unit Training

After basic training, we went into unit training where we learned how our platoon fit together with the rest of the company, battalion, and regiment. The triangular infantry division that fought the war was comprised of three infantry regiments: division artillery of three 105mm howitzer battalions with twelve tubes (designed for each one to support an infantry regiment) and one 155mm howitzer battalion with twelve tubes to give general fire support, an engineer battalion, a cavalry reconnaissance troop, and division service troops—with a strength of 14,043 men. Each infantry regiment was, in turn, made up of three infantry battalions and a headquarters and service company. The battalions each had three companies, each with three platoons made up of three squads, plus a weapons and a mortar platoon. The weapons platoon is a direct support unit to provide additional and protective fire for the rifle platoons.

When basic training was over, we seemed to have more time on weekends. So, Hugh West and I got a pass and headed for Fort Worth, about 40 miles from Gainesville. I didn't have much spare cash so we tried our luck at hitchhiking. We were almost instantly successful and were picked up by an elderly couple who just happened to be going to Fort Worth. When we got out of the car, we walked to the main part of the town, looked around, went to the USO, and at evening time decided to look for a room. We went to a downtown hotel, registered, and as there wasn't much of a lobby—just a couple of chairs, a table, and an old lamp, we went up to our room. It had two beds and an overhead light dangling from the ceiling. The bath was down the hall. We each flopped on our bed. Soon there came a knock on the door, and Hugh opened it and two women in flimsy outfits that revealed about everything they had, which wasn't very attractive, walked in. They then asked if we wanted to "play around." I replied, "What do you mean? Bridge? Hearts? Or what do you have in mind?" They then approached each of us, and we told them in no uncertain terms that they should get their fannies out of there. Hugh said he guessed we should have expected such in a hotel with the name "The Roan Hotel." They were unquestionably a couple of the most unattractive women I've ever seen and met the criteria of the Lee sisters—Ugh and Gast.

The next day we got up and went to a nearby café for breakfast, and after visiting for an hour or so, Hugh said, "There is a church, the same as mine at home. I think I'll go." He did, so I went back to the highway and thumbed a ride back to camp. Later when Hugh got back he said that after the service he had been invited by an elderly couple to their home for dinner. He teased me because I had missed a delicious home cooked meal. And I had the usual Sunday night meal at the mess hall—cold cuts.

One night when we were on a overnight exercise, we set up our tents and were ready for chow. As it was a tactical problem, we had to wait for nightfall. That night was cloudy and dark and it was hard to find our way around the area. One of my men got lost so we all had to look around for him without making any loud noise or talking. We finally found the man, and after chow we bunked down. Soon we were awakened and told to move out. Rolling up the tents and getting all our equipment together was a problem, but we finally made it. The exercise was our first large field maneuver as part of the entire 333rd Infantry Regiment. We were supposed to provide support for a rifle company. I found out how difficult, if not impossible, it is to control men at night.

We had radio contact but that was not enough. It was a good lesson, for I knew it would be worse in combat. From that day on I took extra precautions when trying to move about in the dark.

Early the next day the problem continued. My section was assigned to guard the battalion headquarters. After I placed my two squads in position, I moved a bit closer to the Battalion Commander. The Lt. Col. was trying to run his companies from his position on a hill and was trying to use a "Walkie Talkie." He seemed to think that the louder he talked into the radio, the more information he would receive. During one sequence he was yelling into the set: "S3 [Battalion Operations Officer], come in! What is your position?"

"Right behind you, sir."

"Give me your position again."

"Right behind you, sir."

"Where? What are your coordinates?"

"I am standing right behind you." With that he reached out and touched the CO.

The Colonel turned and continued talking to the S3 over the radio. It was a strange scene, giving orders over the radio to a man standing a few feet from him. The S3 shrugged his shoulders, said, "Yes, sir," and left to follow out the instructions he had received.

(I wondered then how that battalion commander would do in combat. Later, after the war, I learned from friends that there was still confusion with the same people when the 84th went into action in Holland and Germany. A lot of the officers above the rank of major were commissioned through the ROTC system, or came up from enlisted ranks of the regular army, or were regulars who were just trying to stay in long enough to get pensions; they were inexperienced at commanding troops and were not equal to the weight they tried to throw around. But for all the bad, there were enough good ones for, after all, the American Army was essentially a civilian army that did win over one of the greatest armies ever assembled.)

I remember one day when the temperature was about twenty-seven degrees, a horrible one to be doing anything but resting in the barracks. Thankfully, before I fell out in the morning I had put fatigues over my ODs. I was warm in my body, but my hands, feet, and face were cold. The training mission that day was to lead my machine gun section on a drill learning how to creep and crawl dragging the machine guns along with our weapons and ammunition boxes. We were supposed to stay along the ground at all times and keep below the horizon so the "enemy" couldn't see us. That exercise was the toughest that I ever had to do. We made it to the spot where we set up the machine guns while remaining in the prone position—doing everything without standing or kneeling. We couldn't raise our heads except to fire either our rifles or the machine guns. It was a good lesson on the limitation of maneuverability with those heavy guns, but a miserable day otherwise.

Molly found out about the weekend passes and asked if she could come and visit me at Gainesville. Gainesville was not a place for a young lady. I said no, but that I would contact my dear Aunt Annie Forney Newton and see if Molly could stay with her in Little Rock, Arkansas. Annie Forney said of course. So Molly took the train to Little Rock. I arranged for a three day pass and went to Fort Worth and took the train, "The Rocket," to Little Rock.

How wonderful it was to see Molly. We spent two days together with Annie Forney. She arranged for us to meet our cousins, Alice and Anale, and took us around to meet our future sister-in-law, Nancy Dowell. What a beautiful girl. The only problem with the weekend was that Molly had an attack of the asthma. Nothing any one could do for her except to watch her suffer. Annie Forney found a Christian Science Practitioner and drove us there. Molly stayed in with the practitioner for some time. When she came out she was breathing much better. Excitement always seemed to bring on the attacks.

While I was visiting in Little Rock, I got a history lesson from our Aunt Annie Forney. I was relating that in our barracks about half of the soldiers were from the South and the rest from the North with a few from California. I was laughing how I would sit on my bunk at night and get the group going about the Civil War. I said that after they got arguing and fussing with each other I would lay back on my bunk and laugh at them. It was then Annie Forney told me we had relatives who fought on the side of the South during the war.

During the last night we stayed close together holding each other. We spent most of the night just talking. She told me of her fears and how she was making it, living with the Swains and Mother Moranda. She enjoyed staying with them, and our daughter was doing well. She gave me news of our families and friends. Letters are fine but talking is the better way to learn about all the fears and things that were on our minds. The next day we were driven to the railroad station and I departed. As I pulled out of the station I saw the tears in Molly's eyes. With Molly was Annie Forney and Nancy. They all waved. And with tears in my eyes I waved back.

Molly stayed another day in Little Rock. She was wined and dined by our relatives and Nancy and her folks, the Albert Dowells. Molly took the train home without any problems. She said she had a good seat all the way.

It was not long after that trip I was again invited to come to Little Rock. There was to be a wedding, and I was invited to be the Best Man for my brother George. Nancy Dowell had said yes, and she and George were to marry. I really wanted to go back but it was not possible. I asked the CO if I could again have a few days off and the answer came back with a resounding NO! The reason given was that we were in the middle of the tests for the company and they didn't want anyone to be gone at that time. I was saddened, but there wasn't much I could do about it. George forgave me when I called him to advise him. He understood.

During this unit training the squads and platoons were taken to the field and given simulated problems. I was leading my section on a problem one day, and my outfit was in support of a rifle company. We set up our machine guns to be able to provide the support. After a time I was to go ahead to reconnoiter the place where the rifle company had moved forward. Then I was to bring up my men to place them in a new position to provide support in the new location so we could continue with the problem. All went well—the timing was good and the positions I selected were perfect. Watching the exercise were officers who were the judges checking on how well we did the job. After we had finished the problem I heard, "Sergeant, what's your name?" I stood and reported to a full bird Colonel.

"Sergeant Moranda, sir."

"Good job. You are going to go to Officers Training School."

Not do you want to go to OCS. It was a command. So as a good soldier does, I said, "Yes, Sir!!"

It was only a few days later I was called to the regimental headquarters and appeared before the OCS Board. Again they wanted know what I did in my civilian life. I went through the whole thing again, but I again knew it was just a waste of time. I knew the Army needed Infantry officers. So why fight it.

CAMP POLK

Soon after that our outfit was sent to Camp Polk, Louisiana. There we were trained further in tactics. The training was mostly unit training and mainly for the benefit of the officers on how to control troops in the field. It is easy to control a small unit, but getting those the size of companies and battalions is much more difficult. If the Army had a weakness it was leadership of troops in combat. The time I spent in Camp Polk was confusing most of the time. Communication is bad at its best, but in the field it seemed to me no one knew what was going on.

Before we left Texas, just to get away from camp, Hugh and I did get to Fort Worth a couple of more times. On one of our trips I met my brother Earle at a GI hangout. We sat in a bar and talked of home and what each of us had been doing. Earle was in training in Texas at Camp Hood. He looked good. It was great to see him. Also while in Camp Howze I saw my cousin, Leonard "Billy" Edwards. He was stationed across the post from where I was located. He seemed to be doing well. One other man from home was Jack Fulkerson from Somis. We had gone to high school together. He soon left the 84th so I lost track of him.

Speaking of losing people from our company, Rod Munday, the golfer, was placed in Special Services. Dave MDvani, the Georgian Prince, was allowed to leave. He really tried but he was too old to become an infantryman. Two others were Jake the "Fink" and one more enlisted man who refused to shower. The men who slept in the same barracks took him to the shower and gave him a good bath using GI soap and a lot of elbow grease. He went over the hill. When he was caught they brought him back to camp and the Army gave him a dishonorable discharge.

American officers above the rank of captain really needed that field training at Camp Polk. In my opinion real leadership was rarely shown during actual combat. I am not speaking of company grade officers, most of whom did their jobs exceedingly well—they just didn't last long enough in combat.

(To quote from the book about Company K, of the 84th Division, reporting on their action in the World War II, a company that lost 60% of their personnel in their first battle including all of their officers but one: "During our first battle no officer above the rank of lieutenant ever came to see how we were doing. The battalion officers were trying to run the battle from their command post. They had no concept of what was going on. When the front line people needed guidance they could not get it from their headquarters. The only field grade officer they saw was a British Officer who just happened to come by to see if his unit could help. He saw that they really needed help so he got a tank from his unit and assisted the troops get out of a horrible situation.")

We thought Texas was bad but Louisiana was worse. It seemed to rain every day. It poured down day and night. Did the commanders ever call off the problem? No way. It seemed our platoon was forever being attached to some rifle company and the CO didn't know what to do with us. On one occasion they placed two of us guarding a road and said stay there until we relieve you. Well, they forgot about us. We stayed at our post until the problem was over and no one came for us. Finally when they took a check of the men, we were missing and they came for us late at night. They had nothing left in the mess tent for us to eat except six hard boiled eggs for each of us. That with a slice of dry bread was our supper. That night in our pup tent the air was blue from the smell of rotten egg flatulence. My buddy Oberholster was ready to move me out.

On the subject of chow, we didn't have a good field mess. And when they were in the field they were at their worst. After one of the worst meals, one of my buddies said, "Let's explore and see what we can find." We did. We came to an old shack, the home of a black family. We asked if we could buy anything in the food line. The lady of the house said, "I can make you a pan of corn bread." We said great and soon we had a large pan of the best corn bread I have ever eaten. The cost was two dollars. The lady was happy and said come back anytime and I'll cook for you. So we had discovered a source.

Our company roamed over all of the hills and swamps around the Camp Claiborne area. We were broken up into gun sections and then attached to a rifle company. The CO of the rifle company then was to use our weapons to give his company more fire power. That was what we were there for, to learn. In all the times that the attachments were tried I don't ever remember a time we were used correctly. (Sadly, rarely were the machine guns used correctly even in combat.)

During this time I got a letter from Molly telling me that there had been a fire and we lost some furniture and other things. But the one thing that was irreplaceable, and which I was really sorry about, was the loss of my stamp collection. It had been one of my main hobbies before entering the Army. A friend of ours, Ken Winslow's, mother had given me a bag full of stamps that were very old and quite valuable. I had taken them home and looked them up in Scott's Stamp Catalog and discovered that they were of exceptional value, after which I took them back to the Winslows to return them. I told them of their worth, as I knew it, and suggested they take them to an expert for his evaluation. However, they insisted that I take some of them as a reward for being honest, which I did. I wrote Molly back and told her not to worry about the loss and that we could replace most of the things in time. I guess many of us in the service lost more that time.

There is one night I remember vividly. It was payday. We were in our bivouac area, just after chow time. I heard a young male voice singing a sad western song. You know the type, a love song about the woman he had left behind, how the girl of his dreams was missed. A full moon was out. I followed the sound. The moon shining through the branches made my walk through the trees something special. The wet grass with the reflection of the moon shining on the dew made it seem like I was walking on diamonds. I followed the sound of singing to a group of men who were listening to a young soldier who had his guitar and was strumming and singing. What a beautiful voice. The men were laid back and thinking of home, some lying on the ground, others with their backs to the trees, and all had that far away look in their eyes. I joined the group and listened and thought of home. I soon had diamonds in my eyes as well from the tears thinking of home. A nice night.

Going back to my tent I heard more voices from different groups of men. The voices were coming from three different places. Each group was sitting around a blanket spread on the ground. The first group was our company officers who were playing poker for nickels and dimes. I watched for a short time and then I walked to where the non-coms were playing on a blanket. They were playing blackjack. This time the bets were of paper money. I stood there for a time and watched Hugh West try to win a few bucks. I soon left and went to the third group. This time it was the privates with the same setup. Only this time the game was "Craps," and the bets were high. As one lad said, as he threw down a large amount of money, "Shoot the works, what the hell. They feed us and clothe us so what in the hell do I need money for out here in the pucker brush."

Black Jack was the destruction of our First Sergeant Hand. When we first got to camp on paydays, he would come to our barracks and get in a game of blackjack. As he had a lot money he would "tap" the dealer. He had enough money so he could double up his bet until the dealer would go broke. One night just before we left for Louisiana, he came to our barracks only this time his luck ran out. One of the men, Esteridge, was lucky and broke the sergeant. That broke his luck, and he was never able to bluff his way in a game again. And it wasn't long after that our CO discovered the sergeant had been selling weekend passes and also loaning money illegally. For example, he would loan five dollars on the first days of the month for ten dollars on payday. Later in the month the rate would be less. On the 20th of the month the rate would be seven for ten. The sergeant couldn't lose as he was a member of the paying committee, so when the soldier was paid the sergeant would have his hand out to collect. It was an old time caper in the Army, and no one complained. The CO saw the action at the pay table and asked what was going on. Then he found out the sergeant was also selling weekend passes. That was the last of the Old Man, Sergeant U.G. Hand. Better known as Sergeant Ugh!

It was about this time I found out cousin Billy Edwards had been in a wreck. He was in the back of a truck which was involved in an accident and was quite badly injured. They placed him in the hospital at Camp Claiborne where he was kept for quite a time, and then later he was reassigned to the Military Police for the duration of the war.

The chow we had in the field was very, very bad. It was bad enough having to eat from our mess kits with all the food thrown together, but the preparation was never very good. To make the situation even worse, our meals mostly were served as follows: breakfast was before daylight, at noon we were handed our lunch, which normally consisted of two dry sandwiches made from stale Army baked hand-sliced bread. Only three types of sandwiches were served, a peanut butter and jam, a dry bologna Army type that the GIs called "donkey cock," and the infamous dry cheese. When we were eating our lunch we would sing: "Won't you try a donkey cock or a cheese and a jam. It's the driest that ever was in the land." The bread was always sliced unevenly so that on one side of the sandwich a person had trouble getting his mouth open wide enough to take a bite. So we had to break off one half of the bread in order to get it in our mouths.

To make things even worse we were only allowed one canteen of water for the day. Dry sandwiches, hot weather, and limited water certainly weren't dining on the Riviera. The evening meal was served after dark. It really didn't matter because it was bad, and we ate sparingly. But we had found where we could get corn bread at any time, so we knew we were going to survive in spite of the mess.

FORT BENNING

I wasn't long in Louisiana. One day the company commander came into the field in his jeep and picked up Hugh West and me. We were given orders to go to OCS at the Infantry School at Fort Benning in Columbus, Georgia, with a short delay in route. As soon as I could, I called home and told them that I would soon be home for a week before reporting to the school. The family was happy with the news.

The ride home on the train was not the easiest thing in the world to cope with. The train was full of people. In fact I had to stand or sit either on the floor or on the edge of one of the seats. So the first day was a mess. Finally I was so tired, I just laid on the floor and got a couple of hours sleep. What a couple of days! The toilets wouldn't work. We didn't have enough water, and they ran out of food. On the second day I finally found a seat, so the rest of the ride into the station in Los Angeles was better. I had called Molly and she was to meet me in Los Angeles. She was excited with the news and said she would ask Uncle Bill Cummings and Aunt Marie to take her to the station. Bill had a source for gasoline. What a great aunt and uncle. During the war they were always willing to drive the family around and help them whenever problems arose

As we approached the station in Los Angeles, I looked at myself. I was a mess. My uniform was black from sleeping on the floor and just being on the train, I needed a shave, my hands and face were dirty. I then made a decision that the people meeting me were not going to see me in this condition. So as we came in to the station I grabbed my duffel bag and found the way to a restroom where I changed my uniform. I hurriedly shaved and washed. It took a few minutes so when I got to the ramp where Mom, Molly, Tomilyn, Aunt Marie, and Uncle Bill were waiting, I found them wondering why I was not coming up the ramp with the rest of the people from the train. But I appeared and with a lot of hugs and kisses all was well with the world.

I was home for a week. It was great! I saw friends around Oxnard and Port Hueneme. They were interested in what I was doing, and I was willing to talk. I even went by the Draft Board and saw Mrs. Brown and the people who had drafted me. They were pleased I was going to the Officers School. Mrs. Brown really felt somewhat bad they had not been able to send me to the school that I had applied for before being drafted. She was glad I had made it on my own.

I soon had to leave. But this time the trip would be faster and better. I had a ticket to fly from Los Angeles to Atlanta, Georgia. The flight was uneventful. We stopped a couple of times along the way for refueling so I was able to get out and stretch. We arrived in Atlanta early enough, and I was able of catch an Army bus to Fort Benning located on the outskirts of Columbus.

I remember quite well the ride into Fort Benning, an old established Army station with the old red brick buildings on the Main Post. Every rock was in its proper place and painted white. I was impressed. But we didn't stop at the pretty brick buildings; we just kept going on until we reached a group of wooden two story frame buildings. I got out and reported to the company office, where the company clerk told me to report to the Officer of the Day.

I walked into the adjoining office and stood in front of the officer's desk and saluted, "Sergeant Moranda reporting for duty, Sir!"

"At ease, tell me about your last assignment. My name is Lieutenant Jacobs."

With that I told him about the training I had been through for the past nine months. He listened well. He told me the school was tough, but he was sure if I really tried I would make it through the course. He said he would be the Tactical Officer for the platoon I had been assigned to. He really seemed interested in me and asked about my family and background.

With that I went to the supply building and picked up all the supplies I would need during the next four months. From there I found my way to the building where I found my bunk. In the next bunk to me was Ted Ranger. He was a short, stocky man. I could see that he was in good shape. He too was a sergeant. He had been with the division being trained in Colorado and wanted to go back to his unit if and when he graduated. It sounded good to me, and I said that I thought that I, too, would like that kind of a unit. He and I became good friends.

Soon the rest of the new company of candidates filled the barracks. As we were bunked alphabetically, my neighbors around my end of the barracks were Ranger, a young man by the name of Morf, an older man, Sgt McFarland, Sgts. Meece and Meisner from New England, Lassiter from Georgia, Pippen and Lebow from Pennsylvania, and Hogan Lang from California. When everyone had reported in, I discovered the lion's share of the candidates were ROTC men and had just graduated from college. It seemed that half of them were from Pennsylvania University and the other half from southern colleges.

As a person will do, I looked around at the men in the unit and could see the competition would be tough. But somehow I just didn't worry about the school for I knew if I really tried I would make it through.

As we were sitting around getting to know each other, over the intercom I heard, "Moranda, report to the company headquarters."

I wondered what gives? But it didn't take long to find out the reason for the call.

I reported to Lieutenant Jacobs. "Moranda," he ordered, "you are to be the First Sergeant of the company for the first week of the training." Nothing more except that he told me the acting company commander would be Ted Ranger. No other information. I was dismissed.

I went back to the barracks and found Ranger. He and I got busy. By hook or by crook we found out who else had been selected for the rest of the positions needed to operate the student company. Ted and I then gathered them together. Then we set up where we were to form the company, how many platoons we would have, and so on. Ted and I marked off the spots where each platoon would stand and directed each platoon leader to mark their spots so they could easily find them in the morning.

The next morning all went well. The acting officers and non-coms found their spots. The formation was about perfect. I saw a smile come to the face of Lieutenant Jacobs. He watched as I called the company to attention and dressed the ranks. I then turned over the company to the acting company commander Ted Ranger. As I stood at my post in the rear of the troops, I saw Lieutenant Jacobs look at the Commanding Officer of the training company and give him a thumbs up. The gesture was returned to Jacobs. I served one week in that job.

A couple of days later I was summoned to the headquarters. I reported to Lieutenant Jacobs. He gave me a mission that didn't please me, but I didn't know how to refuse it. I was told my job was to watch two candidates in our company who were of German descent. I was to report anything they would do that wasn't in the interests of our government. I wanted to say, "Why me?" But again how does one say no? I asked why they were being watched but didn't get an answer. I soon found out the two men, if they graduated, were to be assigned to U.S. Army Intelligence. The two men were Meisner and Hogan Lang. Both men were bunking near me. As I walked back to my barracks, I thought about the only thing good about the assignment: Lieutenant Jacobs obviously thought I was going to make it through the school.

The assignment made me change my way of going out on my free time. I always tried to go with the two men. Both of them were really good men. Hogan was from Laguna, California, so we did have a couple of things in common. And besides I learned to like them very much. But as so many things happen in the service, and the three of us were separated, I was unable to continue our friendship. And I never did find anything bad about them. They were good, loyal Americans.

It was in December when I really became sick. Only by dragging myself out of bed and going through the day was I able to make it. I should have gone to sick call, but I was not going to give the officers in charge a chance to wash me out. As I look back on it all, I wonder why I was so intense about finishing the school. For two days I forced myself to carry on. On the second day as we finished up training, I suddenly felt stronger. From then on everything went well. I had a cough for a few days but otherwise the fever was gone.

In January I heard from Molly. Her Dad was doing well in the Service Station that he had purchased in Hueneme. Molly and Shirley helped him as much as they could, but he was without real help. Her Dad was getting tired of the station and was looking with keen interest at some property in Lancaster. I was not surprised about his tiring of the station because all the labor force normally available for service station work was gone. Those men were either in the service or at some better paying job in the defense industry. It was soon after that a letter came telling of Henry and Isabelle Swain going into a business arrangement with their daughter and son-in-law, Rozeel and Eddie Gabbert, to raise turkeys and chickens. They had purchased a small ranch of twenty acres in Lancaster that had two houses and other buildings already in place.

The main entertainment for us while in school was going into Columbus. Our favorite place was a famous steak house that was called "Pattersons." Their main menu specialty was steak of any size or shape.

One item was a large steak; if you could eat it all at one sitting you didn't have to pay. I saw a couple of men try, but unsuccessfully. That steak was tremendous. The trimmings that went with the steaks weren't stinted in size either. After the meal we would walk around town for a short time and then go back to the Fort.

We all liked to get packages from home. When the package was brought to the upstairs where we were staying, the receiver suddenly had his bunk surrounded with people hoping for a home treat. I well remember the day I got one of Molly's famous cakes. I opened the package and passed the cake around. A couple of the men decided they would write to Molly and thank her. They did. And it worked because it wasn't long after another cake came in the mail.

The school, for me, was a four months' rest. The studies were easy and the physical part was easy too. The young men from the ROTC units were really in good shape and they helped me keep in shape, especially a young man by the name of Lebow. He would challenge me to do one hundred sit-ups and push-ups nightly. I could do them easily. One of our tests was to run the 400 yard dash. Did it easily—which surprised me too. We did burn the midnight oil on the nights before an examination. The men would test each other to make sure that we could all pass the written tests.

I have always wondered why some of the men were treated better than others. I guess the Tactical Officers saw a bearing or something in their overall appearance to make them good officers, even if the candidates would do some dumb things. We had two such men in our barracks: Kirk and Lassiter. Both good looking men but slow in grasping the different subjects. They had trouble in every part of the course especially in learning the mechanical functions of weapons. For example, Kirk never did learn how to detail-strip his rifle. Twice when the Tactical Officer came to him on an inspection the officer would grab the rifle from Kirk. Then when he opened the magazine the parts would come flying out falling to the ground. Both of them would be on the ground picking up the parts with the Tactical Officer apologizing to Kirk. The rest of us in ranks would do our best not to laugh. When Kirk graduated, the Army placed him in the gunnery section of the school. His assignment was to instruct the candidates on the functioning of the M1 rifle.

Lassiter was just slow in many ways, but he sure looked good in his uniform. He, too, passed and became an instructor at the school. Both of these men, when I heard from them later, said they finally were able to instruct on the things they had problems with when in the school.

Every week some of the men were dropped out of the school. One of the first was Morf. He had the bunk next to mine. He was really a slob and lazy. He would not mop under his bunk nor get his clothes laid out neatly or his shoes shined. But the thing that really washed him out was his performance in the field when we were on a training exercise learning the .81 mm mortar. He was the loader, the man who dropped the shell in the tube. Ted Ranger was on one side of the tube and I was on the other. The shell didn't slip down the tube correctly. One of the instructors told Morf to tap the tube on the side. Not Morf, he reared back and kicked the tube violently. The shell was live, and the tube started to fall with the opening of the tube aimed at the watchers. In the audience, besides our Lieutenant Jacobs, was our commanding officer and his guests who scattered and ducked. Ted and I were able to catch the tube before it fell completely. We were able to hold the tube and aim it down the range. When the shell exploded, everyone breathed a sigh of relief. When we got back to our barracks, Morf was called to the headquarters. The next day he left for his next assignment.

The next man the Army let go was a good friend, Sgt. McFarland. Why he flunked out I really don't understand. He was a good man. He was one of the men who would go with our group on Saturdays to eat at Pattersons. He seemed to do everything correctly but something happened that I don't know about. He may have asked to be let out. The reason I say that is when I was coming home from Europe, I ran into him while I was in Italy. He was coming out of the USO. I spoke to him and Mac came over and we talked for a few minutes. He was with some men so we didn't really get to talk long but he said that he was happy about leaving OCS. He got his old job back in his old outfit. The job he had was safe from combat. I wished him well and said "so long." I never saw him again, but I thought he was a good man.

The lecture I remember the most at the school was given by an officer who had earned the Congressional Medal Of Honor. He read the citations of a few of the men and officers who had earned the award. His he read last. He received the Medal of Honor when he led his men through a mine field, and, after saving a couple of his men, then went on to wipe out an enemy machine gun nest. He had been severely wounded but carried on. I don't know why his award impressed me so much. Maybe it was his almost apologetic attitude as he read the citation.

On 28 November I received a long letter from sister Maye telling me about the seriousness of Dad's illness. In it she told of how crazy Dad was about Molly and the baby, and appreciated so much the visits we made with him which kept his spirits flowing upward. I was so proud of Maye, too, for taking the time off from her nurse's training to be with Dad and hoped it wouldn't jeopardize her progress with the schooling.

One day as we were forming to march to our next assignment, Lieutenant Jacobs called out and said, "Moranda, you are the guidon bearer today." I went to the front of the formation, got the guidon, and took my position. I was standing tall. RIGHT FACE was the command. I did, and when the next command came, FORWARD MARCH, I began to march. We marched about a hundred yards when Lieutenant Jacobs told the candidate in charge to halt the troops. He did. Lieutenant Jacobs relieved me of my job as guidon bearer. His comment was that I rolled when I marched, and no matter how I tried when I stood at attention I always looked at ease. He was smiling so I knew that I wasn't being condemned only that it was not in my make up to be rigidly at attention. He always teased me about my way of walking. I told him that I walked like my father so guessed it was hereditary.

[By May 1943, the German and Italian forces had been driven from North Africa and the Allies started to prepare for an invasion of Sicily and the Italian peninsula which began that fall. Russia had turned from a defensive posture and began to take the offensive. The Americans were becoming battle tested and casualties were mounting requiring a great increase in replacements to fill the vacancies created. Germany began to strengthen forces in the West preparing for an invasion of the British Isles as well as to preserve the sites for their V-Bombs they were raining on England. In August Sicily had been overrun, and the bulk of German forces evacuated to the mainland and took charge of the Italian campaign after the fall of Mussolini.]

I was called to the office one day and was handed a telegram from Mom. It said, "Expect the worst. Dad is dying." I was devastated. What to do. Lt. Jacobs just happened to be in the office when I opened the telegram. He came out from behind his desk and asked what the problem was. I just handed the telegram to him. He was very sympathetic and told me to go to see the Chaplain.

Before going to see the Chaplain, I went to a telephone and called Mom. She said Dad had just died. The funeral would be in a couple of days. Mom was very calm. No tears or emotional outbreaks, she just said what had happened and what was going to happen. She knew death was coming and so had steeled herself to cope. She also said my sister Maye was with Dad when he died. Maye said Dad really didn't want to die but went easily after the priest came and gave him the last rites. Dad had been raised a Catholic, but had married a daughter of a Methodist minister and, after the family moved to Hueneme in 1924, became a member and official of the Community Presbyterian Church there.

With that I went back to the headquarters and discussed the situation with Lieutenant Jacobs. He spelled it out. He could get me the time off to go home, but I would have to join another company and take some of the training over again. When I talked to the Chaplain he said the same thing. He further said, "Your Dad is gone. You would see your Mom, but she must have plenty of help there now."

I then walked to the phone and again called home. I told Mom I had decided that I was going to stay and the reason. She said, "Good, that is what your Dad would have wanted you to do." I went back to the barracks where Ted Ranger and the men all came to me and expressed their sympathy.

The next day we were going to the range to fire our primary weapon, the M1. I was in a blue funk, and on the way said to myself, "I'm going to dedicate my day to my Dad." I did. I had one of the highest scores the Army ever had at this range. When we were at the 500 yard mark firing from the prone position, I maxed the score. All shots were perfect. I looked around when Ted Ranger said, "My man, you have quite an audience." I looked around and saw a large group watching to see if I could make it through the 500 yard series with perfect hits. I did. "THAT'S FOR YOU, DAD!!" At the next formation the company commander announced that I had broken the school record at the rifle range the day before. I was pleased with the honor especially since in my mind the day belonged to my father.

All the next few days Dad was in my thoughts. As I was growing up, it seemed to me that even though he was my Dad, I never did know what he really wanted in life. I wondered if any of the seven of us ever stopped and said to him, "I love you Dad. Thanks for doing for us all your life, and without much thanks from any of us including Mom. From you I learned to accept what is dealt and accept it with calm and, if necessary, bravery. When you were young what did you really want out of life?" So many things that I would like to have known about Dad. How did he feel when his father was killed? So many thoughts of the past. I remembered when Tomilyn was born, and Dad would hold her and play with her. You could see that he really did love babies.

It was only a few days later I was called into the office and was informed that I was to be the company commander of the "Infantry Company in the attack"— a tactical problem. Quite an honor as the role always went to one of the tops in the class. The next day we ran the problem. It was quite a challenge. I remembered how difficult it was to communicate during our Louisiana tactical maneuvers, and I relearned how hard it is with troops especially when they are under your command. There was noise from the different weapons going off. The acting officers of the company were on the radio calling for instructions. With the help of my Acting Executive Officer, Rosensweig, we did finish the exercise. The umpires said they were pleased with our company problem. But I certainly was not satisfied and thought I should have had more control of the men. A lesson learned that I never forgot.

Only about a week later Mom surprised me. I had thought it would be later, but she called me from the railroad station saying she was in Columbus to visit me. Her arrival was on a Wednesday. I really think Mom thought I could get off any time to come to see her. I told her I had not reserved her a room but had talked to the USO about renting a room. I told her to go to the Travelers Aid, and they would let her know where she could find a room and I would be there just as soon as I could get away. I went to Lieutenant Jacobs and told him the situation. He said take off tomorrow afternoon early and go see your mother. I did. I picked her up and took her for a ride on the bus to see where I was located and showed her the rest of the camp. She was impressed. I told her that I would not be able to come into town until Saturday. Then we would have some time together. She said she was going to try to look up some of her distant relatives, the Edmondsons. She did and from her report later they were not very hospitable. So she wasted no more time trying to get to know them. While she was in Columbus she stayed in the room the Travelers Aid had obtained for her. She said it was comfortable, and she enjoyed the women who were also at the house. I was tied up most of the time she was here. But we did get to visit and learn what she was going to do now that Dad was gone.

I remember well that she told me she was going to sell the old house. My first reaction was why? But she said she didn't want to roam around in it with no one else there. I could understand that. She said she would sell the house and live on the interest of the money she would get out of the sale. I smiled as I did the calculations of the money she would have. She also said that she would move in with the girls at 331 4th Street, the house where the Swains lived for years that was now being occupied by Molly, Jeannette, and Lorraine. I was glad she had all the answers. She also said she would work at Dad's office until they found someone to take over for him. Mom had reservations to go to her next stop to see brothers Earle and George in the Washington, D.C., area on Sunday.

I had wished she could have stayed but there was no way I could spend any more time with her, as I was in the middle of purchasing my uniforms, trying them on, going back and forth between the fittings, as well as completing the course work. I had received the $250 allowance to buy the uniforms. The local merchants had set up a large warehouse full of all the items of clothing that a new Second Lieutenant would need. I only bought the bare necessities. My bill came to $200. I did get one dress uniform of "pinks and greens," tailored because of my long waist. I must admit the uniform really fit well. Also I had to arrange to get my tickets so I could fly home. I couldn't fly all the way home, but I could get as far as Dallas. From there I would have to catch the train. Had a hell of a time paying for the tickets as they wanted cash. I had a money order which for some reason the ticket seller would not take. Mom offered to pay, but I said no as she was going to need all her cash. I went back to camp and cashed the check then went back to town and bought the tickets. I said goodbye to Mom as she was leaving that day too.

The next day we dressed in our new officer's uniforms and walked to the auditorium where we were to attend the ceremony of getting our bars pinned on. I was number two in the class. No money for the honor but it was nice that I was chosen.

After the ceremony we walked back to the barracks to pick up our Val Packs and head for the airport in order to go home. On the way I passed the first enlisted man. When he saluted me I gave him a dollar bill. That was the custom. And to be honest I did enjoy that.

From there I went to the airport, and we soon were loaded on the plane and took off. One of my friends was on the same plane—Billy Reinhardt, who had played football and was one of the big names at the University of California. He was in our class. I enjoyed talking with him as we flew together to Dallas. We then got on an overcrowded train and made it the rest of the way to California. When we arrived in L.A., somehow he took my Val Pac while I took his. Thankfully he remembered my name and where I lived so he was able to track me down. The next day I drove with Molly to Los Angeles where Reinhardt and I exchanged bags. That was the last time I saw him during the war. After the war we met at the football camp where he was trying out for a professional football team, the Los Angeles "Dons," and we told war stories to each other.

Again the same routine: we went around the town and saw the family and friends. I again went by the Draft Board and saw Mrs. Brown and "Hap" Maxwell. He was pleased that I had made it as an officer. I had proved his prediction that I would.

We didn't have much time, as we were heading for my first assignment. When I graduated, the Army assigned me to serve with the 176th "Richmond Blues" at Fort Benning. They were the school troops, which did all the demonstrations for the classes at the OCS. To serve with that outfit was an honor. They claimed to be the oldest National Guard unit in the USA and were then commanded by a Colonel Cox.

When the time came we loaded our old 1937 Studebaker with all the clothes and stuff we would need while living in Georgia. Baby's clothes and supplies do take up a lot of the space, but we got it all in the car. And by packing a lot of items in the back seat we were able to place the baby's mattress on top of the boxes of clothes and make a place where she could spend her time. Tomilyn didn't know me at this time and tried her best to ignore me. With patience and persistence I finally won her over. But for a few days it was up to Molly to care for her. This made it tough on Molly, as I couldn't help in the job of tending Tomi because she would cry up a storm whenever I tried to take over.

So off we went, 50 MPH all the way. We only stopped long enough to eat and relieve ourselves and then on we would go. I didn't have much time to get to my new assignment so we had to drive almost continuously. Besides, we had to find a place to stay when we got there. It was a long, tedious, boring drive! Molly could climb over the front seat and get some rest with the baby on the mattress. I just drove and drove and drove. I didn't think we would ever get through Texas. But we finally arrived in Columbus.

The first thing I did was go to the Travelers Aid. They were helpful in finding us a room in a private home. No private bath and no cooking. Molly was able to fix the baby's formula and other like things, but we had to go out for every meal.

We ate at the same place almost every day: a Greek restaurant. The owner of the place took a liking to Tomilyn. The two of them really hit it off. He would come by our booth and take Tomi for a tour of the restaurant. He introduced her to his family and the customers and then when we were finished he would bring her back to us. It was a nice thing for the owner to do as it really gave us a few minutes break.

Daily Molly would take me to the base and then take off looking for a place to rent. About the fourth day of looking around the town she, for some reason, decided that she would take a country road. After driving a couple of miles on the new route, she saw a small house that had a

FOR RENT sign posted. She slammed on the brakes, stopped, and went to the house next door to find out about the house which had the sign in front of it. Thanks to Tomilyn, the lady of the house took an instant shine to her and rented the house to Molly.

What a break. It was two bedroom place. The rent was inexpensive, but there was a condition attached to the rental. I had to mow lawns of both houses. And the area was big. It took me a couple of hours a week to mow both places but I sure didn't mind. I had my family with me. The neighbors loved taking care of Tomilyn, so Molly and I could go out on the town or go to the Officers Club at Benning. We met some really nice couples from the 176th Infantry that I was assigned to. So we had a social life. Our landlords encouraged us to make a garden, which I immediately planted. Our landlady also asked of Molly if she would take her to the store a couple of times a week. Of course Molly did gladly. They also had a piano and asked me to play. They actually liked the few songs I knew. Sometimes in the evenings we would spend a few hours with them—they were nice people.

When I reported to the 176th Infantry, I got the surprise of my Army career. I was assigned as the Motor Officer for the regiment. I went to the motor pool and met the men. I was very happy with my assignment. I went home and told Molly that at last I was assigned to a job that I felt I was best suited for. The assignment lasted for only two days. I was then called into the headquarters and Colonel Cox said that he had been watching me during the past two days. During the noon hour the officers would play a volleyball game. Colonel Cox was always there and watched the games and decided I would be wasted in the motor pool. So I was assigned to Company B, 1st Battalion, 176th Infantry.

My first assignment at B Company was to be the platoon leader in the demonstration for the OCS of "The Platoon In The Attack." The men of the company had staged the problem many times. All I had to do was to be a role player and do what the sergeant advised me to do.

We rehearsed the problem a few times with the instructor from the OCS board. Just as I was ready for our first run through for a live audience, I was called into the office again and was given another assignment. I was to become the Commander of Company B. The Army had a sudden need for company grade officers in the pending operations overseas, which turned out to be D-Day! The only reason I was not shipped out along with some of the others was that I had only been an officer for a couple of months. But I also knew it soon would be my turn to go. And it wasn't long before we got word the 176th was to be broken up.

[Postponed from May, "Operation Overlord," the Allied long-debated invasion of Northern France, took place on June 6, 1944—the war's most celebrated D-Day—when 156,000 men were landed at the beaches of Normandy: 83,000 British and Canadian troops on the Eastern beaches and 73,000 Americans on the Western. By 9:00 a.m. the coastal defenses were generally breached, but Caen in the British sector, timed to fall on D-Day and the hinge of the Allied advance, held out until July 9. Though the heavy fighting in the Caen area attracted most of the German reserves, the U.S. forces in the westernmost sector likewise met very stubborn resistance. Not until June 26 did they take Cherbourg and proceed to clear the rest of the Cotentin peninsula. On D-Day the 7th Armored Division sailed on the Queen Mary from New York harbor for Greenock, Scotland.]

The job of CO was easy. The hardest job I had was spending the company fund. The former CO had allowed the fund to build up to a large figure. The Army wanted it spent before the unit was broken up. I asked advice from the headquarters on how I could spend the money. Their only advice was to spend it for the benefit of all the enlisted soldiers in the unit. It was then the 1st Sergeant and I came up with an idea. Why not hold a banquet for the soldiers, their wives and sweethearts. We formed a committee. They were to go into town, find a very nice place, and arrange for a banquet. As I was a part of the committee, I went along. The place was selected. The subject of cost came up in finalizing the night on the town. The amount of money that we had to spend was told to the owner. We made an agreement: the menu and the price was to be the exact amount of the money in the company fund. All was agreed.

The night on the town was a fine one: corsages for the ladies, a special menu, and a band to play for a later dance. Everything went well. The men of the company really enjoyed the evening with their wives and girlfriends. Molly and I also had a good time. Our good neighbors took Tomi to their house where she stayed the night. So with no baby to worry about, Molly and I really had a romantic night. And at night's end the company fund had a zero balance.

In Combat

Overseas

It was only a few days later that I was called into the office and given my orders to report to Fort Meade, Maryland. I asked about the rule that a 2nd Lieutenant was supposed to have a minimum of six months duty as an officer before he could be sent overseas. The answer I got was, "Oh, you will have it by the time you ship out."

Boy, how I hated to go home and tell Molly I was going overseas. I knew she would really be upset, and she was. But Molly was always stronger than I gave her credit for. We had been so happy being together in the little house with the wonderful landlords next door who really loved Tomi and Molly and with all of our new friends with whom we had so many good times. Those few months were some of the happiest times of our marriage. We kept in touch with those friends for years after the war.

So with great sorrow we again packed the old Studebaker. This time we were better at packing, as we had learned on our first journey across the country. The sad part was to say goodbye to our friends next door. Tomi would easily have been glad to stay with them. The car was serviced and we left for California. Speed limit was still 50 MPH so I knew it was going to take us a long time to get across the country.

I drove from Columbus to Texas and only stopped to eat and gas up. The baby rode well especially with Molly playing with her and talking to her whenever she was awake. I don't remember how many times I heard "See the cow," or "See the horsy."

When we were approaching Dallas, I had to get some rest so I asked Molly to drive and I sat next to her and dropped off to sleep for a few minutes. I awoke as we were going through the main part of Dallas. Molly had the car in the right lane. Ahead was a street car. The street car stopped at the intersection. A black woman leaped off the street car, across the loading zone, and right into the hood of the car. Molly stopped the car immediately. I saw the lady had made it to sidewalk. I told Molly to drive across the street to get the car out of the intersection. I got out of the car and applied pressure to the gash on the lady's head. Her glasses were broken but otherwise she seemed to be OK. All the time Molly was in the car. She was really broken up about the accident. The police came and questioned Molly and me on what happened. We told them what we saw. They talked to the lady and she said the same thing. They asked me where we were going. I told them we were going back to California and then I was going overseas. With that an officer said something that I sure didn't like: "Go on, she is just a nigger." We gave the lady and the police our address. Later on we had our friend Attorney Mark Durley in Oxnard arrange with the lady to pay for her new glasses and the cost of her doctor.

Morandas during World War II

Marine Sgt. Bill and Bob

Lt. Earle

Lt. George and Sgt. Bill

Seaman Paul, Cadet
Nurse Maye, and Bob

Airman Ted in Naples

Molly would not drive again. She was so shook up that it was impossible for me to ask for her help. So the driving was mine to do. Those miles were long and tedious, but we slowly crept across the country. One time we stopped in a small town in Texas to eat at a restaurant that was full of people with large hats and cowboy boots, who were out with their families for dinner. We were tired and the baby was fussing. Our food had been served. All of a sudden the baby up-chucked all over the table and our food. The owner and the waitress were really asses. They made such a fuss about the mess. I was embarrassed, but surely they had seen babies vomit before. I was about ready to pop the owner in the kisser, but instead I went back to the kitchen and got the mop and a couple of wet rags. I told Molly to go out and get in the car. I didn't want her to take any more guff from that staff. After I had cleaned the mess, I went to the restroom and cleaned myself. I returned the mops and rags, then made my reappearance at the cashier's station. There I proceeded to tell the owner how I really felt about him and his staff raving and ranting about the incident. I threw the money for the meals on the counter and walked out. As I left the people applauded my actions. A couple of them tried to give me money, but I sure didn't want that. I am certain most of those people had seen babies get sick before.

From there all the way home I drove and drove, only stopping for food or to relieve ourselves. I got so tired I had to stop once for a couple of hours and sleep by the side of the road. Finally we reached the California border and in a few more hours we drove into Oxnard, California. Man, oh man, I was certainly glad to see familiar sights. For two days I visited family and friends who were glad to see us again. They also knew I was going overseas, so they were very solicitous. They wished me well and sympathized with Molly and Mom.

After the few days at home, it was time for me again to leave my family and depart, this time for Fort Meade, Maryland, where I would be processed for overseas duty. D-Day had happened and the Army had a great need for "Cannon Fodder"—better known as first and second lieutenants infantry. I really didn't believe any lieutenant in the infantry who fought in the war for any length of time escaped either being killed, captured, or wounded. So I thought I knew what I was getting into. But I also knew the family was placing me in God's care, so I would have plenty of prayers going on for me. When I left Molly she said to me that she would ask God to place me within a shield of love. Molly also had a Christian Scientist Practitioner, a Mrs. Reedy, work (pray) for me all the time I was overseas. And I prayed for the same thing.

This time I went on a plane so I didn't have to drive across the country again. We stopped a couple of times flying over the states and landed in Washington, D.C., where I was the guest of my older brother Earle. He took me around the city to see the sights and where he worked. We talked baseball and went to a game, for at that time in our lives we followed the baseball "stats" closely. He was addicted to baseball. I remember his discussions about baseball with his barber, as I sat and watched him get a haircut and listened to the two of them tell each other what the Washington Senators should do to improve their team.

Washington was really a city of haste. Everyone was in a hurry. The war effort was at its height. Everyone had someone in the service, so it seemed they were looking, listening, talking, and praying for a quick victory. Brother George was stationed at the Engineer School at Fort Belvoir on the faculty teaching Officer Candidates and lived in nearby Alexandria, Virginia, with his wife Nancy and their newborn son. I spent one afternoon with them and caught up on their news.

After a couple of days with Earle it was time for me to report to Ft. Meade. Earle took me to the bus line. We said so long and I departed. When I got to Fort Meade I got out of the bus, entered the headquarters building, reported to the Officer of the Day, and there, waiting in line ahead of me, was my enlisted buddy Hugh West. We were so glad to see each other. He had been sent to an Army unit in Texas. We were together for the next few days and later sailed on the same ship to cross the Atlantic.

They sent us to Camp Shanks, New York, located about an hour away from the Big City. We were only there for about a week, during which Hugh and I went to see the sights. He took me to a night club where he knew the *maitre d'hotel*, who gave us a special table near the stage. The girl singer came to the table and asked if she could sing us a special song. We thanked her and she honored our requests.

We had to take a variety of modes of transportation to get to the city. First an Army truck, then a bus, and finally the rails. I was fascinated with the underground system. Hugh and I got pretty good at getting around the town. On one of my trips I was hustled by an UGLY. She wanted me to get off at the next stop for a good time. I thanked her and she cursed me, "What's the matter with you. Don't you want a freebie?" That was my first time to experience the neighborliness of New York.

Everyone in New York seemed in a hurry. If you asked directions from a person walking in the opposite direction, he would give you the instructions as he walked away from you. And as the distance got farther between the asker and the responder, the voices got louder. So in just a few minutes the two people would be yelling at each other. I'm sure the people around were certain there was bad blood between the two and really all the time they were just being friendly.

At the end of the week it was time for us to depart from Camp Shanks for the harbor and load onto the ship taking us overseas. They trucked us to the Hudson River. There we were loaded onto a large river barge which took us down to the New York harbor. After sailing for an hour or so we arrived, unloaded, and after milling around for a few minutes on the pier, we marched to the waiting ship and boarded the HMS Mataroa, an old English passenger ship converted into a troop ship. Hugh and I were in quarters with a group of officers, all of them company grade officers heading for the war.

ENGLAND

We were quite comfortable. We had a steward who took care of our bunks and kept us abreast of the happenings aboard the ship. He would wake us in the morning and as he did so he would announce in his British accent what was on the menu. Seemed the breakfast for most of the days was Kippers. Kippers are fish. Fish for breakfast? No way! When announced there was always a groan and most of the men would stay in their bunks. We soon learned if we didn't eat kippers for breakfast we would get them later at another meal.

The only way we could bathe was with salt water. A tub was filled with warm salt water. After soaping with a special soap and rinsing with the salt water, our orderly would bring us a basin with unsalted water to get a final rinsing. As there was no way to really exercise, we really didn't have to bathe every day.

Daily Hugh and I went to the salon, found a table and comfortable chairs, and spent most of the day playing Gin Rummy. I didn't know how to play the game when we first started the voyage but I soon learned. The stakes were 25 cents a box and 50 cents a game. We played hundreds of games and as we were within a convoy it took us a long time to get to England. When we debarked Hugh paid me two dollars. So I guess we were pretty evenly matched.

The convoy was made up of a large number of freighters. Our ship was in the middle of the convoy, while on the outside of the convoy destroyers from our Navy patrolled for submarines. We thought we were fairly safe with the U.S. Navy nearby, but we also knew the Germans had sunk many of our ships going to England. Our biggest danger came not from the Germans but from Old Mother Nature. Near Newfoundland our convoy had to fight through a scary storm with waves that seemed fifty feet high. I went to the upper deck and watched the waves break over the bow of the ship. What power! The ship's captain slowed down and sort of "laid to" by turning into the waves at reduced speed and held there while plowing ahead.

The ship never varied from its course. I learned later the convoy had lost a freighter during the storm. I am sure if a person ever went overboard during that storm there would be no way to rescue him. But after that storm the sailing was fine: smooth seas, fleecy clouds, and a friendly breeze.

The morning we arrived the steward came into the cabin and announced that England was soon to be visible. We all got up and ate our breakfast and then took places at the rails where we could observe the coast line. And there it was: green and pretty. Slowly we approached the harbor, and soon we were docked in Bristol, a very large harbor with a lot of activities. It wasn't long before Army personnel came aboard and welcomed us to England.

We debarked and were loaded on trucks which took us to Warminster Barracks located near Bath. This time there were no barracks for us. When they dumped us off, we were guided to our new homes—permanent tents. We soon were greeted by the commander of the base, who told us we would only be in England for a few days. The war was going great, and they wanted us to get there in time for us to participate in the victory. What a yuk!! He was, in his way, trying to be cute. One of the officers in our ranks asked, "If it's so wonderful, how come you are still here in this camp?" No answer was forthcoming.

Our quarters were tents complete with Army cots, which never were really comfortable but were adequate when you were tired. Our toilet facilities were located about fifty yards away from the tents. I guess the Army wanted us to be so miserable that we would enjoy going into combat. Our group was made up of all 1st and 2nd lieutenants. The morning muster was really a mess. Many of the officers would go to town and get a little drunk and then at the morning call they just didn't want to make muster. The captain in charge would not dismiss us until everyone was accounted for. He was forever saying, "Shape up or you will be sent overseas to combat." That somehow didn't faze any one in our group, as we knew we were already headed there, so that threat was ignored.

The city of Bath was nearby so we would catch a ride into the town on an Army truck of some kind. It was easy to get into town but tough to get back to camp. Not many trucks from the Army would travel during blackouts. On the first day, one of the regular cadre told me there was a mail truck that came back to camp at 10 o'clock every night. He told me where to find the post office. So I would go to town and then come home on top of the mail bags containing love letters from the wives, mothers, and sweethearts of the men in our camp.

One night I went into town and into one of the numerous pubs. I sat next to a family of three. Mom and Dad and a young girl about fifteen years old, a beautiful blonde girl. I found it was customary for families to go to their favorite pubs in the evening and visit. I talked to the family and told them where I was from and about my family. We visited for quite awhile. I asked the young girl what she really missed most because of the war. She thought for a short time and then said, "An orange. In my mind I can still smell the scent of an orange. It has been four years since I had an orange." I stayed there for some time visiting and watching the continuous game of darts and thinking to myself what rotten things wars are. The people who really suffer are the kids. It certainly was not their fault a war was going on. I asked if she came to the pub every night. She said yes, we come here nightly to visit with our friends.

When I got back to camp I made it a point to go to the mess sergeant to see if I could get a couple of oranges for the young lady. When I asked he said sure and gave me six of them. He smiled and said, "That is certainly a new story." I just smiled, for if he wanted to believe it was for other things then that didn't bother me. I took the oranges to the girl the next night. I assumed she would wolf them down. But no, she just sat and took one of the oranges and smelled it. Never in my life was a gift I gave appreciated as much as those few oranges. Sadly I never saw the young girl again. But this much I know, she will forever remember the lieutenant who gave them to her.

My assignment for the next couple of days was one I didn't enjoy. I was assigned to teach a group of enlisted men the art of bayonet fighting. The night before I found the manual and brushed up on the proper way to teach the subject. Then I got Hugh West to practice with me. The men I had to train were prisoners who had been court-martialed and were in the guard house. They had been given the choice of going overseas and joining an Army outfit or staying in prison. Their choice was the guard house or combat. Those I was assigned to train were the ones who decided that they would take their chances in the war by going overseas and joining a combat unit.

The next morning the men were marched to the training area and the training began. The Military Police stayed around all the time watching the training. I was glad they stayed. Some of the men were really tough looking, and I wondered if I would ever get some of these men when I was in combat. But the training went well. I seemed to get them to actually try. I guess that I did too well: when I got through with them I went back to my quarters but was soon called to the CO's headquarters. There I was informed I would be the officer in charge of the prisoners until they got to France and had turned them over to the Replacement Center. But the good part was I would have the weekend off.

Friday I went back to Bath. I sat in the pub and visited for a time with friends I had made. But I was tired and decided that it was about time for me to get back to camp. I had to first make it back to the Post Office where I could find the man who drove the mail truck. I went outside and darkness descended on me. The moon was not out, and clouds covered the stars or was it fog? Whatever it was I was really having a difficult time finding my way. I knew it was a couple of blocks one way and then a couple blocks another way. So I bumped along the sidewalk sort of keeping my body next to the walls. I stumbled into a couple doing their thing in the standing position—practicing the art of standing seduction—known in England as the "wall job." I said, "Sorry," and continued on my way. Finally my eyes became adjusted to the darkness and I found the Post Office. I paid the man the few shillings and climbed on top of all the mail sacks. There I relaxed until the truck arrived at our camp.

The next day I decided I would go to London. So I found the highway and started to use my thumb to hitchhike. I was soon picked up by a lady—I mean a real Lady driving an open roadster. She said to me, "I say there, would you like to ride with me for a while? I am going almost to London." I thanked her and came on board. She reminded me of Mrs. Richard Bard, a friend of our family's in Port Hueneme. She introduced herself as Lady so-and-so, but I do not remember the name. She questioned me about where I was from and kept up a banter until she came to the driveway where she lived. It was a manor. She said goodbye and told me where the best place was to pick up another ride. I did get a ride and was soon in London.

When I arrived I wandered about and came to a large park. On the lawn were hundreds of couples sitting on the grass listening to music. A lot of love was being displayed, many GIs with English girls. Romance was in the air. I listened for a time and then moved on and ran into Hugh West. He was going to a party and asked me to go along. I did. But I was soon aware I was a fifth wheel, so I left and went back to the highway. It was only a few minutes before an Army truck picked me up and took me back to camp. My experience in London was not one to remember except for the friendliness of the people.

The day soon came when it was time to move out. The MPs marched the prisoners to waiting trucks and loaded them aboard. The MPs saluted and said, "All present and accounted for." My instant thought was I hope that I can say the same thing when we reach the shores of France and will have turned my charges over to the replacement center.

FRANCE

The trip to the waiting ship didn't take long. I was in the first vehicle and saw where many of the ships had been loaded for the great invasion. The harbor was still busy with ships loading men and supplies for the troops in France. The trucks drove us to the loading area, and the prisoners were unloaded, assembled, and counted, and then taken aboard the ship. My group was taken to an area where they could be guarded easily, though it wasn't a problem. The men were quiet and seemed to be thinking of their next assignment. Soon the blast from the ship's horn was sounded and the tugs pushed us out. We were on the way across the English Channel.

There were all kinds of ships around us—ships carrying supplies to the Allied Forces. Ours seemed to be the only one that was carrying troops. I could only think how much time and planning must have gone into making the first attack on D-Day. Most of the men were playing cards or writing letters, but there didn't seem to be much joy among the troops. They were just quiet. I am sure they too were impressed with this trip, and they too were thinking of D-Day. I wondered whether some of them would have been on the first waves of the attack if they had not been in prison. I wondered if they had a sense of quilt about that. Some of the men became seasick and made trips to places where they could relieve themselves. For me, my time was spent watching and thinking of what was to come next. I did manage to write a couple of letters to Molly and Mom.

The next morning we could see the shores of France. We were coming into the area of Utah Beach, and we could see the remains of the great battle. We were approached by LSTs. They came along the side of our ship. A net had been installed on the side, and our group was supposed hold their duffel bags and climb down the net into the waiting LST. I now found out how brave some of the men were. They were afraid and didn't want to climb down. After trying persuasion I decided I would show them how easy it was to take the trip. I grabbed the first man in line and made him place himself at the top of the net. Then I placed my body in position around his so he could not fall. Down the side we went. When we got into the waiting ship, I noted the rest of the men were following. I got quite a hand from the watching men. We were finally loaded and started toward the shore. I was really into thoughts of what those guys on D-Day had gone through. We can read about them, but we cannot ever understand what they went through that day. We will never know of the many heroes because there were so few left to write up all the citations that could have been written. Each minute must have seemed like forever. I guess I was so emotional about the scene, I wrote a poem about how I felt about the day:

REMEMBERING D-DAY 1944

You see the waves
That flow toward the shore
You hear the music of the waves
As the tides flow and the sands reach for more.

You hear songs
Of gulls that are screeching
You smell the sweet scents
From the tides and sands that are reaching.

I see Red waves
Carrying the blood of the wounded and the dead
I hear the blasts of the guns
From the ships behind and guns ahead.

I hear the moans
Of the wounded and the dying
I smell the Death
Of the bodies floating and no longer crying.

Those who were there remember
As thoughts blast through their minds
And bring tears
That are not possible to leave behind.

I could see how the Allies suffered so many casualties. I visualized the carnage and the bravery of many of the participants. I could also see the many who would not move from a safe spot until someone booted them along. There were many, many heroes that day no one will ever know about because there were not many left alive to write about the heroic actions of the day.

The Navy still had the blinkers working to guide the landing crafts to shore. We soon reached the landing area. Each man reached down and hoisted his pack on his back and we took our first steps onto the shores of France.

I did a lot more thinking about those men who braved the day. You could still see the burned out tanks, the gun emplacements, the sunken landing craft. We passed hundreds of underwater obstacles. We did see some Germans, but they were no longer fighters. Instead they were prisoners under guard, and some of them were loading trucks—which I thought was odd. They didn't seem to be under any stress. Rather they seemed relieved.

We continued up the hill on the hastily built roads. The place was really busy. Trucks were being loaded with rations and supplies. There were thousands of "Jerry" cans filled with gasoline waiting for someone to load them into the trucks. I wondered what a German airplane could do with a small strafing job. Thank God that the Allies had the upper hand in the air war. It was then that I heard that the Army had run out of gasoline; that stopped their drive. After the war many hours and words were spent discussing what the outcome would have been had the supply of gasoline kept up with the charge across France.

I followed the signs to the replacement center. When we arrived, I halted the group of prisoners and said to the officer in charge, "All present and accounted for." And then I said to myself, "Self, you and the two sergeants did a good job." With that I turned to the two sergeants and said, "Thanks for a good job." Which reminds me of a situation that happened in Texas. We were in the field and the colonel in charge said to one of his officers, "Get that platoon to come over here." That officer yelled at the platoon leader, "Please bring your platoon over here." The colonel really chewed out the officer and told him, "You never say please or thank you in an Army command." So I broke the rules. But I was not sorry. Those men had had a tough couple of days and I sure appreciated their effort.

[In July, 1944, the American Army on the Allies' right, newly supported by the landing of the Third Army under Lt. Gen. Patton, broke through the German defenses at Avranches, the gateway from Normandy into Brittany. Though some of the U.S. Forces were then swung southward in the hope of seizing the Breton ports, others were wheeled eastward to trap in the Falaise "pocket," a large part of the German forces retreating southward from the pressure of the Allied left at Caen.

Meanwhile, more and more Allied troops were being landed in Normandy. On 1 August two Army Groups were constituted: the 21st (comprising the

*British and Canadian Armies) under General Montgomery, and the 12th
(American) under General Bradley. General Montgomery was given oper-
ational control of both groups until General Eisenhower arrived in France.
From August 10-14, the 7th Armored Division landed at Utah and
Omaha Beaches in Normandy and was made part of the XX Corps, com-
manded by Major General Walton Walker, a part of General Patton's
Third Army. The 7th spearheaded the XX Corps drive from Chartres to
Metz between August 14th and September 25th.*

*By the middle of that month, an eastern wheel, wider than the one that cut
off the Falaise pocket, had brought the Americans to Argentan, level with the
21st Army Group on the left front so that a concerted effort could be
launched eastward. On the 19th, a U.S. division crossed the Seine. Orleans
was taken on the 17th, and after the French Resistance-led uprising in Paris,
the capitol city was entered by General LeClerc's French force on the 24th.
The U.S. 7th Army under General Patch and the French 1st Army under
General de Tassigny landed on the French Riviera on 15 August, advanced
rapidly up the Rhone valley, and joined the Americans north of Lyons early
in September.]*

When I landed in France, the front lines were almost to the German
border. The lead units were near Verdun. I remembered that name from
the first World War. A large battle was fought there—trench warfare at
its worst. Being so far from the front in Normandy, we were pretty
much safe from shellings. The only worry was an occasional fly-over by
a German plane.

I reported to the headquarters of the Replacement Center. They
said it would only be a couple of days before I would be assigned to
a unit at the front and that I could relax and enjoy the rest. I pitched
my tent—first class accommodations! But I had plenty of company.
Most of the officers I had come over with from the U.S. arrived about
the same time. Lieutenant Kinnebrew was made the officer in charge
of the officer group. Somewhere along the line, I was separated from

my long-time buddy Hugh West. He did not come over at the same time as most of the others did. In fact when we parted in England, it was the last time I ever saw him. Sad. The soldier and friend that was on every promotion list with me from Private First Class to 2nd Lieutenant was gone. Why I never tried to see him after the war I don't know.

While I was waiting for my number to come up, I took walks around the area, saw the remains of the war, watched the hustle and bustle of the ships coming in and the cargo and men coming up the slopes—quite a sight—and the small children who hung around the camp who were hoping for a candy bar or a cigarette. The French adults just went about their daily lives. They were happy to have the Germans gone. I am also sure they were very unhappy, for their homes were pretty much destroyed. They appeared to be still in shock. The battles of D-Day and the subsequent actions for the territory must have scarred them for life.

At night we sat around and talked and played cards. There was always a blackjack game going on in one of the tents, if you can imagine five or six men crowded in a small tent playing cards. I remember the many types of money in the pots. A mixture of francs, pounds, and dollars. We soon learned the exchange values. The game was usually played by flashlight, as blackout was ordered. Amounts grew in the pot when we were gambling with francs or English pounds. We knew the exchange rates but we didn't seem to mind losing foreign money. I was soon finished as I never seemed to have money to gamble with. I still hung around because the chatter was interesting to hear and I enjoyed watching the action.

One night two of us walked into a French bar. They did have wine. We each had a glass of wine from the owner's private stock. I was never a wine drinker, but never since that day have I tasted a better one. I really do not know all the things that good wines are supposed to have, but this wine had it. We tried to pay for it, but no luck. The owner accepted a package of Chesterfields, but no cash.

We were advised one night that we were to leave at 0700 the next day. We would be going to the front. There we would join an infantry unit already in combat. To tell the truth when I heard the news I got a twinge in my belly. Fear? I guess so. But the term "combat" seemed to be like a dreaded final exam. For two years we had been practicing, and now was the time to see how it really would be. No more of our own Aggressor Forces play-acting the enemy roles. Now the real thing, where the enemy will try his best to kill you. But I soon cleared my mind and said, "Here we go. Dear God, I place you in charge."

The morning came. We were twenty infantry officers and two hundred enlisted men. The officer in charge was still Kinnebrew, the young man from Georgia. Nice guy and wise enough to see he had a group of men who would do what he wanted, and he didn't have to play the role of tough guy. He just told us what to do and we did it. After it was over and we had reached the point of our assignments, I wondered why no one out of the large group had disappeared. After the war was over I heard that over ten thousand deserters had left combat and stayed in and around Paris for the duration. But I don't remember any mass court-martials for the deserters.

We were loaded into the old French railroad freight cars of the first World War vintage: the 40 and 8 cars. You could get forty men in the car or eight horses. We soon took off. The engine pulled the cars easily. The tracks were somewhat smooth so the ride was comfortable and we rode with the doors open so we could see the countryside. France was colorful. The green was a rich green and the other colors were vivid. We also saw the results of the drive of the armies that had preceded us by a few weeks. We got a look at the Hedge rows. I capitalize the "H," because what a great defensive weapon they were. There was no way to fight against them except by the old World War I command, "Over the Top!" They were too steep for tanks, so they were rarely used. The infantry would be exposed for a hundred yards or so between rows. If the infantry did try to attack over the open ground, they would be mowed down by machine gun fire. The best way to overcome the problem was by mortar fire—and both sides used their mortars effectively. Its trajectory fits the bill. With their high angle of fire the shells can drop just over the row's edge and cause havoc.

One thing I noted during my ride across France was that the women were working the fields. Lots of the crops were being harvested. While the Germans were in control, the French were very reluctant to harvest any crops. The reason given to us was that if they had brought the crops in the Germans would have taken most of them to "Der Fatherland."

When we passed through each town or city, the one obvious item we noted was how few steeples were left standing. The tanks and artillery would always zero in on the steeples, as either army always assumed the enemy would be using them as observation posts. And I suppose they were correct.

Our route followed that of the allied forces when they went across France. The one city that I remember was Chartres. In that town the steeple was still intact. The Americans knew the church was a treasure so they took pains not to knock it down. We didn't stop, but we did get a good look at the city as we passed by.

VERDUN

Finally, we crossed the Moselle river and the train came to a stop. We had arrived at the historic French town of Verdun.

Verdun. I remembered the stories told about the Battle of Verdun in World War I. For some reason Mom had saved pictures of the great battles of the first World War. I think she obtained the pictures from magazines. I remember reading about the trench warfare, and the trenches were still visible. Trenches that stretched for miles during that war. Of course, the barbed wire is no longer in place. That war killed so many on both sides by shells, bayonets, gangrene, and poison gas. The continuous bombardments by both sides lasted for months. And now here I was at that historic place. I imagined I could hear the sounds of artillery in the distance. Was it still going on? Or was that the ghosts of war still practicing their arts? Why Mom of all people saved war pictures I cannot understand, for she was so against all wars. The only explanation I can think of is that her brother Basil Newton was in the Army and in training in a camp in Texas, but he was never in combat; he was still in training when World War I ended. He became a prominent member of the Arkansas National Guard following the war and stayed with it until his death in 1941. Other than that I know of no other reason.

[In the north there was discord. Montgomery argued with the Supreme Allied Commander General Eisenhower for a single main thrust northeastward through Belgium into the heavily industrialized Ruhr valley—an

area so vital to the German war effort. The U.S. Generals wanted to con-
tinue the advance on a broad front in accordance with the pre-invasion
plans. Eisenhower, by way of compromise, decided on 23 August that
Montgomery's drive into Belgium should have the prior claim on resources
until Antwerp was taken, but that thereafter the pre-invasion plans would
be resumed.

Consequently, the British 2nd Army began its advance on 29 August,
entered Brussels on 3 September, took Antwerp the next day, and went on
to force its way to the Albert Kanaal. The U.S. First Army, supporting the
British on the right, took Namur on the same day Antwerp was taken and
was nearing Aachen. To the south Patton's Third Army, having raced for-
ward to take Verdun on 31 August, was attacking to cross the Moselle River
near Metz hoping to achieve a breakthrough into Germany's economically
important Saarland.]

We unloaded from the train, boarded Army trucks, and were taken to
a field near the Verdun trenches. The two hundred infantrymen and the
twenty officers would soon find out where each of them would be
assigned. Naturally we were a bit anxious. As soon as we were in the
field and positioned in a semi-horseshoe formation, a jeep came on the
scene. It brought the commanding general of the 7th Armored
Division, Major General Sylvester. He was a large man who stood tall,
with gray hair—a good looking officer. Along with him were members
of his staff. When the jeep was close enough to the troops, it stopped
and the general stood in front of the troops and spoke to us.

Bob joined the 7th Armored Division at Verdun

His talk went something like this: "Welcome to the 7th Armored Division. We have just come across France liberating the land that had long been in German hands. We are now preparing to move into Germany. Each of you will be assigned where you are needed." Then he turned to the twenty officers that were formed in a group at one end of the formation and continued, "As for you officers, you will be assigned to infantry companies. I want each of you to look to your right and left at the officers who are next to you. After the next battle there will only be a few of you left to carry on." I looked right and left and said to myself, "You unlucky bastards." And he was accurate. After the first serious battle there were very few of us left; over half were lost in their first battle. I remember thinking, when the general was talking, that is one hell of a way to greet inexperienced soldiers. We were all filled with anxiety and were concerned about what was going to happen. The odds quoted by the general certainly were not good for morale. As we stood there waiting, we heard a gun shot. Everybody ducked. Our eyes followed the sound, and we discovered that a soldier had shot himself in the foot, better known as a SIW or "self-inflicted wound." I guess the speech by the general had made a deep impression. To cap off our introduction to the division, as we were waiting for the next thing to happen, a truck drove slowly past our position. Inside the truck was a load of bodies—American soldiers that had been killed in the last battle.

It was while we were standing around the area that I first heard the far away rumblings of artillery firing. The sound, though not close, seemed to be foreboding of things to come. From that day on until the end of my experiences in the combat area, the rolling rumble was there. I have no knowledge of how many rounds of artillery and other explosives were used during the war on all sides, but it must have been tremendous.

After that the enlisted men were assigned. As their names were called, the men were loaded into waiting trucks. The trucks then delayed to see if there would be officers assigned to the same groups. One by one the officers received their assignments, and they too climbed aboard the trucks. Finally there were only two officers left, Lieutenant French and myself. French had been a machine gun instructor at Camp Roberts for two years. I had worked at a service station for several years. There were two jobs left. A motor officer and a machine gun platoon leader. French had never had any experience in motors, while that had been my civilian job. So he became the motor officer and I was assigned as the leader of the machine gun platoon of the Headquarters Company, 38th Armored Infantry Battalion.

The Division, like almost all Armored Divisions, had three Combat Commands (CCA, CCB, and CCR[eserve]), three Armored Infantry Battalions (23rd, 38th, and 48th AIBs), three Tank Battalions (17th, 31st, and 40th TBns), three Armored Artillery Battalions (434th, 440th, and 489th), a Cavalry Reconnaissance Squadron (87th), an Armored

Engineer Battalion (33rd), an Armored Medical Battalion (77th), an Armored Ordnance Battalion (129th), a Signal Company (147th), a Band, a Military Police Platoon, and a Division Trains (for maintenance and supply). They also normally had one Antiaircraft Battalion and a Tank Destroyer Battalion. The AIBs were made up of three Infantry companies, a Headquarters Company, and a Service Company. The Headquarters Company, besides the Commanding Officer and his staff, contained a Reconnaissance Platoon, a Mortar Platoon, an Assault Gun Platoon, and a Heavy Machine Gun Platoon. I was assigned to command the Machine Gun Platoon

The authorized strength of an Armored Division was 10,500 men and 168 medium tanks, 77 light tanks, 450 half-tracks, 54 self propelled 105 mm howitzers, 35 assault guns (105 mm), 54 armored cars, 1031 motor vehicles, and 8 light aircraft. In my Machine Gun Platoon, I had four heavy machine guns organized into two gun sections. Our job was to have sections go out with Infantry units and provide fire support for specific operations.

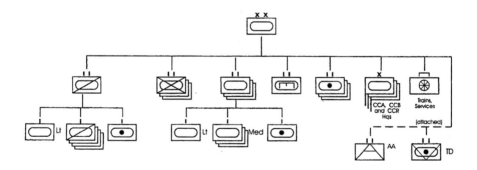

I was given a brief run down about the 7th Armored, which had come across France and made an excellent record but had not suffered many casualties. They were a rapid moving force and had

been successful in exploiting the hole made in the German defense line. It was in XX Corps, commanded by Major General Walton Walker, and a part the General Patton's Third Army. It had liberated many towns and cities and must have thought this war is easy—you know, "bring on the Germans." Then they ran out of gas, and for seven days they had to wait for the supplies to catch up with them. The units had a short rest and caught up on maintenance and sleep. I learned that the largest battle the 7th Armored had fought going across France was the Battle of Chartres, which is located about sixty miles southwest of Paris and through which we had passed on our train ride to Verdun. At that battle my new commanding officer, Captain Carl M. "Rusty" Mattocks, distinguished himself. His unit had come across a company-sized German force that was apparently trying to get back to their own forces, and the two companies clashed. After a sharp fire fight, the Germans put up a white flag and Rusty's outfit won. Rusty and his men took forty-two prisoners. For his gallantry in action, he was awarded the Silver Star.

From Chartres the 7th continued on the march and had arrived at Verdun so fast the Germans did not have time to blow out the bridge leading into the town. They had captured the town intact. It was there that a warehouse full of Wehrmacht cognac—and other alcoholic beverages—was found by one of the soldiers who was looking around the town and just happened to go into the warehouse and found it was full of liquor. The news didn't take long to get around the division, and soon cases of liquor were on almost every tank and half-track. It was issued out to the units with the stipulation that it was only to be used during inclement weather and for snake bite. It must have rained a lot, because no snakes were ever seen.

The Division's next objective was to get across the Moselle River. One evening the mess sergeant, after imbibing in a few drinks, decided that the crossing would be easy. He said, "You damn doughfeet don't know how to fight. I'll show you how to get across that damn river." So he talked another cook into driving a half-track, on which he had mounted a .50 caliber machine gun—he was going to show the GIs how to get the Army moving again. Off they went toward the river, and as they came close to it, a German 88 opened up on them. After a near hit the sergeant quickly decided that the life of a front line soldier was much more dangerous than that in the kitchen, and crossing the river was not as easy as making a stew. So he hightailed it back.

When the gas supply finally got to the front, the attack commenced again. The 38th Armored Infantry made it across the Moselle at West Arnaville and later took over the town of Lorry. It cost the units a lot of casualties, but they were successful. The Germans were really getting tough. They knew the area and had every crossroad covered with mortar and artillery fire because they had been operating an artillery school nearby and had every key place plotted. The town of Arry was our next objective. The area was with hills and forests. On one day during the battle for Arry, the 38th lost five battalion commanders—three were killed, two seriously wounded and evacuated. When I heard of the loss of all the battalion commanders, I wondered if they ever thought of moving their headquarters. Seemed to me that the Germans knew the position of the battalion command post and were playing, "Let's shoot the colonel." The last commander, the one who survived, spent all his time in his foxhole digging it deeper. He was given another job after that fracas.

I learned that the lieutenant I was replacing had been captured. He had been assigned to the company, and on his first combat mission with his new assignment he was captured along with the commander of the headquarters company. It was quite apparent why there was the great need for infantry officers. Left in the headquarters company was Rusty Mattocks, recently promoted from lieutenant to captain. During the time I was getting acquainted with him, I wondered how I would be received by the men of my new platoon—the weapons platoon. After meeting Mattocks and his staff, I asked where my new platoon was located. The first sergeant, Alvie Davis, pointed to a group of men who, with their half-tracks, were located on the side of the hill about 500 yards away. I got my stuff out of the truck and started up the hill. It had been rainy for days, so after a lot of slipping and sliding I finally made it to where the platoon was located. I remember at the time wondering why none of the men came to help me. But that is the way of war. It was then I reminded myself I was a new officer and the men were only testing me. I fooled them. I didn't ask for help nor did I give them hell for not helping. The immediate problem of a replacement officer is to prove himself. His new men would size him up quickly. The first experience in combat would do the proving and nothing else. I had to wonder how I would behave when the fighting was going on. We all would soon know.

A big sergeant stood up when I approached. He came forward, saluted, and said, "Sir, Sergeant Sicari reporting." I gave him my name and then after a few minutes of conversation, he assembled the men and introduced me. They were a group of men of all sizes and shapes and from all races except blacks. With that I took my bed roll and other baggage to my half-track, pitched my tent, and started around the area to get acquainted with the men: Sergeants Sicari, Simoneaux, Curtin, and others. My driver was Corporal Cox. Cox helped me get my stuff into the half-track. The next man I met was Maurice Conover, who was to be my runner and who proved to be a Godsend to me for the rest of my time in combat. Conover was from the small town of Broadview, Montana, where he had a large wheat ranch. Most of the other names in the platoon have disappeared from my memory. I can see them vividly, but the names are gone.

After meeting with my men, I went back to see the other officers and enlisted men of the Headquarters Company. It was practically a re-staffed unit with Captain Mattocks as the Commanding Officer and Lieutenants Kinnebrew, French, and myself as platoon leaders. Over a cup of coffee, Captain Mattocks gave us a run-down of his experiences during the race across France:

The 7th's first mission was to seize the cathedral city of Chartres, about sixty kilometers southwest of Paris. The twin spires of the Cathedral were seen as we approached the city. The 38th AIB was assigned to by-pass the city to the north through the village of Leves and seize a small German airport on its northeast perimeter. A small task force made up of a reconnais-sance platoon, an infantry platoon, and my assault guns [75mm guns mounted on light tanks with an open tur-ret] fought the first battle the 38th was in.

As the task force took the east road from the center of the village, it came under direct machine gun fire from some place near a large church located in the eastern side of the village. No casualties were sustained by the Recon Platoon, however the platoon leader, Lt. Frederikson, had become separated from his unit and took refuge with a group of nuns at the church. The infantry platoon leader was hit and had to be evacuated. So I took command of the task force and deployed the assault guns in a wooded slope just west of the town from where we could fire into the church area. First we demolished the brick wall, which then allowed us a clear field of fire.

A German armed with a *panzerfaust* [bazooka] came out from the ruins of the wall and became our first pris-oner. I told the rifle platoon to move into town after my guns had finished shelling, which would be signaled by a smoke shell. The troops advanced and seized three of the four corners of the cross roads near the village center. However, the Germans in the fourth part were able to fire into the turret of one of the assault guns and wounded two of my men. I had moved with the infantry and was in a house looking eastward towards the burning church. While doing so a lone German, unnoticed by me, came out of a building in the unoccupied fourth part of the town. He shot at me, striking the window frame, which got my complete attention, and I took him down with a quickly borrowed M-1 rifle.

The infantry advanced to the east side of the village to a point near the burning church, where we found a Renault car that the Germans had abandoned when they apparently withdrew through some heavy woods nearby. We proceeded east for approximately one-half a mile then turned right, crossing over an abandoned stone quarry which had probably been used during the construction of the church. We then approached the air strip and came under artillery fire from the southeast. We withdrew to a point overlooking the quarry, where we spent the night. We thought the artillery fire came from our own forces which were part of the pincer movement around the city.

We captured several Germans that night who were trying to break out to the east, but when we heard a burst from our ring-mounted .50 caliber machine guns, we heard them yell *Kamerad.* We didn't close the gap that day, but did on August 17th.

Captain John M_____and a platoon of riflemen were ambushed in the city, and John abandoned his men, which didn't endear him much to his men, but we were able to get the men back safely. After that I went back to where we had lost Frederikson. I found him as he was coming back to our lines after hiding out with the nuns in their domicile.

We had a Colonel by the name of Wellborn Griffith, the Operations Officer from XX Corps there monitoring our action, who came down into Leves to check things out after we had passed through. He was riding in a light tank and when he stuck his head out of the turret it was promptly shot off by one of the many Germans we had by-passed.

Our next major engagement was at Melun, located on the Seine River about thirty kilometers upstream from Paris. We forced a crossing of the river on August 24th and sustained several casualties doing so.

Our route of advance took us northeast through the World War I cities of Soissons and Verdun. Our next assignment was at Reims in the champagne district of France. The city had been liberated by the 5th Infantry Division, who was working with the 7th Armored across France. Our outfit was located on the extreme right flank of the division. We seized a fort by the name of De Brimont, which overlooked a small German airfield about three kilometers northeast of Reims. The Germans had stored a lot of planes in this underground fort—which we destroyed. While there, my assault guns intercepted and captured forty-two Germans who were trying to make their way back to Germany. We hit them really hard and our medics had quite a time treating their wounded.

From there on and into Germany we encountered heavier enemy resistance, especially as we neared the West Wall. At the town of St. Prival, we had a real donny-brook and lost quite a few men, including our S2

[Intelligence] officer. 1st Lieutenant John Cornel of Company C of the 38th won the Distinguished Service Cross there.

We crossed the Moselle River at Thionville in coordination with the 5th Division, but it proved untenable and we withdrew. We were in the Metz area which had twenty-six forts, some of which were nine stories underground. There we again made a river crossing over a pontoon bridge at night with the rest of the Combat Command following, and we ran over towns named Arry, Lorry, Mariellies, and Bouxiers-Froidmont.

My assault guns passed through Lorry and traveled to a small cross roads where they parked and turned off their engines. After doing so, we heard some noise in a nearby clump of bushes, and we threw a concussion grenade into them. We didn't hear any further noise after the explosion. But just as dawn arrived we heard a groan from that area and we found a German soldier with a *panzerfaust* who had been hit by the grenade and his testicles were hanging out by a shread of skin. We took him to the aid station, but he died shortly thereafter.

At daylight, a German short-barreled anti-tank located on the edge of Mariellies opened fire on our tanks. Every gun in the Combat Command brought fire down on the AT gun, and I saw Germans running to our lines, all crouched over, wanting to surrender. Throughout that day, September 18th, our division engineers labored to clear a road through the dense forest located just to our front. All that day we had received heavy shelling; one of the barrages killed my supply sergeant, Charles Schenk, who was so mangled it was impossible to identify him.

The next day, the 38th advanced to the eastern edge of the heavy woods after the road had been constructed. We received a new commander that day, Lieutenant Colonel Henry Rosebro who, I believe, had been assigned previously to Division Trains. On a personal reconnaissance, he apparently discovered an 88mm gun emplacement near a small crossroad on the eastern side of the village of Sillegny. He was shot through the head. Next our S3, Major Tom Wells, came forward and was immediately hit by a 150mm shell. His body was also destroyed beyond recognition. Shortly thereafter, Lieutenant Colonel Ted King arrived from division headquarters. He too was hit by a bullet through his helmet and evacuated. The next commander was Lieutenant Colonel Robert Rhea. He too didn't last long. His main contribution was to return the remnants of the battalion from the woods which we had attacked that morning and to enlarge the slit trench he occupied. He was relieved at dusk. We then got our present commander, Lieutenant Colonel William H. G. Fuller.

My first assignment came the next day. I was to take a section of men in one of our half-tracks, on which we mounted a machine gun, drive it to the Combat Command Reserve headquarters, and meet the commanding general. At that time the 38th was with CCR. We arrived at its headquarters and were met by the aide. He showed me the vehicle the commander was going to ride in which we were to guard. So on one of my first days I was able to see a lot of the division, as the commander wanted to visit with a number of his units. It was a good quick introduction to my new outfit and was the first time I had ever been in a half-track. The job lasted for a couple of hours. When we were dismissed, we returned to our bivouac area. On the way back to our area, as we were driving through woods, I suddenly had an urge to relieve myself. I had the sudden "gripes" and I knew I had better take the time to do something about it. When our vehicle stopped, I got out and walked a short distance, stopped, and did the job. I stood up and started to pull my pants up when I spotted, deeper into the woods and on the ground about thirty yards away, a German soldier. I ducked behind a tree. I kept looking and the soldier didn't move. After a short time I decided the man was dead. I walked over and verified for myself: dead he was. As I stood looking at him I wondered about the man. He was somebody's son or husband. I got back to the half-track and told the men about it. They asked if I had searched the body, and did he have a Luger pistol? I found out then that Lugers were a real prize and that I had goofed. I said no and that I would tell the graves registration officer about the body, which I did.

The next two days were spent doing our wash, cleaning our equipment, and, of course, writing home. I had continued to try to write every day, and suddenly it came to me that I was really homesick, for I had not received a letter since I left home to come overseas. I knew there were letters in the mail pipeline, but no one knew where I was or where to send my mail. I wondered about the family. The only member of the family in harm's way at the time was my brother-in-law Tom Swain. I took comfort that the last I had heard everyone was okay.

The 7th Armored Division was decimated trying and finally making it across the bridge over the Moselle. When the division finally made it, the casualties were counted, and the powers that be in the Third Army decided that it was necessary to bring the 7th back to strength. At this time General Patton ordered our General Sylvester to continue the attack. Gen. Sylvester answered, "With what? Most of the squads in my infantry only have two or three men left." With that "Old Blood and Guts," (our blood and his guts) relieved him from command. Subsequently Sylvester was reduced to his permanent regular army grade of colonel. The men in the division never really forgave General Patton for that action. We were alerted and advised that we would soon move from the Third Army to another major command. Of course I did not know much about other Armies, but everyone had heard of General Patton. By hook or by crook he was going to be the hero. I think the personnel of the 7th Armored Division were really glad to leave his command.

HOLLAND

[On 24 September orders were received for the 7th AD to shift from the Third Army to the First Army in Holland.]

The weather had been rainy for days. When we got the order to move out, we did have a bit of a problem getting the half-tracks down the hill again from where they had been parked. The half-tracks would slip and slide, but by skillful driving, Corporal Cox and the other drivers made it down. When we reached the road, we were met by Sergeant Curtin. During the night he had gone absent without leave exploring the area. He had been roaming around in the nearby town, had confiscated an old twelve cylinder Packard, got it running, and wanted to join the convoy. He said one of the villagers had given the car to him. It didn't take me long to get him back into his half-track and leave his prized possession. I thought about breaking him back to private for going AWOL because he had been gone without permission, but Sergeant Sicari talked me out of it. He said that Curtin was the best combat leader in the platoon. He would goof off when there was a lull but he never missed a formation and was always there when needed. I decided then and there I would test Sicari. I told him that he was to talk to Curtin and tell him the next time he wandered off he would be broken back to private and that no one in the platoon was to leave without his permission. It worked out well. Sicari knew then and there he was to be the boss of his men.

[General Montgomery attempted a thrust to the Rhine at Arnheim. The British 1st Airborne Division and the U.S. 82d and 101st Airborne Divisions were dropped ahead to clear the way for the British 2d Army, but the Germans were able to check the thrust, thus isolating the airborne troops, many of whom were taken prisoner. By this time the German defense was rapidly stiffening as the Allies approached the German frontiers. The U.S. First Army spent a month grinding down the defenses at Aachen, which fell on 20 October (the first city of pre-war Germany to be captured by the Allies), and the Canadian 1st Army, on the left of the British 2nd, did not clear the Scheldt estuary west of Antwerp, including Walcheren Island, until early November. Likewise, Patton's Third Army

was held up before Metz. Regardless of the Allied advance of about 350 miles, the Germans in November still held both the Ruhr Valley and Saarland.]

We were on the move. I had never been in an armored convoy. With the jeeps, half-tracks, assault vehicles, and tanks, the rattle of the vehicles could be heard for miles. Our route was through Belgium and a part of Holland. Little did we know we were soon to return to Belgium for one of the most critical battles of the war. At every town we motored through the streets were full of people watching and waving. Some appeared to be happy to see us and others certainly did not have a look of joy. But I must admit that for the most part there was a look of happiness on their faces. The men in our half-tracks all had their heads above the side plates. They were enjoying the sound and the appearance of the people. Most of the men in my platoon had been on the break-out from Normandy after D-Day and had participated in the march across France so they were not as excited as I was. Never had I seen so many friendly waves. I hadn't earned and didn't deserve the reward of these masses, but I must admit I enjoyed the reception by them. At one of the towns we were going through, the convoy for some reason came to an abrupt stop in the middle of the city. Standing on the corner was a beautiful blonde girl. She was waving an American flag and cheering. Sergeant Sicari was going nuts! He was yelling at me. I was in the lead half-track, and he was in the following one. He was shouting, "Hey Lieutenant, how would you like to hold that girl close and love her? Isn't she beautiful?" and so on. He raved to me for about fifteen minutes how he had fallen in love with the girl. All the time the girl kept waving and smiling. Finally the convoy started again. As it began to roll the girl called out to Sicari in perfect English, "Why didn't you come over sergeant?" We laughed at the crestfallen look on the sergeant's face. We soon learned most of the people of Holland could speak the English language.

We came to our new area. The division was now a part of the First U.S. Army. Our new assignment was to clear out the Peel Swamp, west of the Meuse River. It was soon after we arrived in the area I received my first combat duty. My platoon was to guard some tanks during the night—tanks that were going to make an attack in the morning. The armor unit had moved close to the front lines waiting for dawn. So I took the platoon to the area and placed the machine guns defensively where they could be used in case of an attack by the enemy. What struck me, when I reported to the officer in charge, was the men in the tank were trying to see the terrain from their small openings. It was then I began to understand why the infantry really hated tanks: tanks are so vulnerable. They can't hide, they make a lot of noise, they attract artillery fire, and all it takes to stop them is one bazooka or anti-tank gun of any type. The night soon passed without incident, and we were relieved and returned to our area. Later that morning we were given a new task—we were to be a part of the combat team trying to clean up in an area where a disorganized group of Germans was supposedly ready to surrender. We got that kind of intelligence all the time, and most of the time the German ability to fight had not diminished very damned much. As I was leading my men following the infantry unit my platoon was assigned to, I was aware of a glint of a bullet that whizzed past my head. It just missed me. Odd as it might seem, I knew right then I was going to make it through the war; that bullet had my name on it and it had missed. "Yea though I walk through the valley of Death," came to my mind.

It struck me that there were not as many men in my platoon as there would have been in a regular platoon in an Infantry company. By the time the driver and assistant driver remained with the half-track, I noted there were not very many ammunition bearers. I wondered about that at first but later understood that an armored infantry unit is not supposed to stay in the front lines as long as in an infantry division. Our infantry was supposed to follow the tanks and exploit their efforts. I soon learned it was designed to be that way, but it just didn't work out.

When the tanks and the infantry took off toward the enemy, it wasn't long before the first tank was hit and exploded. Then the Germans hit the rear tank. Then one by one the tanks were knocked off. It was like a shooting gallery. In some cases the men got out of the tanks, but most of the men inside the tanks that were hit were killed by fire or by shell fragments. When a shell penetrates a tank, the shell tears up the insides of the tank and pieces of metal fly around causing fire and hitting all of the personnel. Rarely do any of the members of a tank crew survive a penetrating hit.

I think that is when I became aware that our tanks were so easily destroyed, and it was quite a shock. For some reason I was under the impression that our tanks were almost indestructible. In talking to the Tankers in our division, I found they were very unhappy to have to fight the German Panthers and Tigers, with their better guns and armor plating, and had to beat them with numbers and by out-maneuvering them. And I soon discovered that the Allies had a number of weapons that were inferior to what the Germans had, such as the *panzerfaust* which was much more powerful than our bazooka. The German mortars were bigger and more effective, and their machine guns had a higher rate of fire. We had better rifles, the M-1 (Garand), and artillery. But our greatest asset, besides the quantity and superiority of our arms and equipment, was primarily the leaders in the front lines: the captains, lieutenants, and non-coms—the guys who were pulled together from our population, given some training, and sent to fight a war with men who never knew each other before entering the army, who were drawn from all parts of the country and yet developed a closeness that is most difficult to describe.

The battle continued. Finally our troops knocked out the anti-tank gun that had caused all of the problems. It was a rough situation for the infantry, as the GIs had to go across an open field to reach the Germans. My platoon was committed, but we didn't have to do much firing as our fields of fire were full of our own men. But we were able to help on the flanks.

[Early on 27 October, the German Army launched a vigorous attack against the 7th Armored Division, which was guarding the right flank of the British 2d Army in southeastern Holland. For three days two Panzer Divisions clashed with the 7th in an attempt to force a diversion from the Allied drive on the Scheldt Peninsula to the west, or to cut lines of communication and supply along the salient into Holland toward Arnhem. At that time the 38th AIB was with CCA near the town of Meijel, Holland.]

The next engagement was the attack toward Meijel. I had to break up my platoon. Sergeant Sicari took one of the sections to support a combat team, while I took the other section and took a position in the small town of Nederwert. My mission was to protect the flank of the operation. We placed our guns. Then we found a tall building used for the storage of grain. We could see the surrounding area from the top floor of the warehouse. We were there for a couple of days and could see most of the terrain. I even called for some artillery fire from that observation post. We had heard the German mortars popping as they dropped shells in the tube. I don't think we hit the spot exactly, but we did silence the mortar firing from that position.

On the second day I was called to one of the lookout windows. The men had spotted a German soldier about 500 yards away. He was either a forward observer or a sniper. The men had heard I had made expert on the M1 rifle. They challenged me to hit the man. How do you back down from that kind of challenge, especially from men who did not want to fire their weapons for fear their position would be given away? I set the sights on the weapon, squeezed off the round, and the man went down. He got up and then fell again. I knew I had wounded him. Soon the Germans came with a stretcher and carried the soldier away. I was looked on with more respect after that, but, to tell the truth, I have seen that German soldier fall every day since. Why only that one I do not know.

After we were there for three days, Captain Mattocks came and told me to bring the men back to the headquarters. So we packed and followed the captain's jeep back to battalion headquarters. I went in to the maps on the wall of the S3 (Operations) room and asked where Sergeant Sicari's section was located. The S3 pointed out on the map where it was supporting a combat team just outside a small town about a mile away. The town could be reached either by the road the combat team had been following, or, I noted on the map, there was a shortcut which went along a road by a canal where it joined another road. There I would have to take a left turn and go across a field about a thousand yards to the town. As the section had been following on foot, I knew they did not have their K rations and were probably in need of some sustenance. I went out to my half-track, placed a case of K rations on my shoulder, and said to my runner, Conover, "Let's go." We started up the road by the canal. When we reached about half way to the road we were going to take to the town, we decided to take a short cut across the field. When we reached the road, we took it toward the town. As we approached it we heard a fire fight going on. As we were almost to the town, we continued on. Conover, who was my eyes said, "Hey Lieutenant, that's Sergeant Sicari waving his arms at us." Sicari was by arm signals telling us not to stay on the road but to go behind the town. The task force was still fighting for it. So the two of us took the circuitous route to enter the little town. There Sergeant Sicari took the rations from me. I checked around to see how the men were and went close to the front, where the fighting noise was coming from, to observe. The firing had quieted down, so I told my men I would see them later. Conover and I left taking the same route back. We walked the road rather than taking the short cut across the field. As we got close to the canal, we could see American soldiers aiming their weapons at the two of us, but we continued on and came to the canal. A lieutenant stood up. I recognized him. It was Will Rogers Jr. He was the officer in charge of the men along the canal. He said, as he chewed on the end of a piece of straw, "Where have you been?" I told him where and why I was on the road. I asked why they were guarding the road and why he didn't stop us when we went across the first time? He said none of them had seen us. They must have been asleep, as we sure didn't creep and crawl along the road. Rogers was a member of the Reconnaissance Company of the 7th Armored Division's 87th Cavalry Squadron.

I returned to the headquarters and told them there were no enemy along the area of the road. They didn't really believe me because the Combat Team had been fighting to clear that area for some time. I told them Conover and I had just returned from walking the road. I would further be glad to show them again. Conover and I said later that we had freed more land with a case of K rations than the task force had done with all their combat team.

K-Rations! There were three types: one each for breakfast, dinner, and supper. I liked the one for breakfast best, for it had a can of eggs, some kind of meat, a couple of cracker biscuits, a bit of toilet paper, and about ten cigarettes. When we got a package that had Raleighs in them, we gave them away to civilians, but they actually were not even good trading material. The dinner ration had some kind of spread that we could put on our package of crackers, and the usual paper and cigarettes. It also contained a candy bar that was made so that no one could eat the damned thing because it was so hard, but we saved them for rainy days. The supper box was about the same as the dinner one, except it had more biscuits and the worst cheese ever concocted. But, in all fairness, they did keep us alive.

The battle continued. My platoon was again assigned to another task force consisting of tanks and an infantry company. This time the objective was some small towns. If I remember correctly, the name of one of the towns was something like Dork. The attack started at 0600. We knew there were enemy tanks in the towns ahead, as we had heard the WHOOMP of their 88mm shells going by. No use ducking when you hear the WHOOMP because the shell has already passed. But scary it is. We had questioned an elderly couple who had just come from the town, and they confirmed there were a couple of tanks and other soldats around. Most of the civilians had left the town and had made their way through our lines when the Germans appeared on the scene. I think everyone in the town had a bicycle and those that could came riding toward and through the lines of the Allies.

We positioned our heavy machine guns so we could give maximum support to the attacking infantry. The attack started. First the tanks sped ahead into the town. Then we watched the infantry take off across the open field ahead. I admired their guts, especially the leaders. They would yell at one man and the man would take off for a few yards flop on the ground, then the next man would take off, run and flop and fire toward the enemy. A mine exploded killing one of the men. The cry of "Medic!" rang out. The medic crawled out and looked at the man and saw there wasn't a thing he could do; he stuck the man's rifle in the ground and continued on. All this time I had my men in position behind a pile of dirt that was about two feet high and twenty feet long. The dirt covered a crop of sugar beets that had just been harvested. Sgt. Simoneaux was next to me sitting with his back to the mound. We heard a splat and then the WHOOMP of an 88. Simoneaux quietly called to me, "Lieutenant, look." He pointed at a shell that had come to rest between his outstretched legs. It had not exploded. I said, "I don't know about you but I am moving out. Pass it down to your men that a mine field is ahead. Follow me. Only step in my tracks or other footsteps that you can see. Don't panic. Carefully step around the unexploded shell. We must get through the mine field. The infantry got through it with only one casualty so maybe we can get through safely."

I led off. The men followed. I could see they were carefully watching every step they took. Suddenly we began to get machine gun fire so we dropped to the ground. What a hell of a deal! Where was the damn gun located? I couldn't see the machine gun, but I knew the firing was coming from the left. I also knew that one of the tricks the "Jerries" used was to pin the troops down with machine gun fire and then lob mortar rounds into the pinned down soldiers. I heard the horrible sound of the plop of the mortar round going into a tube. I yelled to the troops, "Let's go. No use staying here and getting killed. Run for the buildings ahead. Watch your step." With that I took off running toward the nearest building.

Those damned mines scared the hell out of me. Most of the time they were hidden and set to bounce up just high enough to really clobber the victim. Usually the damage was a very severe wound, which then required more personnel, especially medics, to care for the wounded. They were a very cruel weapon. Tiny prongs from them protrude just barely above the ground, and who in the hell has time to look? I guess it must have looked odd to see us trying to run fast while attempting to step where the guy ahead had stepped before.

I took off running for the nearest building. As I came to the farm building, I saw an opening into the barn. I dove in and landed next to a sow's ass. She was lying on the ground grunting every time a shell landed. The mortars' rounds were coming in regularly and with every WHOMP of a shell the pigs rear end and my nose came closer together. Neither one of us seemed to mind.

The enemy stiffened and was giving us all kinds of weapons fire. The commander of our force requested artillery support. Boy did we get it. TIME ON TARGET followed. Every artillery piece in the division and the supporting artillery guns of the corps laid the barrage down. The earth actually shook! It was very effective. During the middle of the barrage an elderly woman came out of a nearby cellar and ran for the house. I saw her and tried to stop her but she wouldn't stop until she got to the kitchen where she reached into a closet and grabbed a handful of food and then scampered back to the cellar. At the entrance to the cellar I saw her husband looking out to see if she was going to make it. She did.

Right after the barrage we were able to get our team together, move out, and take the objective. My platoon continued to assist with the drive, and the tanks started to clank on with our infantry following close behind. I talked to the sergeant and asked if I could be of any help, but he replied, "No sir, this is my platoon now and we have them on the run." With that, I congratulated him on his performance in handling his platoon coming across the open field. He nodded his thanks. I wish I knew his name, but it was such a brief encounter and I never worked with him again. There were a lot of examples of great actions by individual soldiers that were never recognized with medals—probably because no one had time to write up the recommendations. And when it was over, all we wanted to do was forget those minutes of hell.

While I was still in the house with the stable, waiting for the troops to get on their way, I walked to a large window and stood there looking out. Suddenly the window was shot out. Bullets from a machine gun raked the window. How the rounds missed me, I don't know. But never again did I give the enemy such a good target.

My platoon again started to follow the infantry, each time shifting our machine guns to support them. When the objective was reached and all was calm we were relieved. I took my men back to the company bivouac area where we rested for a day. The time was spent cleaning our weapons and getting ourselves washed up and shaved again.

About that time Captain Mattocks was rewarded with a trip to Paris and a three day pass. He deserved the time off. After he left, the company continued doing a bit of training. When he returned he came in with an empty cognac bottle. With a grin on his face he waved the empty bottle and said a bit sheepishly, "I tried to bring back this bottle to you but the ride was long and we got thirsty. Guess what? We drank your bottle." We all laughed and were glad to see him back.

The next day I asked Rusty about his trip: what did he see, where did he sleep, and was there anything back there in Paris that was worth the trip? He told us that Paris was so crowded with Army people that a person coming in from the front was lucky to find a bed. He had run into a buddy and the two of them stayed together. He did get loaded. But what bothered him most was that all the soldiers there had never seen combat and never would. He saw a lot of officers dressed in pinks and greens. We all agreed that it took a lot of bodies to win a war, but only a few ever saw combat. Even in a Division less than half are involved in actual front line fighting.

And later I came to the realization that no one in our outfit ever saw any of the USO entertainment, I guess because we were so far forward. Most of the entertainment was provided to the rear echelon people, who probably didn't need much as there was plenty around for them. At the time, though, we were too busy trying to stay alive to even think about such things.

It wasn't long before my platoon got its next assignment to be under the command of Captain Johnny M___'s task force. We were to support an action to take over a village near the town of Meijel. After passing through our force's road block, Captain M___'s task force was to clear the swamp near the town of Weert. All was going quite well. We ran into some mines but soon got around them and then continued on. The task force next took the town of Horick. Just before we started, I had received two men back who had previously been wounded, Sergeant Totoni and a man whose name I can't remember. I told them to join with their previous sections. About that time as we were passing through a small village whose buildings were along the right side of the road, all hell broke loose. We were blasted by artillery from the left. I mean it was an intense barrage. But the damn stuff was coming from the friendly side. Our force took cover behind the buildings and in the ditch that ran along side of the road. That was where I wound up, in the ditch. When the barrage lifted we reassembled. The private who had just joined my platoon was still in the ditch and was shaking all over. I tried to get him up and with no success. He was just mumbling and completely out of control. I learned then that the reason he had been sent to the rear the first time was for combat fatigue. I had never seen a man act like that before, and I sure didn't want him with my men in that condition. So I sent him back to the command post and told him to check with our medical officer, "Doc" Jell. The task force continued up the road. Suddenly a fire fight broke out ahead. It was going on hot and heavy. My platoon was looking for a place to set up to help. We looked ahead and saw our forward infantry troops streaming to the rear. I yelled at my four sergeants, "Stop those men. Have them dig in place." My sergeants literally had to tackle some of the men to stop them.

Captain M___turned to me as he hurriedly started to walk to the rear, "Moranda take over. I am going back to the headquarters and tell them what's going on." Why the man broke I do not know. He had communications with the rear, so he didn't have to leave his command in my lap. His two platoon leaders came back to me and asked what they were supposed to do. Me, a brand new lieutenant. Luckily I knew both of the men. One was a good friend, Lieutenant Corbin. The other young lieutenant was one who had come over with us from England. Again my memory of his name is gone. I said, "I guess we must go on and take the objective." They left, assembled their units again, and we all proceeded again toward the objective. Hell!! It wasn't but an hour later the lieutenant, whose name I can't remember, returned to where I was, only this time on a jeep. He was without a leg. As he saw me he said, "Bob, guess I'll beat you back to the States." Damn! Damn! Damn! I really felt bad. I was the guy who had told him to continue the attack.

The attack went on for a time. The turning point was when Lieutenant Corbin led his troops across the field into the town. After we had been under fire and pinned down for some time, he got mad about the situation. He just stood up and said to his men, "Let's go." With his weapon firing at every step he led his troops to the town. After we had reached the town, the two of us sat in a barn, after posting sentries to the outposts, and reviewed the day. Corbin and I just enjoyed talking about anything that would take our minds away from the war for a few minutes—mostly about home and family. We later found out the first intense barrage had been from the English artillery unit that was supporting us. They had seen us and didn't think that we could be so far toward our objective so fast. They gave us the "sorry old chap," bit, which didn't help much.

It was at this battle I saw something that I have wondered about ever since. A corporal from one of the leading infantry units came back to the place where I was doing my best to keep things running. He had two German soldats, prisoners, ahead of him and was marching them back to the rear. Our S2 (intelligence officer), Captain Fredrickson, always wanted to get information from captured enemy soldiers as soon as possible. The corporal asked how far back the command post was. I gave him the directions, and he left for the rear with the two Germans. It wasn't long before the corporal was back. I knew he could not have taken the prisoners back that quickly. I asked him what had happened and how he could get back so fast. His reply was that they tried to get away so he had to shoot them. I didn't believe him then and I don't believe him now. I felt badly, but there were no witnesses so I couldn't do much about it. But I'm sure he knew I didn't believe him.

(I didn't see Captain M___ again until long after the war was over. I was sent back to the Pentagon for some training when I was a member of the National Guard 40th Infantry Division. I was visiting with Colonel Boyer who had been the S3 of the 38th AIB. Captain M___, then a lieutenant colonel, was stationed at the Pentagon, and Boyer asked if I would go and see him. I said negative, that I never wanted to see the man again. But when he asked the second time I did go down to where M___ was working. I talked to him. He said he was sorry. And with that I left. He had suffered enough years of remembering his mistake. I'm certain a person does not forget his cowardice ever.)

[General Montgomery persisted in his concept of widening the salient in Holland and had given priority of supplies to the British 2d Army. After pressure from Eisenhower to switch emphasis to taking Antwerp, a prime target so the port could be used for the logistics necessary to support the main effort, Montgomery finally promised an all-out effort to do so. On 16 October, he altered his supply priorities to the Canadian 2d Army, who proceeded to move to Antwerp, and after heavy fighting took the port city in early November]

During the month of October it seemed we were in the line fighting most of the time. Our headquarters units were assigned to one command after another, usually small task forces, most of the time around the town of Meijel. Our division was protecting the left flank of the First Army. We had large gaps between our forces. On one of the nights we were in the town of Meijel, it was time to bed down so we placed our security guards around the area and went into an unoccupied house. We never took advantage of the houses other than to sleep in a bed or sit in the chairs. We did not want to hurt any of the Dutch people. This night we had eaten our rations and just gone to bed when we heard a loud bang and something clanged against the front door of the house. We jumped up when we heard the rattle of a machine gun and the whirr of the burp guns. I opened the door. There just a few feet away from the door was a *panzer-faust* shell. It had hit the door but must have hit it on a slant and didn't go off. Had it exploded some of us would have been injured badly or killed. We called the engineers, who came and took the shell away and destroyed it. We then learned that a German patrol had come through our lines and tried to wipe out the command post. While fighting in Holland, we had become somewhat lax as we thought everyone in Holland loved us. Not so. Most of the citizens did, but someone had told the Germans where we were sleeping and that it was the command post. We had a Dutchman with us who was one of our guides. Since he was with us at the time, we knew he had not told anyone.

The night after the fire fight, when I got back to our battalion area, I was going back to my tent and as I passed the medics' tent our Medical Officer, Doctor Jell, called out to me, "Lieutenant Moranda, don't you ever tell me that a man is shell shocked. That is the job of the medics."

I retorted, "OK, Doc, it is your decision, but don't send that man to me again. He would only be a continual problem, and it's a bad thing for the rest of us to observe. And furthermore he shouldn't have been returned to the platoon where he had broken down before."

The doctor grumbled a bit and then to get in the last word said, "And don't call me doc."

I replied, "Why not? It is a term of endearment."

To which he responded, "I don't like the name because a 'dock' is the strap on the harness that goes under the tail of a horse."

"Hmmm," was my response that he didn't hear as I continued to walk around the area.

One job I had was to read all the mail that was written by my men. I really only had one man who wrote almost daily, Private First Class Miskowski. He knew the rules of censorship, so I never had any problem with him. As I was reading the outgoing letters one day, I came across an envelope that was addressed to a Mr. L. S. Moranda in Chicago. It had been written by Sergeant Totoni. So I went over to where he was sitting and asked about the name, because it was the same name and initials of my own father. He said he wondered about my name when he first heard it and wondered if I would happen to be related to the Morandas that he knew. I found out that the Morandas he knew were from Albania, while our name came from southern Switzerland.

I didn't care for the job of reading someone else's mail. Reading mail from a frontline infantryman was certainly not revealing to the enemy, even if they wrote about those we were fighting. By the time we got around to writing about any battle we were in, and the mail reached the people at home, the fighting was long past. And an infantryman only knows that he survived another round. He wasn't going to tell the rotten story of the life of a GI. Miskowski wrote about the scenery and the churches. He had a good eye so he wrote what he saw and about the people of the area. He was a good writer, and I did enjoy the scenes that he described. But I still hated to read the personal things. This may be difficult to understand, but a lieutenant infantry officer is a lonesome man. He cannot get too close to any of his men because he may have to give the order that would cost a man his life.

We would get the *Stars and Stripes*, "The Armed Forces Newspaper," about a week after an action. The paper wrote about the various skirmishes and battles at the front, and in so doing that newspaper told the world about the war but we couldn't. Dumb! I think the reason we were a little mad at the write-ups in the papers was that they didn't really know what the hell was going on. I remember reading the *Stars and Stripes* after we had been trying to get to our objective for a couple of days. The paper said how the fighting had been slow. Hell! A hundred yards gained in a fire fight, at times, is a day's, sometimes a week's, work. Usually more casualties happen in that kind of action than in the ones where the gains are much greater. If we got by with only a couple of men wounded or dead, we thought we were indeed fortunate.

After being assigned to the 38th, it took a long time for mail from home to start reaching me. But it finally started and was a welcome relief. It seemed everything was going along okay there. The baby was growing, and Molly kept me posted on the family. The Swains had moved to Lancaster, California. They had entered into a venture with the Eddie Gabberts on a farm where they were also raising chickens and turkeys for a money crop. Mom and the girls still lived in the house on Fourth Street in Oxnard. I am sure they all looked forward to the daily run of the postal carrier, Mr. Pell. They shared the letters received from the members of the family who were away serving in various places.

Overloon and Meijel

During the month of October we seemed to be in some kind of a skirmish with the enemy almost daily. I don't remember the exact sequence, but one of the toughest battles that I remember was the battle for Overloon. My platoon was a part of the task force headed by Lieutenant Colonel Fuller, the new commander of the 38th. During this battle he was near the front most of the time. He was positioned on a small hill where he could observe the front lines. I had my men set up close by so I could watch the actions of the front line troops and had positioned our weapons to protect their flanks. My platoon was being held nearby as a reserve for the front line troops. The infantry got pinned down so he called to me, "Moranda, take your men forward and help them get out this mess." I got my men and we crawled down to the front on our bellies with our carbines and M1s and helped the riflemen. Finally the battle was over and the leading infantrymen were successful in reaching the objective. I was a bit concerned when given the order, for we had to go down the hill to the front lines dragging our machine guns. When we reached the front lines we were only able to use our rifles. Since the heavy weapon .30 caliber machine gun is fired from the sitting position, there was no way my men could sit behind their machine guns and fire as they would have been exposed to enemy fire. But we helped and it was enough. I remembered the time during training with the 84th Division when we had to crawl forward with the heavy machine guns and the limitations I found existed in such a situation.

When we got back to the headquarters, I had a chance to talk to Colonel Fuller when he was alone. I went up to him and had a discussion on the positioning of the machine guns. I was surprised that he listened so intently. After it was over I saluted and left. The next day I had my platoon behind a hedgerow. I had the guns in position standing behind an embankment so they could help the leading infantry get across an open field. Suddenly a mortar shell came right over my head and exploded right behind me. The concussion knocked me to the ground. I felt a sharp hit in the back. All the buttons on my overcoat were knocked off. I got up and called to my runner Conover to come and look me over. I thought I had been hit with shell fragments and wanted him to see how bad the wounds were. He pulled up my coat, shirt, and undershirt. He said there wasn't a mark on my back. A couple of the men had been hit but none seriously.

We had close air support at this battle. Twice our planes came over and strafed the enemy positions. We were being held up by enemy anti-tank and machine gun fire. The first time they made a pass it didn't do the job, but the second time they knocked out the problem guns, and our troops were able to reach the objective. After the battle we discovered the reason the enemy resistance was so strong: our objective was defended by elite German paratroopers and former German air force men. And for the next few days we were really busy.

One day as I was in the command post, the intelligence officer, Captain Fredrickson, told me the story of what happened to him during the battle of Chartres. He was out looking for intelligence material. He got out too far in his searching, and suddenly he looked around and the friendly troops were not with him. He had wound up behind the German lines. So he hid in a cellar of a nearby house and decided he would wait, hoping his unit would come back his way and retake the town. For three days he waited. He had to sit through a couple of the barrages from our artillery and mortars, but being in the cellar he was safe as long as the Germans didn't come down to his hiding place. They didn't, and finally he took a chance and escaped back to our lines. He was so happy to see the men from the 38th when they did come back. He said he had no food or water for the three days and because of that he had lost about 10 pounds.

While I was in the command post I was told to work the radio because the radio operator had been wounded. My men were stationed around the Battalion headquarters, and the CO saw me and said, "Moranda, come in and take over the radio for awhile. We lost our radio man." So into the headquarters I went. I really had never worked a radio before, but it didn't take long to grasp the knowledge required to operate it. My job was to pass on the reports received from the troops in the front line and from the supporting troops. I would listen and then pass the word on to the CO. I stayed on the radio for twenty-four hours straight. It was at this operation that Conover was worth his weight in gold. Somewhere, somehow, he found a source of potatoes, eggs, and a hunk of bread and brought me a hot meal.

After a couple of days of heavy fighting we were to be relieved by the British. We were still on the front lines trying to beat the Germans into submission. The Germans had a different idea so the battle was almost a draw. As we had been on line for some time, higher headquarters decided it was time to give our outfit a rest and resupply us with arms and men. We were told the relief would be done at night. We were in our positions watching the front and being careful not to show any light. The area was quiet. Suddenly we heard a convoy of vehicles coming from our rear. They had their lights on and were certainly drawing our attention, so we knew the Germans were also aware of what was going on. A British officer came on the scene. He told us we soon would be relieved. We then discovered how the real relief would happen. A lorry drove up a few yards behind our position and a British non-com came up to us and said in his English accent, "I say there. You chaps can take your guns now. We will take over for you." And with that the British troops came up and a contingent of them took over from my men.

Then the rest of their men sat down and with the lights on from their lorries started to boil some water for their tea. I asked the non-com in charge, "How come you are so careless with the noise and your lights?" His answer was, "We want them to know that we are here, so why should we hide?"

[*On 27 October, the German Army launched a vigorous attack against the 7th Armored Division in the vicinity of Meijel, Holland, with two Panzer Divisions. The 7th Armored's task at the time was guarding the British 2d Army's right flank. The Germans were obviously attempting to force a diversion from the Allied drive on the Sheldt Peninsula to the west, or to cut the line of communication and supply along the Allied salient toward Arnhem. The Germans made only slight progress, but the fighting was bitter. The 7th Armored contained the drive. After three days, reinforcements arrived to shorten the 7th's front, and British forces combined with them to push back the Germans to their starting positions. More British units arrived, and the 7th Armored was relieved and reassigned to the American Ninth Army. The 38th AIB was part of CCA holding the southern sector near Nederweert during the action.*]

I guess the things that foot soldiers most treasure are: mail from home, a good meal, a good bed, clean socks and underwear, a bath or a shower, and to be no closer than a thousand yards from the action or, better yet, to be in back of our own artillery. But for the most part just to be away from direct fire was great. Being in the house with the commanding officer was just like being at the Ritz-Carlton. For thirty-six hours I was almost safe. Finally at the end of the skirmish I was relieved of my job. I got the men of my platoon into our half-tracks. Cox, the driver, took off. I placed Sgt. Sicari in the observer's seat and I sat between the driver and the observer and in an upright position fell sound asleep. And I slept in that position for at least two hours. When I did wake up I really had a stiff neck, but at least it was some rest.

Back in the bivouac rest area we were cleaning ourselves and our weapons when I decided to take a walk around the area. When passing the motor pool, a chicken was clucking and scratching around the men who were working on their vehicle. I asked about the hen. They said they had named her Henrietta, and she gave them a fresh egg every day and was a treasure for the motor pool. A couple of days later I again walked past the same group. I didn't see Henrietta so I asked about the chicken. The answer came back as they pointed to a pot boiling over a burner, "Oh, Henrietta didn't lay an egg for a couple of days, and we found some potatoes so we are having Henrietta chicken soup."

It wasn't long after when I was in my tent and was awakened out of a sound sleep. There were no moon or stars, so the darkness was like being in a closet with the door shut and no light. I wondered what in the hell could be so important that they would call me out in the middle of the night. The sergeant who woke me up said he didn't know. He led me to the command track. I ducked my head and entered it. Standing around a map were the brains of the 38th Battalion: the commanding officer, the executive officer, the S1 (personnel officer), S2 (intelligence officer), and S3 (operations officer). Only the S4 (supply officer) was missing. The overhead light was really bright. I reported to the commanding officer. Lieutenant Colonel Fuller said, "Moranda, we have a mission for you. We need your machine guns to support an infantry company." (I think it was company A). Your guns will support the company in an attack to eliminate a small force of Germans occupying some strategic ground and giving us a problem. The attack is slated to go off early in the morning."

I asked where the rifle company was located. They pointed out the position on the map. I noted aloud that since it is so dark, could they point out an easy way to get there. The CO then said, "We have thought of that. The sergeant that brought you to the CP has been to the location before, so he will lead your half-tracks to the assembly area." With that I saluted and went out into the dark night. And I do mean dark, especially after being in the bright lights of the command half-track. I stumbled around for awhile looking for the area where my tent and my men were bedded down. Finally after trying to get back to my tent for awhile, I knew I was lost. I was completely turned around in our own bivouac area. But I stopped and stood still and listened. Then I heard the rattle of some pans. I headed for the noise. It was the kitchen truck cleaning and getting ready for the next day. I asked them where my tent area was and they pointed out the direction. Finally my eyes became adjusted, and I could see the tents and my half-tracks.

Before I left for the CP I had alerted Sgt. Sicari, and he had the men up and ready, so we loaded. The Company A sergeant came by in his jeep and I got in. With the jeep in the lead and the two tracks following close behind, we proceeded to the assembly area. We were very close to the German lines so I wondered how safe we really were. I know as we rode along I was really scanning the area. Our little convoy was quite noisy, and it wouldn't take much of an effort to hit us with anti-tank weapons. But we reached the assembly area just at the first light of dawn. I met the infantry leaders, and we looked over the terrain and discussed how best to attack. We decided my guns would set up and fire at the objective with continuous fire. The infantry troops would go along the tree line on the left and along the railroad tracks on the right. We agreed. So I took my men to the area where we were to locate our guns and selected the gun positions and alternate positions, so that if the Germans came at us with mortars or artillery we could quickly move to a new position. When we were ready to fire I waved at the platoon leaders and the attack was on.

The plan worked. The continuous fire kept the heads of the Germans down, and our troops soon reached the objective. The operation was a success. The front line riflemen captured quite a number of Germans. When our troops reached their objective, I then moved the machine guns forward so we could set up and, if needed, help the infantry again. That didn't happen. No help was needed as the Germans didn't send relief. The company commander thanked me for the support, and we were dismissed. My men were happy with their work as were the officers in the 38th, especially the S4, Captain Watson. He was pleased that he had to bring us more rounds of ammunition. As he said, he wanted the troops to fire a lot so he could go home to his wife and family. He was a great guy, full of life, and I enjoyed our talks together.

Looking back on the war I now realize that for Hitler and the Germans, October was a crucial time. They had lost France, and now for the first time they were really defending "Der Fatherland." When our attack started at Aachen, Hitler ordered his soldiers to hold at all costs. The German command needed time to prepare for a counterattack. He ordered that the ground must be held, and there would be no surrendering no matter what the cost. Aachen was the first large city in Germany to be attacked. I remember the first time our unit crossed over the line into Germany. I had all my men get out of their vehicles, and we stood in line and pissed on Hitler's land—his "Der Fatherland." We relieved ourselves in two ways—both mentally and physically.

It was not long before our outfit moved back to an area near Nederweert and Weert. In that area we did a lot a outposting and patrolling. We would usually be assigned to a infantry company and would help them out when needed, but for the most part it was an easy time for my platoon. I do remember one night we were on an overnight patrol. We put out guards around us, and I found a feather bed in one of the houses. I was tired, and for the first time in a long time I got a really good night's sleep. I took my boots off, climbed in, and, as they say, "slept so deeply I was on the bottom of the mattress." What a great night!

It was about this time that I heard from Daisy Wood, the mother of our dear friend Wannie Wood. Wannie had grown up with us boys in our family—he was almost another brother. Diasy asked me to join with other men from the Port Hueneme area in establishing a branch of the VFW (Veterans of the Foreign Wars). She was contacting every person from our hometown serving in the war.

Naturally she contacted all my brothers, and I guess we all joined. The branch was to be called the "Wannie Woods Post." Wannie, another infantry lieutenant, had been killed in Italy while leading his men in battle. He only lasted a couple of weeks in combat. (Oh, the great life of an infantry officer.) I wrote to Molly the next day and asked her to give Daisy the money for me to join the post.

Nederweert, the place where Conover and I had taken the rations over the road and liberated the land, had been recaptured by the Germans. So again our outfit had to retake the place. It was tough to do, and by the end of the month of October we were in that area doing battle. The Germans came at us a couple of times, but we were able to hold the ground gained. In fact, on the 31st of October the Jerries hit just one more time, but they were repulsed and suffered a large loss of men. On the 1st of November we were again trying and succeeding, for the most part, in ousting the Germans from Holland. We were to clear the area from Zuid Willems Vaart Canal. For some reason the Jerries didn't want to leave. But slowly and surely the 38th was able to clear the area. Actually my platoon was not used as much during that operation. One reason the attack went so slowly was the mine fields. The Germans must have known that they were out-gunned, and in order to slow down our attack they had scattered mines around the fields, and in most instances they were not buried. That made it even tougher, because as we gingerly walked through the mined area we couldn't help but wonder if there were more of them buried. We used tanks and engineers to do the difficult and delicate work of removing the mines. Finally on the 3rd of November we reached the canal—our objective. The 38th withdrew and when relieved, we went to an area to again reorganize and to be able to continue the attack.

[The 84th Infantry Division had recently arrived and had been assigned to General Simpson's Ninth U.S. Army. Shortly after getting there the Ninth was given the mission of seizing the high ground east of Geilenkirchen,

some twenty kilometers north of Aachen. They had the British 21st Army Group on their left flank. British General Horrocks made a surprise visit to the 84th units at the front to see conditions. Stephen Ambrose, in his Citizen Soldiers *told of this visit: "The 84th struck him as 'an impressive product of American training methods which turned out division after division complete, fully equipped, composed of splendid, very brave, tough young men. But he [Horrocks] thought it a bit much to ask of a green division that it penetrate the Siegfried Line, then stand up to counterattacks from two first-class divisions, the 15th Panzer and the 10th SS. And he was disturbed by the failure of the American division and corps commanders and their staffs to ever visit the front lines. He was greatly concerned to find that the men were not getting hot meals brought up from the rear, in contrast to the forward units in the British line. He gave the GIs 'my most experienced armoured regiment, the Sherwood Rangers Yeomanry,' told the American battalion and division commanders to get up front, and returned to his headquarters.*

"The problem Horrocks saw was becoming endemic in the U.S. Army in ETO. Not even battalion commanders were going to the front. From the Swiss border north to Geilenkirchen, the Americans were attacking. SHAEF put the pressure on Twelfth Army Group; Bradley passed it on to the First, Third, and Ninth Armies; Hodges, Patton, and Simpson told their corps commanders to get results; by the time the pressure reached the battalion COs, it was intense. They raised it even higher as they set objectives for the rifle company COs. The trouble with all this pressure was that the senior officers and their staffs didn't know what they were ordering the rifle companies to do. They had neither seen the terrain nor the enemy. And unlike the company and platoon leaders, who had to be replaced every few weeks at best, and every few days at worst, the staff officers took few casualties, so the same men stayed at the job, doing it badly."]

After being relieved, the battalion left for an area near Zomeren-Maarheeze. For the next few days we spent a lot of time retraining the outfit. We had a new battalion S3, Major Don Boyer. He was determined to make our 38th a better fighting outfit, so he put the 38th through a few field exercises. These involved the tanks and infantry working together, which has more drawbacks than benefits. The damned tanks are so noisy, and they do draw fire. They can't protect themselves, so the infantry had to guard them at night, which we continually bitched about. But, on the other hand, the armored infantry normally does not stay in the front lines as long as the regular infantry. Like it or not, we had to rehearse.

My troops found an abandoned house which became our base. They made it as comfortable as possible, but being inside has its pitfalls. If one man gets a cold, the whole outfit comes down with it, and that is what happened. The weather had changed and we were now in the late fall of the year. We were having a lot of cold weather. My men were warm at night, but I soon learned it was healthier when everyone was outside in their tents. Every one of my men came down with a terrible cold. I had a minor cold, but not the kind that they suffered with. After a few days, though, they had all recovered enough to function. As for me, I was billeted with Captain Mattocks in a different house.

While in the rest and training area, Captain Mattocks, Lieutenant Kinnebrew, and I left for the rear. The division had located a working coal mine that had a building with showers and a real tub. Not that I needed a bath. Hell, it had only been sixty days since I had taken one. Our normal bathing while in the field was done out of the helmet. Shave, bathe, and wash your underwear and socks in that order. We would use the water from our canteens to brush our teeth. Not that there was a shortage of water, but when the need for it arrived, you always seemed to be too far away from the source. We drove first to a quartermaster supply point, where we all purchased new clothes. I bought everything new with the exception of my boots and jackets. Two items that I purchased were really life savers later on: a wool scarf that was over six feet long and a pair of silk pajamas. The PJ's were to take the place of woolen long johns, as I have a problem with wool when worn next to my skin.

From there we drove to the mine. There were hundreds of bicycles parked around the main shaft. It seemed everyone in Europe rode bicycles. No one drove automobiles, as gasoline was not available for civilians. We went to the area where the baths were located, and the attendant asked whether we wanted a shower or a tub. I chose the tub. A man filled the tub to the brim, handed me some soap and I was soon covered with the warm water. I soaked for quite a long time relishing the wonderful, relaxing feeling. I hated to leave, but soon the other two men had taken showers and were ready to get going again, so I reluctantly toweled off and joined them.

The rest of November was the easiest of my experiences in combat. We really had a soft time compared to the previous month. For the first eight days of November we were only called up a couple of times, and those times were quite easy for my machine gun platoon. For some of the time we were stationed in the small town of Terlinden, which is located in the Province of Limburg in the panhandle section of Holland. The company troops were spread out in the town. Capt. 'Rusty' decided the best place for his command post would be with a Dutch family, the Prickens. Momma, Papa, and the kids Willie, Henrietta Leone, Arthur, Sophie, and Josie. They welcomed us with open arms. The ages of the family ranged from the two older children who were about twenty to the baby in the family. We were given the run of the house. First Sergeant Alvie Davis ran the headquarters. Three of us were bunked in one room upstairs, and the captain and Davis were bunked in the downstairs living room. Alvie also had his clerk and records of the company in that room.

While there I received a letter from Molly, which I kept with me, along with the New Testament, throughout the remainder of my service (and still have them):

Nov 20, 1944

Dearest Bob,

Well honey, we are up at the ranch, we arrived about 6:00 last evening. Loraine, Tommy, Tomilyn, and I left Oxnard about 2:30, but we had so many drawbacks that we didn't get here until pretty late. First of all the Saticoy bridge was out as per usual in the winter, next I smelled something burning and stopped the car and looked under the hood and a piece of felt lining up under the hood had fallen down across the motor and was blazing away. Boy it scared us silly with two babies in the car, anyway we pulled the felt out and went on our way, then last of all the road up to the folk's house was all full of mud puddles and I had to go about a mile out of the way to get to their place. Well, we were all well received. Tiny [Rozeel] and Mom knew we were coming, but the rest were surprised, especially Daddy because he had never seen little Tommy before and he was sure tickled.

Boy is it cold up here, snow all around on the hills and frost all over the ground this morning. I slept with Daddy's robe on, I'm always cold at nights. Sure wish I could snuggle up to your big, warm body. Oh boy, would I love that, in more ways than one!!! I sure hate this business of not having a husband—we girls here at home all agree that it is sure a dull and lonely life without your husband with you.

Tiny and Eddie are going to take a turkey up to George [her uncle] in Bakersfield, he lives in a boarding house and wants to give the turkey to his landlady.

Nona won't be lonely while we are up here because Jeanette is bringing Marion up to spend a few days with her. And it will be much nicer for them if we aren't there because it is really very hard to have three babies in a house at once, especially when they aren't all one family. You can imagine Tomilyn showing Marion around and them all crying at once and trying to bathe and feed them all at nearly the same time. Oh me, I'm afraid that will be the problem too when George [my brother] and Nancy come with little George. They asked Nona to get them a crib so I guess they expect to stay at our house although I'm afraid it will be rather crowded, but we have managed so far so I guess we'll continue to get by. What we need is a few more bedrooms!!

I'm writing this letter in the morning as we will probably go to town pretty soon. I know I won't have a letter from you because Nona wouldn't have had time to forward one until tomorrow at the earliest. Sure hope to get one soon as I haven't heard for about a week, but I know you have been busy.

I'm sending you a poem cut out of the Journal, it did me a lot of good and I know it will you too.

I was just browsing thru your last three letters and even if I have read them a dozen times it always makes me feel good to read them again. You're a darling, and I love you so much! Seems like I can almost hear your voice and visualize what you are doing when I read them.

Pumpkin told me to tell you that you are the best Daddy in all the world and to take good care of yourself for your two girls.

Molly & Robin

We love you!

Sergeant Davis was from Mississippi, and spoke with a southern accent. He was the perfect "First Soldier." When Rusty was promoted to company commander, there was an opening for an officer to head the

Assault Gun Platoon. Rusty tried to get Alvie to take over the platoon and become an officer—a field promotion. Alvie really tried for about two weeks, but then he came back to Captain Mattocks and said that he was out of his element and requested to be returned to his previous position. His request was approved, and he again became the 1st sergeant. That's the time when Lieutenant Boyd arrived as a replacement to take Rusty's old job, leading the mortar platoon, and Kinnebrew became the assault gun platoon leader. For the short time that Davis was gone we had a sergeant that took Alvie's place. He was a gung ho, tough talking, rough riding first sergeant. He was 180 degrees different from Alvie. Alvie was a kind gentleman who got the men to do their jobs by exerting leadership qualities. The new man was just a bastard, determined to "shape up this outfit." His attitude was that he would show them how to be a brave and a great leader of men in combat. The men listened and grumbled and really wondered about how tough he would be. It didn't take long. We started to receive German artillery fire on our position one day. That tough talking first soldier ducked into the waiting cellar, and we couldn't get him out to do his duties. It wasn't long before the CO got rid of him, and I know the men in our company were glad to have Alvie back as our First Soldier.

The cast of characters in the company were: Captain Carl Mattocks, the commander, a tough man (by that I mean at times he talked like he enjoyed the war, and he was a good leader of men); 1st Lieutenant Kenny Kinnebrew, executive officer and mortar platoon leader; 1st Lieutenant Hugh Boyd, assault gun platoon leader; and I running the weapons platoon. Kinnebrew was from Georgia. I asked if any of his relatives were of the Newton name, as that was where Mom's relatives originally were from. He said no. He was a short man with a blonde butch haircut, friendly to me, and we had some good talks about home and fireside. Boyd was also from the South. He was very religious and read the Bible at every opportunity. He was a tall man with a gangly frame, spoke when spoken to, but rarely started a conversation. 1st

Sergeant Alvie Davis was a tall southern man. I enjoyed his southern drawl. He loved his men and took an interest in each and every one of them. He was considerate and kind and yet tough—a rugged looking man with a soft heart. The men loved him, and he watched out for them. He and Captain Mattocks made a good team

The one thing we did at every opportunity was to talk of home and family, though most of the time no one really listened but would grunt at the right time, and the talk would go on and on. Each of us would get that far away look in our eyes and continue with thoughts of home. I put the "we" in here because I know I did the same as the others.

As a replacement officer I did not know the history of each man. I had to learn by listening to the men as they talked and conversed with each other, and as I had to censor each man's letter, mostly to their loved ones at home, I learned a bit more about them. Some of the men wrote often and others rarely. As time went on I began to get a grasp of their lives and their homes—where they came from, marital status, and the make-up of their families.

The nights were spent listening to the Buzz Bombs fly over us. We would hear the motor of the bomb chugging along and knew if the motor would only keep running until it passed over us we were safe. But when the motor quit the bomb would head straight down. One night one of them did come down about a thousand yards away—quite a bang! It really shook the house where we were staying. The next day we went to the crater and saw the results of the bomb. It made a huge hole in the ground. Thankfully it caused no damage other than to the earth.

While billeting with the Pricken family, a really clean and well-scrubbed family, every morning the two older girls would put on their wooden shoes and scrub the courtyard. Mama was in the kitchen most of the time doing her chores, and papa tended to the farm. No one loafed around with nothing to do. All the family could speak English, so we had some good times talking to them. Alvie Davis was able to get some rations from our mess which he gave to the family, and we were rewarded with some fine Dutch cooking. I fell in love with a couple of the youngest children, towheaded and pretty. They could have passed for my Tomilyn's sisters. While we were with the Pricken family one of my men received one of those "Dear John" letters. He was really shook up and got rip-roaring drunk. He had been engaged to the girl and thought everything was going well at home. But the girl had found someone else and was going to get married to her new-found man. Before long he was over the shock, and he said that he was glad to find out the girl really didn't love him. I remember wondering how many other "Dear John" letters had been received. What a blow! I had heard about the letters before, but that was the only one I saw first hand.

[By the early autumn, even Hitler knew that the Germans were in serious danger of losing the war after suffering huge and costly defeats on the eastern, western, and Italian fronts. The Allies had reached and crossed into his Fatherland at the Holland and Belgium and French borders, and his troops were fighting on their own soil. By this time his mind was not reliably clear, and many of his actions were illogical. After all, he had nearly lost his life and suffered injury in a bomb blast in July. However, he seemed to regain some of his strategic vision, and in mid-September he began to formulate a plan that might avoid defeat by forcing the Allies to agree to a negotiated peace. He recognized that the huge Russian army precluded any offensive on the eastern front as there were no apparent weak spots. The Allies, on the other hand, were much more vulnerable. Their logistical support depended on long supply lines which meant water shipments and the capacity of several ports, and Antwerp was the most important at that time. Hitler's plan was to concentrate forces in the west in order to break through a weak, American-held sector, and retake Antwerp, which would separate the Americans from the British-Canadian 21st Army Group. He wanted to attack the Americans because he believed they were less capable soldiers than the British and unlikely to put up much resistance. That may

have been true for the American Army during the North African cam-
paign, but not so two years later.

At least, Hitler planned, even if the British and Canadians escaped encir-
clement, the Allies would be back where they were in late August, and
Germany would have three or four months' grace to deal with the
Russians. In the best case, the rout of a major element of the U.S. 12th
Army group and the loss of Antwerp might create such a rift between the
British and the Americans that the western Alliance would fracture, and
Germany would then face only a one-front war by early spring of 1945.
Hitler chose the Ardennes region as the target for the offensive. This was an
area of winding river valleys and steep hills, covered with dense conifer
forests. The Ardennes was thinly settled with many small villages but few
significant towns. It was the region through which the Germans had rup-
tured the French defenses to win the Battle of Flanders en route to winning
the Battle of France in May 1940. He also knew from battlefield reconnais-
sance and communication intercepts that the area was thinly held by the
Americans, and he believed that an immediate breakthrough would be rel-
atively easy. His generals were reluctant to accept all those goals and tried
to limit the effort, but to no avail.]

We stayed with the Prickens from the tenth of November until the
38th was returned to an American army. We had been with the British
Army commanded by the famed Field Marshal Montgomery, doing our
bit in freeing the Holland area from the Germans. The division's next
job was to receive replacements and be rehabilitated, after which we
would be assigned a new mission. For a week we had trained around
Terlinden, then we moved to Schimmert, Holland, and were now quite
far away from the front lines and back far enough so that we felt secure
and safe.

[By early December, SHAEF had two airborne divisions, the 82d and
101st, as an immediately available strategic reserve and additional divi-

sions in the pipeline in England or en route from the States. Also there were operational reserves available to the armies and corps: the Ninth Army had the 30th Infantry and 7th Armored Divisions,; the First Army had all or parts of four divisions, the 1st and 9th Infantry, and the 3rd and 5th Armored; and the Third Army also had all or parts of four divisions, the 26th and 80th Infantry, and the 4th and 10th Armored]

At the end of the month we, the 7th Armored Division, were placed in reserve so that we could support the 84th and 102nd Infantry divisions. Being assigned to help the 84th Division was a special few days for me. The 84th was where I started in the Army, and I was with them when they trained in Texas and Louisiana. Now they were in combat, and there was a possibility that my platoon would be assigned to support them with my machine guns. My first assignment was to help the 334th Infantry Regiment of the 84th in one of their first combat missions. The 84th was trying to take the town of Pummeren, Germany. When we arrived, the commander of the 84th decided he didn't need our help. Though I could hear firing of small arms to the front, their commander decided our men could go back to our own area. I didn't understand that decision then and I still don't understand the refusal now, especially after reading of that operation in their history book.

During the month of December we hoped that the war would soon to be over. In the infantry the men always look for clues as to what was going on in the world by using the Army's emphasized special training. When the Army started to hold meetings with the officers and non-coms on how to conduct ourselves with the civilians when we arrived in Germany, it led to much discussion and hope. They told us that above all we were to live by the rules of warfare and the Geneva Convention. The way the Army was talking, we in the infantry only had to win the next big push and then the Germans would give up. Somehow, though, the ground-pounders knew rumors come and go. We knew there was a lot of fighting left to do. It was a nice thought, though. The only way for a infantryman to really be away from the front lines was either by a wound, being in a bag, be captured, or for the war to come to an end. But it wasn't all lost time, as the Army did conduct a lot of other specialized training. It was during one of those meetings that we were introduced to our new commanding general, Brigadier General Robert Hasbrouck. He seemed like a good soldier. I think he was a West Pointer.

About then, the 7th Armored Division moved to Bach, Germany. There we were rested and went into another training mode. For the first time in a long period the troops were able to rest and repair and again receive personnel replacements. The tanks and other vehicles needed a lot of work, and the men needed time to get themselves rested and cleaned up. They also needed a time for letters to be written and to get mail from home. Mail seemed to come in bunches, so in the rest area a person could sit back and think of home and write and reread the letters from wives and families. It was in November that I received a letter from brother Earle announcing he and "Becky" (Lorene Becker) were to be married soon. That was good news. Earle had been fortunate in that he had been able so far to stay in Washington, D.C., and was assigned to Army Air Intelligence. It wasn't long after that a letter came from sister Maye telling that the wedding of Becky and Earl had happened.

I wrote to Molly on Dec. 13th, and Molly kept it:

Hello Darling,

Well honey I'm in the chips as I got four letters from you, two from Mom and one from Maye. Thank you darling they were certainly well received. I've read each one of them three times so far and will reread them a couple more times before burning them.

You asked me a few questions and I'll try to answer them the best way I can. First I'm not a big shot having a C.P. but just a Lt. A C.P. is a command post and every leader has one even in the field. It's a place to meet his non-coms and direct his men. As you go up the ladder, a C.P. is of more importance. A Company Cmdr has one for his officers & non-coms. A Battalion Comdr has one for his staff officers, in other words a command post is where orders are issued and the unit is run from (clear as mud huh!).

You asked too about Overloon and I'll try to answer that by telling you it's close to Venray. We were all over that part of the country, and if you have a map showing the boundaries of the British 2nd you can see where we were. I guess you know by this time where we were tho so I'm not telling any news.

Today was spent in the usual way so there is really no news from here. We hear now and then some planes flying around and big guns in the distance but other than that we would never know there was a war going on.

Lt. Boyd and I are now in our cellar and he is shaving and dripping water on me. Of course he is cussed out but no one minds that over here. We're really not crowded but I doubt if we could get any more in here without a shoe horn.

This is really not much of a letter as its hard for me to really concentrate with people talking. When I write to you I like to be by myself so I can concentrate, it's more like talking in person.

So you're still dreaming of me, well honey keep it up and maybe soon I can make them come true. Boy I sure wish I were home and could be holding you in my arms. Sure am in love with you and my love grows every day—
Your
Bob
Hi Pumpkin, I sure am glad you like my little letters to you. You're my little sweetheart
Daddy

[Hitler had assembled on the Western Front all that was available as a consequence of his second "total mobilization." A decree of 18 October had raised a "volkssturm," or home guard, for the defense of the Third Reich, conscripting all able-bodied men between the ages of sixteen and sixty years. While the Allies had reached the Rhine in Alsace, the Germans had *meanwhile been building their own strength up for a counterstroke. Under the overall command of the reinstated Marshall Rundstedt, this stroke was to be delivered through the wooded hill country of the Ardennes against the U.S. sector of the front, between Monschau (southwest of Aachen) and Echternach (northwest of Trier). The plan called for the Fifth Panzer Army on the left, under General von Manteuffel, with its left flank covered by the German 7th Army, to wheel north westward after the breakthrough and to cross the Meuse south of Namur in a drive on Brussels. The 6th Panzer Army on the right, under SS General Sepp Dietrich, was to wheel more sharply northward against Antwerp, its own right being protected by a supporting thrust westward from the Roer Valley. Thus it was hoped that the British and Canadian forces at the northern end of the front could be cut off from their supplies and crushed, while the U.S. forces to the south would be held off by the German left.]*

Our next mission had been planned by our higher headquarters. The 38th was to aid in the attack into the Rhineland over the Roer river, to drive the Germans farther back into their own country. Daily our officers would head to the front line and observe the terrain and plan for our assignment. The 38th was to pass through friendly lines and attack through the lowlands and to seize the high grounds where a dam was located. We were to get control of the dam before the Germans could release the water and flood the lowlands. If successful, the war would be shortened and the powers that be thought Hitler would give up. Boy, were they fooled.

I was interested to see in advance what we were going to do. For the first time in my Army experience company grade officers in combat really knew what was supposed to happen. Usually it was: take "that hill," "that town," or some other limited objective; then wait for further orders for the next hill or town we were to take. The information was, usually, that there were a few disorganized enemy to our front—and normally that "disorganized" enemy would stubbornly fight for each and every yard of real estate. Infantry company grade officers apparently didn't warrant deep intelligence briefings. Somehow we found out by the rumors that came down to enlisted men from the division and combat commands. Rusty did try his best to keep us posted, but there was a lot he did not know. Typically, when we motored to the front lines in our jeeps, supposedly through safe routes, we had to pass through areas under surveillance by the Germans. And when they observed our vehicles approaching, they would lob mortars and fire artillery at us. Once at one location where we had to make a right turn, it turned out to be particularly dangerous. So as we approached the driver said, "Hang on, here we go!" and he revved up and at a high rate of speed rounded the corner and drove to the shelter of some houses nearby. It was sort of like playing Russian Roulette. But, though we were shot at, luckily, we weren't hit. That kind of thing happened to us several times.

We noticed one morning that one of the haystacks in enemy territory seemed to have moved. We called in artillery. We then discovered there had been a vehicle under the haystack.

One incident that happened in the rest area was during a poker game. A group of the officers had a game going in the kitchen of one of the houses. Captain Fredrickson, Captain Mattocks, Lieutenant French, and a couple of others. The game had been going on for hours. Fredrickson had had nothing but bad luck. A new hand was dealt. The ante was in and the openers had been bet. Fredrickson was about to raise the bet when all hell broke loose. We heard a German plane approaching our area, and it soon came over and dropped a bomb. Then the pilot maneuvered his plane around and came back down the road strafing the area where we were all billeted. The poker players were under the table, in a closet, in the pantry, or on the floor. I dove toward the outside and watched the plane from behind the open front door. No one was hurt so I went back in. The players were gathering themselves together, picking up the cards and chips, and placing the chairs around the table. Fredrickson was on his hands and knees and still had his cards and was crying, "Come on let's go. I've still got my hand." The others didn't so the hand was called off. "Damn! Damn! Damn!" he moaned, "I have four aces." Somehow none of the other players displayed any sympathy.

On one of those days, Lieutenant Corbin and I were driving to see what we were soon going to be doing when I saw the sign on the road announcing that my old outfit, Company M of the 84th Division, was billeted nearby. I wanted to see my old friends, so Corbin and I took a detour and drove to where they were training. As we came into the area, I saw my enlisted friends from the 84th. They were in formation standing at ease. I asked permission from my old company commander, Captain Burns, to visit my former bunk mates. He gave me the permission gladly, so I had a few minutes with Sallee, Marshall, Emeterio, Ashford, Klein, Bird, and others. One of my old friends had just received a battle field promotion; Sergeant Esteridge was now a second lieutenant. So for a few minutes we were enjoying each others' stories. They all asked about Hugh West. I told them I had come overseas on the same boat with him, but we parted in England and I hadn't heard from him since. The most asked question was, "How is combat?" What do you tell them? You don't want to frighten them, but you want to be honest. All I could do was to tell them to be aware of everything—to keep their eyes and ears open. But they knew what I was trying to tell them. The sad part is I never saw them again and wonder how many of my friends made it through the war. At times I have wished that I had remained as a sergeant with the 84th. With those men I belonged. As a replacement officer you have to, time and again, gain the respect of your men—men whose capabilities, strengths, and weaknesses were unknown to you and whom you had no experiences with. Even over fifty years after the war, in many respects, it is still the same. The men who served throughout the war with the same unit have more to talk about. For example, when they ask if you remember the training in the desert, and you come back with, "I wasn't there," the conversation stops.

THE BATTLE OF THE BULGE BEGINS

[At 1730 on 16 December, Brigadier General Robert W. Hasbrouck, commanding general of the 7th Armored Division, was ordered to get ready to move south to an assembly area near Vielsam, where he would be assigned to VIII Corps of the First U.S. Army. The 7th Armored Division had been located near Heerlen, Holland, and in Scherpenseel, Germany, northwest of Aachen, and was then an element of the III Corps reserve as part of the Ninth U.S. Army. The First U.S. Army commander, General Hodges, had planned an attack and was not about to "let the Germans dictate the timing of my attack". And said he did not need the 7th. Knowing that General Hodges had not wanted the 7th, his staff did not give them road clearance immediately. General Hasbrouck was told to move out as soon as he received information about his route of march. At 2000 he called Brigadier General Bruce C. Clarke, commander of his CCB, and told him to go to Bastogne and report to Major General Troy Middleton the VIII Corps commander for instructions and information.

Shortly before midnight, General Hasbrouck was told to take two parallel roads behind two corps of the First Army. The western route went through Heer, Verviers, Stavelot, and Trois Pont to Vielsam; the eastern route went through Aachen, Eupen, Malmedy, Recht, and Poteau to Vielsam. He then issued orders to elements of the division: the western road was to be used by the 87th Cavalry Reconnaissance Squadron, CCB, CCA, the 814th Tank Destroyer Battalion, Main Division Headquarters, the 33rd Armored Engineer Battalion, and the division trains; the eastern route was to be

used by CCR, Division Tactical Headquarters (TAC), Division Artillery, the 203rd Antiaircraft Battalion, and smaller units. The units using the eastern route were to commence at 0800, 17 December. Hasbrouck had not been told that VIII Corps had told General Jones, commanding general of the 106th Infantry Division, that the 7th Armored Division would reach St. Vith and the 106th Division by 0700 on 17 December. However, the information given to the elements of CCR did not indicate that it was anything more than an administrative move, and the unit commanders could not understand why the move was being made, since VIII Corps had the 9th Armored Division already assigned to it as the corps reserve. Some surmised that either General Patton's Third Army had made a breakthrough and was screaming for more armor to exploit the penetration, or that Patton had borrowed the 9th AD and the 7th AD was to replace the 9th as corps reserve. It wasn't until they saw the heavy stream of traffic of American forces going west that the realization came that it was more than an administrative march and that there was a serious emergency facing the American Army in this area.

After three false starts, because the Ninth Army's Military Police had trouble clearing the roads, the 7th Division's western column started moving at 0430 and covered the sixty-five miles quickly. They reached the Vielsam assembly area without difficulty at 1100, where orders were waiting for them from General Clarke. On the eastern road the column had trouble. Colonel Peiper's spearhead elements for the 1st Panzer Division hit the column just south of Malmedy. The Germans captured Battery B of the 258th Field Artillery Observation Battalion, which had inserted itself into the column between TAC and Division Artillery unbeknownst to the 7th Division—which led to the Malmedy Massacre. The last few vehicles of TAC were also hit, and Colonel Church M. Matthews, the division chief of staff, was killed.]

On December 16th rumors started to go around that our division was going back to General Patton's Third Army or back to the British we had fought with at Overloon, Holland. We knew our present mission, which was to support the divisions trying to capture the dam on the Roer River, had been changed. Now we waited for our next orders. But rumors were really flying.

The Combat Command Reserve (CCR) commander called a conference that night. I saw our company commander, Rusty Mattocks, go to battalion headquarters about 0300 on the 17th. There was an anxious feeling going around, but we company grade officers didn't know why. Lieutenant Boyd read his Bible even more. Me? I thought of home. For some reason I had a real down deep fear of some pending action.

Sgt. Sicari asked me, "What's up Lieutenant? The men want to know."

"I don't know but something's up. Get your men to bed and get rested. But have your half-tracks ready to move out soon."

It wasn't long before a runner came and said, "Lieutenant Moranda, we are moving out. Report to the company command post." When I did, Captain Mattocks gave me the word that we were to move out. The 38th Battalion was to be attached to CCR and proceed to St Vith, Belgium. I remember asking, "Where is St. Vith?" but I never got an answer.

[Hitler planned the "Wacht am Rhine" (the term used for the cover plan— the actual operation was called "Herbstnebel" or "Autumn Smoke") to use the Sixth Panzer Army to deliver the decisive blow in his Ardennes offensive. Commanded by General Sepp Dietrich, the Sixth Army contained four SS Panzer divisions, a Parachute division, and four Volksgrenadier (Infantry) divisions. The infantry formations were to tear holes in the American lines between the Losheim Gap and Monschau for two Panzer divisions to advance over five pre-selected routes to seize the bridges over the Meuse River from Huy northeast to Liege. A powerful task force under veteran tank commander Lieutenant Colonel Jochen Peiper, containing more than half of the armor of the 1st Panzer division along with supporting panzer-grenadier, engineer, and artillery troops, was to lead the exploitation. The plan called for the breach to be made within twenty-four

hours and for the lead units to reach the Meuse that same day. Then the panzers were to push on rapidly toward Brussels and Antwerp, leaving the volksgrenadier divisions to hold the northern flank. Once Antwerp had been taken, the Army was to hold a line from that port city eastward to the Meuse around Maastricht.

The Fifth Panzer Army, on the Sixth's southern flank and commanded by General Hasso von Manteuffel, was assigned the task of isolating and destroying the American 106th Infantry division in the Schnee Eifel massif and seizing the critical crossroads of St. Vith immediately west of the Eifel. Farther south other divisions of his force were supposed to break through the American 28th division, isolate and bypass Bastogne if defended, then advance through Houffalize toward the Meuse crossings around Namur. Once the initial breakthrough had been achieved and the immediate geographic objectives had been seized, the Fifth Panzer Army was to shield the southern and eastern flanks of the Sixth Panzer Army along a line roughly from Antwerp to Givet. But the key to the whole operation was St. Vith. Without the communications center there, the focal point for highways, and the rail lines, the armored, infantry, and supply columns would be practically immobilized because the rugged, hilly terrain was heavily forested and permitted very limited cross-country movement. St. Vith was to be captured on the first day of the offensive, for it was to be used as an advance rail depot for both the Fifth Panzer and the Sixth Panzer Armies.

The southern positioned Seventh Army under General Erich Brandenberger was to protect the southern flank of the Fifth Panzer Army and hold a line between Givet and Echternach.

The breakthrough was to be aided by "Operation Greif," led by Colonel Skorzeny, in which German officers and men dressed in U.S. uniforms (worn over their own German uniforms so they could discard the outer garments after the breakthrough) would seize the bridges across the Meuse and, as a secondary mission, spread confusion and panic.

On the 16th of December at 0530, the attack began with a massive artillery barrage in the 6th Panzer Army zone. The volksgrenadier divisions were repulsed initially by the American 2nd and 99th Infantry divisions, but on the 17th, Peiper's Task Force found a hole and advanced, in three and one half hours, nearly ten kilometers into the American lines near Bullingen. His column then pushed westward to Moderscheid, on to Schoppen, Ondneval, and Thirimont, but had to backtrack when he found an impassable quagmire and turned northwest toward Malmedy. There, at about 1300, his men ran into an American convoy moving south, and the Germans shot up the vehicles.

To the south, the Fifth Panzer Army did not use an artillery preparation, as General Manteuffel preferred to infiltrate his units without giving any warning. This penetration was made through the American 28th and 106th Infantry divisions. The 106th, with a squadron of the 14th Cavalry Group (Reinforced), were positioned across the Losheim Gap at the western foot of the Schnee Eifel and on 16 December had been there less than a week. The Our River meanders through the Gap, which is cluttered with abrupt hills, some bare, some covered with fir trees and thick undergrowth. Two main roads were of macadam construction and ran through the American positions directly to St. Vith. The division's front was about eighteen air-line miles, but when traced on the ground it was actually more than twenty-one miles. The 106th's northern neighbor was the 99th Infantry Division while the 28th Infantry Division was on its southern flank.

The 106th division's units and the troops of the 14th Cavalry were so sparsely situated that when the attack came before dawn, the German forces moved through gaps, many of which were undetected by American units until after daylight. By nightfall on the 16th, the German attack had gone according to schedule and had penetrated through the Losheim Gap, had overrun American artillery units and the troops of the 14th Cavalry to reach Auw, and were preparing to send through heavy armor units the next morning on its drive to St. Vith. Two regiments of the 106th Division and an artillery battalion were surrounded, while its 424th Infantry Regiment and its neighboring unit, CCB of the 9th Armored Division, halted the German advance along the line from Neidingen-Maspelt-Hiereberg.

The American High Command, meanwhile, were reacting to the German offensive. Among other changes made in the dispositions of the 12th Army Group, General Bradley ordered the Ninth Army to send the 7th Armored Division from its position about fifteen miles north of Aachen to Bastogne, some seventy miles to the south. The division was preceded by Brigadier General Bruce C. Clarke of CCB, who reported before the dawn of December 17th to the Corps Commander in Bastogne for further orders. General Troy Middleton, VIII Corps commander, was told that the 7th Armored Division, already on the move, would report to St. Vith to help the 106th Division, which had two regiments marooned on the Schnee Eifel. General Clarke proceeded to St. Vith, arriving at 1000 and reported to Major General Alan W. Jones, Commanding General of the 106th. General Jones told Clarke that he wanted an immediate counter-attack towards Schonberg to relieve the two regiments of the 106th Division.

The 7th Armored Division, which had been expected around 0700, was at that time fighting its way across muddy roads clogged with vehicles fleeing westward. Lead elements of the division did not arrive in St. Vith until late afternoon. About 1530, General Jones turned over the defense of the St. Vith sector to General Clarke who, at that time, still did not have elements of his command. Included in the scattered units given to General Clarke was the 275th Armored Field Artillery Battalion (Separate), a Corps Artillery battalion that had remained in place despite the panic and the fact that there were no friendly units between it and the enemy. He also assumed command of two engineer headquarters' companies and a platoon of infantry. And at that time the Germans were only three or four thousand yards from the town. East of the town, several critical roadblocks were being manned by the engineer troops across the road near Prumerberg.]

The route for our march went through the following towns: Aachen, Eupen, and Malmedy, to Vielsalm. All I saw that night were the dark roads, black night, and shadowy people along the roadside. Cox, the driver, and I were in the front seats of the half-track. I stood up as the observer to help him drive. It was snowing, blustery, cold, dark, and difficult to see anything but the small red lights of the jeep in front of us. The weather was cold and damp and there wasn't any moon. It took a lot of stamina to stand. My nose was cold, my eyes continually watered, but, because it was so dark and the lights could not be on, it was necessary I continue to help guide the half-track. As we drove along, a ghost of a vehicle or a man would suddenly appear beside the road. No words were spoken just a wave of a covered flashlight and the convoy continued.

My men seemed exceptionally quiet. They seemed to know we were marching toward doom. The questions were, "What's going on, Lieutenant?" I couldn't answer, but I too had a very bad feeling in my gut. Infantrymen seem to know when a battle is pending and what the odds were going to be before they ever get to the line. There is something in the air that spells out in advance how tough the battle is going to be. And from the actions and quietness of the men, I sensed they were worried. Infantrymen know they are the expendable parts of the war, and one of their jobs is to stop the enemy and plug the hole in a line if there has been a breakthrough. From the attitude of our command, we knew something serious had happened.

The farther we went, the more traffic we saw—but not going forward. They were going fast westward to the rear. This caused more concern among my men. The one person I saw the most during the march was our S3, Major Boyer. He really seemed to be everywhere, picking up stragglers, keeping the march going, and doing a great job. He commented to me during a rest break, "For the life of me I cannot understand why some persons of higher rank can't see what's going on and stop a few of these fleeing officers and make them form some kind of defense. No, those guys all just seem to want to run and get out of the way. They just don't think about stopping and defending. I can't help from being proud and thrilled at the spirit of you guys and the rest of my men for what you've done—loading vehicles, spinning tracks, gunning motors, and taking off for a fight which others are running away from, when all we know is that somewhere down there are krauts and that there is going to be a fight. And here we run into all these guys bugging out. I'm really proud of belonging to the 7th Armored, a fighting outfit."

[Near Stavelot, CCR ran into more of Peiper's German units, who apparently were as surprised as the Americans by the meeting. CCR brushed them aside and arrived at Vielsam with no serious damage late in the afternoon. German air was more active than usual, and the column was attacked several times.]

Somewhere along the road we were alerted to man our machine guns, that it was thought German paratroopers had been dropped into the area, were disrupting the march, changing road signs, and that snipers were shooting at the troops. So now my men were really awake. We placed another head above the side armor to have more eyes observing. I went back to the following half-track and advised Sergeant Sicari to do the same.

My God, but it was dark. As I was without my glasses, I had trouble seeing fine details but by squinting I could get by. It was snowing. It was cold. It was scary. One of my men, I think it was Conover, (who was my eyes) said he saw a parachute hanging in the trees. Now we believed the rumor. Now it was a fact. The men became even more questioning. We were now passing a forest and any minute we feared a burst from a machine gun or a bazooka (German type they called *panzerfaust*). We were certainly easy targets—they could see us and we couldn't see but a few feet at any time.

We continually met vehicles coming from the opposite direction. What was their hurry? My men were very quiet. Funny, we never saw any civilians. The farther we went the colder it got. We saw Military Police on occasion and they seemed very nervous. I couldn't seem to get a grasp on what was happening. All I knew was that we were in convoy. We saw many vehicles going in the opposite direction and my men and I wished to know what in the hell was going on.

Finally on a break I found out more news. Germans were in the area dressed in U.S. Army uniforms. They were disrupting traffic, changing road signs, killing people, and generally stirring up trouble. Their mission was to do anything to stop or slow down the functioning of the our Army.

Captain Mattocks told me all he knew: "There has been a breakthrough by the Germans and the vehicles we are seeing rushing to the rear are Americans in flight. No one's in charge and they are trying to save their asses."

[The heavy stream of westward moving traffic, which was a disorganized rout, caused Lt. Col. Fuller, commander of the 38th AIB, to divert Company A and Headquarters Company from the route and ordered them into an assembly area at Rodt. B Company was also diverted, but Company C and Service Company got separated from the battalion column and were snarled in the traffic jam. This concentrated the battalion, minus C Company and Service Company, about three miles west of St. Vith. Meanwhile CCB, with the 31st Tank Battalion and the 23rd Armored Infantry Battalion attached, had been all but immobilized by the traffic maelstrom which jammed the Vielsam-St. Vith road. Lt. Col. Fuller and Major Boyer of the 38th AIB helped Lt. Col. R. C. Erlenbusch, commander of the 31st Tank Battalion, clear a path for one medium tank company and one armored infantry company before the western bound traffic double-banked each other and again closed the road.]

We convoyed for most of the day and finally pulled off the road near a small village of Rodt. There was a school house where we all got out and relieved ourselves. Rusty came by to see us and offered me a drink of cognac. I saw an old upright piano, so naturally I had to sit and play a couple of tunes. Must have been quite a scene: men listening to me while waiting, concerned about what they were seeing—trucks, jeeps, tanks, and command cars fleeing from the direction we were going. In those vehicles were all ranks. And there I was playing the piano. The song I was playing was "My Blue Heaven." The words went, "A turn to the right, A little bright light will lead you to my Blue Heaven. Just Molly and me and baby make three the reason for My Blue Heaven." When I look back at my piano playing then, it was dumb of me. The piano is one of the easiest things to booby trap. Lucky for me it wasn't, or I might have gone immediately to "My Blue Heaven."

I remember on December 17th, as I was waiting with my platoon in the school house, I looked out on the main road full of our troops fleeing the battle, completely out of control. Their vehicles were packed with men who were yelling at whoever they saw, "Run the krauts are coming!" They were throwing away their weapons, but what surprised me most were the many officers among them who could have exerted some control but made no effort to do so. One man jumped off one of the trucks when he saw our unit and yelled that he came to fight and wasn't going to bug out. I don't know what outfit he hooked up with, but he didn't join our unit. It was a sight that I never dreamed I would ever see: a U.S. Army unit completely out of control.

ST. VITH

[As the first units of CCR of the 7th Armored Division crept towards St. Vith, two hours had passed since General Clarke assumed command. The final traffic jam at a crossroads several hundred yards to the west of the town was cleared by General Clarke himself. When the first column of Sherman tanks arrived, Clarke directed them towards Schonberg, until they met the engineers. Thus began the defense of St. Vith. The initial plan for a counterattack by CCB had long since been scrapped because of the delay caused by the congested roads.

The Corps of Engineers trained its engineer combat battalions not only in the primary role of facilitating the movement of troops and supplies by keeping the road nets open for rapid advance and creating obstacles to the enemy forces, but also to fight as infantry when necessary. That training and experience proved itself many times but especially in the Battle of St. Vith. On the morning of 16 December Lt. Col. Thomas Riggs, commander of the 81st Engineer Combat Battalion of the 106th Infantry Division, whose headquarters was in Heuem, learned from a messenger from his Company A, which was supporting the 422nd Infantry Regiment, of the German attack. Col. Riggs checked in at the Division headquarters at St. Vith and learned that it was a concerted German attack; he was given orders to assemble his unit and serve as infantry. Riggs' B and C Companies were already committed within their respective combat teams, and one platoon of A Company was also involved with its assigned infantry troops. Those elements of his command were fighting a delaying action and were slowing the enemy in the various places where they had been assigned. He rushed to Schonberg and evacuated most of the bulldozers and other heavy equipment. Then back at division headquarters, Riggs learned that the 7th Armored Division and CCB and the 9th Armored Division were en route and scheduled to arrive at 0700 on 17 December, and that he should withdraw from Heuem to just west of St. Vith. Three hours later he was told to assemble all available men from his battalion and the 168th Engineer Combat Battalion, a VII Corps unit commanded by Lt. Col. W. L. Nungesser that had been operating saw mills and maintaining the rear road network. He was able to scrounge up slightly more than two companies, comprising his Headquarters and Service Company and about one third of A Company and elements from the168th Engineers, commanded by Lt. Col. W. L. Nungesser. With these troops, Lt. Col. Riggs established a defensive position along a wooded ridge about one mile east of St. Vith, near Prumerberg. Mines were laid to their front and the troops dug in. Several German tank and infantry attacks were repulsed during the day. During the night German patrols were stopped, but the lines were anything but clear as both American and German troops became commingled. Major Boyer checked in with Col. Riggs that night. At a meeting with officers of both engineer battalions, Troop B, the 87th Reconnaissance Battalion, and an attached platoon of medium tanks of the 7th Armored Division, it was decided that Company B, 38th Armored Infantry Battalion, would relieve the 168th Engineers troops.

Col. Riggs had his platoon leaders tell his troops about the incoming infantry of the 7th Armored Division and instructed them to lead the new arrivals into position and to avoid firing on them as his engineer and the German troops were intermingled on the ground.]

Finally, by a superior leadership job, Major Boyer and Captain Mattocks got the convoy rolling. My platoon was again loaded and on the alert. I don't know whether Boyer and Mattocks were ever decorated for the job they did on the convoy, but they should have been. I remember one incident: I had walked from the school to the road and was watching and helping where I could. We were trying to get our troops back on the road. A command car came down loaded with some of the high ranking officers of the fleeing troops. They apparently wanted to continue to get away from their responsibility. We needed their space to get our vehicles back on the road. They would not move, so Major Boyer told them to get off the road or he would get one of his tanks to push them off. I am sure they didn't like the order from a Major, but they got their vehicle out of our way.

Now my men were really wondering what kind of hell we were getting into. I could read their minds easily because I was thinking the same thing: Why are we going forward when all those troops and officers are leaving? But then it didn't take long for me to come to an answer. We were going up to the front. We were the infantry, and it was up to us to do the messy jobs. We didn't know what we were getting into, but we knew it was going to be a dirty mess of some kind. Some one had goofed up again and it was up to our troops to stop the enemy somehow, some way.

[It took CCR six hours to get to get from Vielsam to St. Vith—a twelve mile run—because of the disgraceful traffic jam caused by the fleeing Americans, a delay of combat units which might have saved elements of the 106th Infantry Division if they could have reached St. Vith earlier. During the night General Clarke supervised the extension and thickening of the thin line of Engineers that ran roughly from Hunningen, north of St. Vith, through Prumersberg to Weisenbach, where it loosely joined the left flank of CCB of the 9th Armored Division. To the south he knew that the 422nd and 423rd Regimental Combat Teams (RCT) of the 106th Division had been cut off and completely surrounded; that to the southeast, CCB of the 9th Armored Division was attacking to retake Winterspelt; and that the 424th RCT of the 106th south of the 9th AD was retiring to take up new positions. By 1630, Clarke was in his command post in a school house in

*St. Vith—also the CP of the 106th Division—and only three units of the
7th AD had been able to enter the town: one cavalry Reconnaissance
Troop, one medium tank company, and one armored infantry company.
When Lt. Col. Fuller and Major Boyer reported to him, General Clarke
told Major Boyer to, "Go in town and get B Company of the 23rd, which
you will find in the main street. Have them take up positions here," (pointing to the southeastern approaches to St. Vith). Boyer asked who would be
on his right and left. Clarke answered the only way he could: "We don't
know about the right; CCB of the 9th is there somewhere. On the left,
some engineers from a Corps Battalion, farther to the left, a reconnaissance troop from the 87th." General Clarke then told Fuller to coordi-
nate the defenses of St. Vith with the commanders of the engineer units
then in position about 2400 yards east of the town and in the woods to
the right of the Schonberg road, and at the same time he attached the
reconnaissance troop, the armored infantry company, and the tank company to the 38th AIB]*

By early evening we finally arrived at St.Vith. It was dusk. My men
unloaded and went into a vacant building to stretch and wait for
orders. I wandered about the town for a short time trying to find out
what the hell was going on. There were a few civilians. They didn't
seem to relish the idea that Americans were in their town. A young
lady at the rest stop we had just left was crying, "Le Boche. Le Boche."
We tried to understand her, but no one in our group understood
German or whatever she was speaking. But to be honest we saw that
the town was in one hell of a confused mess.

When Major Boyer first got into town, he was fired at by a sniper
from one of the windows overlooking the street. The sniper missed. It
just happened that one of our armored vehicles was passing at the time
and had a .50 caliber machine gun mounted on it. The gunner adjusted,
aimed, and fired. The sniper was killed with one burst and was left
hanging out of the window.

Soon after our arrival in St. Vith, a Military Police motorcyclist raced into town from the direction of Malmedy. He skidded to a stop against a building on the other side of the street from where Major Boyer was directing traffic. The MP's uniform was ripped and torn, and he was bleeding from surface cuts apparently sustained from a spill. He was highly excited and out of breath, but he was able to gasp out the news that our Division Chief of Staff, Colonel Matthews, had been ambushed by a German tank about two miles north of St. Vith. Colonel Matthews in his jeep and escorted by two MP's had left town about 1730 en route to Recht with orders for CCR. As they rounded a turn in the road, they came almost face-to-face with an approaching German tank. In an attempt to get away, the vehicles got stuck. The driver and Colonel Matthews bailed out and tried to escape on foot. The MP said he stayed in the area of the incident for more than an hour but had not seen either his buddy, the other MP, Colonel Matthews, or the driver. As soon as he caught his breath, Major Boyer directed the MP to the school house to report to General Clarke what had happened to the Chief of Staff.

That report about a German tank being just two miles or less from town, needless to say, meant the road to the north was cut, and that the krauts would probably try to force the town from the north sometime during the evening. It sure wasn't a comfortable feeling, for I knew that Captain Anstey of Company A was not yet in position. The only troops that were in line were a few engineers of the 106th Infantry Division.

I ran into First Sergeant Alvie Davis, who was trying to organize the command post. No officer was around. Davis said Captain Mattocks was out trying to find out what the new mission was and how long we would be able to rest—and would we have time to feed the troops? We hadn't had a good meal for a couple of days. No, he found out, we didn't have time and besides the mess truck was not with the forward elements of our group. In fact he didn't know where the truck was.

I went back to my men. They too were waiting and wondering. I had been back for only a few minutes when a runner from the CP came and said, "Lieutenant, you are wanted at the CP." So again I found the command post. My orders from Captain Mattocks were, "Moranda, take your platoon up this road (pointing) about a mile or so. You will come to a small house on the left. Report to either Lieutenant Colonel Fuller or an Engineer Lieutenant Colonel Riggs. One of them will give you the mission. Good luck!"

"Strange," I thought, "what's the 'good luck' bit? He had never said that before."

Back where I left my men, I called Sergeants Sicari, Simeneaux, Totoni, and Curtin and gave them the word, "Let's move out." We loaded the half-tracks and drove to the house. When we arrived there, I looked at the men sitting around the command post. They seemed to be in a daze. Not many smiles on their faces. They were milling around, just waiting. They didn't seem to be anxious to continue what they had been doing, whatever that was. By now it was dark. I went inside and found Lieutenant Colonel Fuller, Lieutenant Colonel Riggs, and a Lieutenant Holland conversing. As I approached I saluted and said, "Lieutenant Moranda reporting."

Colonel Fuller introduced me to Colonel Riggs and Lieutenant Holland. Colonel Riggs gave me a brief history of the previous action. They were from the Engineer Battalion of the 106th Infantry Division. Their division had been broken through and the division was in a full retreat. Colonel Riggs and Lieutenant Holland were ordered by General Jones of the 106th Infantry Division to make a stand on the outskirts of St. Vith. St Vith was an important hub on the route the Germans had to take for their operation. When the 38th Armored Infantry arrived in St Vith, Col. Fuller was ordered to join Col. Riggs' men. As Col. Fuller was the senior Infantry officer, he was to be in command. The 38th

Battalion was to join with the engineers and stop the attack of the Germans. My mission was to go with Lt. Holland and support his men. Col. Fuller had no more information except to say the enemy was only a few hundred yards away.

(I discovered later that Lt. Holland and a few of his men had been in a series of skirmishes before our troops arrived. When the 106th Infantry Division had been overrun by the Germans, some of the American soldiers broke and ran. Holland came across some of those men that were trying to save their skins, and as he watched some of them throwing away their weapons, he stopped them and made them members of his unit. Soon after that, on the 16th of December, he and his men stopped the Germans by first knocking out an enemy tank and the infantry following it. Holland's men had used some of the discarded American weapons—a .50 caliber machine gun and a bazooka.)

While walking to the forward troops, we held our conversation to a minimum, and what was done was in whispers, for the enemy was near and we certainly didn't want to draw their fire before we even got to the front lines.

DECEMBER 18

[The defensive cordon around St. Vith was established piecemeal with units placed in line as they arrived. Some such as Troop B, 87th Reconnaissance Squadron, had to fight its way into its assigned position. Another example as related by Lt. Col. Erlinbusch who commanded the 31st Tank Battalion: "Company A, 31st Tank Battalion, was ordered to take up a defensive position on the high ground about 2000 yards east of St. Vith. Lt. Dunn, the leading platoon leader, preceded his lead tank in a quarter ton to reconnoiter for positions. About 1500 yards from St. Vith, upon rounding a bend in the road, Lt. Dunn spotted, about 800 yards to his front, three German tanks and about one company of infantry moving

in the direction of St. Vith. He turned his vehicle around, issued instructions to his platoon by radio, climbed into his tank, and led his platoon to the point where he saw the enemy approaching. The German force and his first platoon met head on at the bend of the road. The fight was short and at point blank range. We destroyed the enemy tanks and killed or wounded about fifty of the enemy with no loss to our own forces. Company A secured the high ground, blocked the road, and extended its position north from the road along the ridge."

Traffic jams on the St. Vith-Vielsam road were still increasing as those American forces who had been in the area before the German break-through were trying to get as far west as they could as fast as possible. It took Captain W. H. Anstey with his Company A, 38th AIB, two and one-half hours to cover three miles. By 0700 on 18 December troops were dug in along a U-shaped arc from the Prumerberg road on the south to the Malmedy road on the north—the sector assigned to the 38th AIB by General Clarke. On the left of the 38th was, at first, the 87th Cavalry Reconnaissance Squadron and later the 31st Tank Battalion. On the right was CCB of the 9th Armored Division. During the night of 17 December there was some probing by the Germans and some small arms fire, but no major attacks. The weather, which had been bitterly cold all day with gray, overcast skies, turned into a cold, drizzly rain late that night and the ground was muddy and soggy, making vehicular movement almost impossible. Even so three German tanks and two of their 75 mm assault guns were destroyed in front of the 38th's arc.]

After about 500 yards we came to the front edge of the forest. Lieutenant Holland and I trooped the line. His men were dug in and were really glad to see some help arriving. After walking around the area, Holland and I decided we would split our forces. He would take Sergeants Sicari, Curtin, and Totoni with a section of machine guns with him and bolster his defense on the left side of the road. Sergeant Simeneaux and his section, along with a few of Lt. Holland's engineers, would come with me and establish a defense on the right side of the road. It was very dark that night and difficult to establish fields of fire. While we were moving forward we could hear the rattle of machine gun fire to our left and Lt. Holland remarked, "Sounds like the Jerries are still trying to break through the line."

I walked back to the CP with Conover, who had accompanied us. As we were walking through the trees we heard the clop of footsteps coming toward us. Conover went to the side of the road so he could cover me as I challenged the man. It was an elderly civilian who kept repeating "Le Boche, le Boche," while pointing toward the east. My interpretation was that the enemy was very close. We continued to the command post where we placed the half-tracks nearby. With the platoon in tow, we all went forward. No words were spoken. The men all sensed the situation was serious.

Capt. Carl K. "Rusty" Mattocks

Sgt. James Totoni

Pfc. Maurice Conover

Cpl. Glenn Fackler

We placed our .30 caliber machine guns on either side of the road so their fields of fire could cover our entire front. The rest of the squad and the engineer troops were dispersed so they could also fire their weapons through gaps in the trees. We then placed the other men back into the woods for cover and protection from the enemy in front, and they still could have fields of fire.

I told each soldier, "Dig in, as we will be hit early in the morning." They understood and began. Few of them had entrenching tools, and those that didn't dug with their helmets or whatever they had, and soon all had foxholes. I didn't dig one as I usually jumped into the nearest one when the need arose.

[*At 0800, 18 December, medium small arms fire broke out along the front of Company B, 38th AIB, along with close direct fire from two German tanks and one assault gun. This firing decapitated trees causing limbs and chunks of wood to fall into and behind the foxholes. One light machine gun was destroyed and its crew and one rifle squad annihilated by Panzerfaust fire. This heavy fire overwhelmed the center platoon of Company B, and the platoon withdrew about 300 yards. Tech Sergeant J.P. Revels, the platoon sergeant, quickly rallied his men and launched a counter-attack. There were no reserves available. The attack shifted about forty-five minutes later to the right platoon of Company B, commanded by 1st Lieutenant J. H. Higgins and the engineer troops under the command of 1st Lieutenant W. E. Holland. The German troops were very aggressive in trying to widen the breach and this showed that seasoned troops were involved. By 0920, contact was broken and the Germans withdrew, leaving one tank and one assault gun as burning wrecks.*]

Early in the morning we heard troops moving in to our left. I soon learned that it was Company B, 23rd Armored Infantry Battalion moving in. This made the line almost continuous for a few hundred yards. All of the American troops were on the edge of the forest.

I met with Lt. Holland and discussed our plan, and after that I went back to the right side of the road and for a few minutes I got a short rest. But it wasn't long before we were awakened by an enemy patrol probing our lines. A few rounds came in. A tank was seen near a small house to our front. It was rumbling but not advancing toward our position. It was then I discovered that being back in the forest had its benefits but also its drawbacks. The artillery coming in hit the tree tops and we suffered casualties from tree bursts. The incoming shells exploded and the fragments of steel did their best to find you and kill or wound you.

Someone said the damned fragments seemed to have eyes. We soon learned that the safest thing to do during a barrage of incoming artillery that hit the trees above us was to hug a tree. We soon placed our foxholes near one, but even then we had to don our helmets—even while trying to sleep in the hole. We found the best way to build an emplacement was to establish a field of fire, then build yourself some overhead cover, and have it near a tree.

I was hit on the nose and above the eye by a shell fragment, and another piece hit me on the right leg, none very serious. Then it dawned on me, we didn't have a medic with our bastard outfit of half 106th Engineers and half of our 38th Headquarters Company machine gun platoon. When we first got there we used a medic from one of the other nearby units.

The first real attack occurred at about 0800. The Germans hit first along the entire front of Company B/23 and our team of engineers and machine gun platoon. Attacking were two tanks with accompanying infantry. One of the light machine guns of B/23 was destroyed along with its crew, and the enemy fire had annihilated the men of the adjoining infantry squad. Their front line withdrew about 300 yards, but the officers and non-coms soon got their men reorganized and retook their positions on the defensive line. In the Infantry School at Fort Benning they had called the line the FPL—Final Protective Line.

The second attack came at about 1100. The Germans still had not given up trying to come through us and again hit the front of our position, this time with two platoons of infantry supported by a tank. As I was going toward the rear in order to get to my other men and not expose myself too much, I came close to our battalion CP. I saw Lt. Col. Fuller and Lt. Col. Riggs talking to a captain with a tank destroyer crew. Just what I hoped for. I went to them and I asked the officer in charge of the TD if he would take on the tank in front of our position. He said he would. With that the tank destroyer rumbled up the road; he got the weapon into position and with a couple of shots knocked out the enemy tank. The tank destroyer departed right after the firing as its commander said he couldn't stay and left. It was a short term relief because we soon heard more tanks to our front and to the right of our position.

[About two hours later the Germans tried again and hit the right platoon of Company B and the Engineer troops, this time using two platoons of infantry supported by a tank. The tank section of Company A, 31st Tank Battalion, took care of the German tank with a ricochet shot that left it burning about twenty-five yards in front of the defense line. The attacking infantry were unable to stand up against the withering hail of rifle and machine gun fire which was poured into their ranks and they soon broke and fled.

Meanwhile Company A, 38th AIB, and Troop B of the 87th Recon were having a rather quiet time, except for an incident in B Troop of the 87th, according to Captain Anstey who described one action: "One of his armored car crews was in a concealed position near the boundary of Company A and the 87th Recon when a Tiger tank approached at right angles and ran along a trail in front of the Main Line of Resistance; the armored car slipped out of position and started up the trail behind the Tiger, accelerating to get closer; the German tank commander saw the armored car, and started traversing his gun to bear on it; it was a race between the Americans in their vehicle with a puny 37 mm gun trying to get close enough to be effective in the Tiger's vulnerable rear armor, and the Germans who were desperately trying to get its main gun to bear in order to blast the 'fools' who dared to fight a sixty-ton tank with their little 'pop gun;' suddenly the armored car got to within twenty-five yards and quickly pumped in three rounds; the lumbering Tiger stopped, shuddered, and a muffled explosion was heard followed by flames which billowed out of the turret and engine ports."

At 1300, Company A, 23rd AIB, under Captain J. R. Foster arrived and was put in line between Companies A and B of the 38th AIB to relieve B Troop of the 87th. From 1445 to 1730 the Germans attacked again, and this time they meant business for they slashed into Lt. Higgin's platoon and Lt. Holland's engineers with an estimated battalion of infantry on a two company front, with direct support from four tanks and eight assault guns. Two of the tanks and two assault guns attacked with the infantry, while the rest of the armor placed direct fire on the Americans from the vicinity of Wallerode. Initial penetrations were made, and it was only the heavy enfilade fire poured into the assault ranks by the Machine Gun Platoon of the 38th AIB, commanded by 2nd Lt. R. E. Moranda, and the direct fire placed on the attacking tanks and assault guns by Companies A and C of the 31st Tank Battalion which broke up the attack. After almost three hours of vicious fighting, much of it hand-to-hand, the Germans were forced to withdraw. The American lines still held, although several gaps had been opened and some German patrols filtered through. B Troop of the 87th was pushed into line to plug a gap between Company B of the 38th and the engineer troops.]

About mid-afternoon we were hit again by infantry and tanks. It was during this fray that one of my gunners on a machine gun broke and ran away from his gun. Conover and I stopped him. He was just a young blond kid, twenty years old and scared to death. I talked to him and told him the seriousness of his running away. Then I talked to Sergeant Simeneaux and we decided to put him back as the gunner.

During one of the attacks, one of the squads in Lieutenant Higgins' platoon reported they got word one machine gun section was seen taking off. Higgins asked them to check, but they never found them. No one knew whether they had been captured or killed.

Normally, when the infantry is under fire from artillery, mortars, Nebelwerfer rockets (we called "Screaming Meemies"), and tanks and they are also in range of small arms fire, the best way to overcome the fear of the enemy is to attack. We couldn't do that. We had orders to hold at all costs, so stay we did. And we always had to fight the urge to withdraw.

At 1745 we were kept on the alert, the enemy was still probing our lines looking for a weak spot. Their mission was, obviously, to push through our position and capture St Vith.

[*The night was reasonably quiet except for the ever present probing attempts by the Germans patrols, but a lot of vehicular movement, including tanks, could be heard by the Americans to their north in the vicinity of Wallerode. German 88s and artillery concentrations were placing continuous harassing fire on St. Vith and all roads. The weather was bitter cold, overcast, and there were snow flurries during the day. The rain had stopped, but the roads were slick and covered with a thin coating of mud. The actual count of German losses included five tanks, two assault guns destroyed, one assault gun damaged, and 249 killed.*]

During many of the lulls I made all of my men take their shoes off and massage their feet. There was some grousing but the men followed the order. The weather was really cold and we sure didn't need to have any frostbite cases. The hardest thing to do was to keep warm, as we only had our regular outfits which were inadequate for the weather we were experiencing. I was fortunate in having bought some silk pajamas to wear underneath and that long muffler I could wrap around my head and body which kept old Jack Frost away. But the men were not so lucky. Most of them had only one pair of socks and no "long johns" so it was very difficult for them to keep warm. During the breaks between action, they would usually pair up, two men to a foxhole, and position themselves back to back so their body heat helped some. Sleep? I don't think I had more than an hour's sleep at a time for five days, and that seemed to be with one eye open for a foot step or any unusual sound would cause me to be wide awake. I think all of us there were in the same state of alert.

DECEMBER 19

The next day there were more probes. We heard German tanks to our front. One of our left flank units broke and withdrew farther into the forest. Their leaders were soon able, however, to control the men and get them back into position.

About that time, Captain Mattocks told me about the U.S. Army Searchlight Company. As we were making our way to St Vith, their commander had asked the commander of our convoy, as we were leaving Uback, if they could follow behind our convoy. Our CO said yes and they did. But when we were coming into Rodt, the searchlight convoy took the wrong turn and wound up in Malmedy. The unit was captured and massacred. Word got around about that slaughter, and I think it was one of the reasons our outfit and others fought so well at the Battle of the Bulge, for it did not take long for the news to spread about the killing of Americans who had surrendered. It was understandable that my men were concerned. For two days they had observed American troops fleeing from the front, who probably had not heard of the Malmedy massacre. Even so, it is questionable whether it would have made a difference in their attitude or whether their fears could have been overcome and caused them to stand and fight. Yet here we were, doing our job and doing it well.

One of our problems was that we didn't know anything about the enemy, or where we were, or who or what kind of units we were fighting against, nor who the people were that were retreating. There was supposed to be a friendly unit on our right flank. In all the time we were in the line the right flank unit never materialized. At one time we did hear some tanks clanking around on our right but we never did see them. And for one brief period we heard some tanks firing their weapons, but they never came near us. So we knew we had no help from the right and were really exposed. It worried me—knowing we had no friendly troops there to protect our flank. I wondered if another of our own outfits had bugged out on us?

Engineer Lieutenant Holland was my main source of information. To me he was one of the many heroes of the Battle of St Vith. There were many heroes, and most were the lieutenants and sergeants. I saw but one field grade officer in the front lines after we were in position. The one field grade that we saw at the front during all of the battle was Major Boyer. He was with B Company on my left most of the time. The right side of the horseshoe was still under the Holland-Moranda group.

The third attack of the day came about 1700 hours. The enemy really meant business this time. They came down the road with tanks and infantry—it seemed like an army of tanks to us. But the decision to have our positions back into the forest trees protected us somewhat from the tanks, and our machine guns and infantry with bazookas were finally able to stop the Germans. Even so, it seemed like the battle would never end.

When Company A's line had been broken, I saw that Sergeants Curtin and Totoni and their sections were withdrawing deeper into the forest. Curtin had his men under control. To get to him I had to go back about fifty yards and then across an open area to the other side of the road, and Curtin had his men standing behind trees and firing into the oncoming enemy. Curtin was in his glory. He must have thought he was playing cowboy and Indians. But with the tanks knocked out it wasn't long before this German attack was over. I then remembered what Sergeant Sicari had told me earlier about Curtin: that when the chips were down he would be the platoon's best leader during actual combat.

On the right side of the road my gunners were firing into the advancing Germans. The young lad who had fled the first fire fight, and who we had turned around after stopping him, was firing his weapon even after being wounded with a shot through the arm.

[In Major Boyer's After Action Report he wrote: "The devastating effect of the enfilade machine gun fire was aptly demonstrated along one fire break in 'B' Company's area. Yesterday the Krauts broke through the line and had immediately pushed a platoon of paratroopers through to exploit the gap. They quickly dodged down the reverse slope, but as they broke through the trees one of the machine gun sections of Second Lt. Moranda's platoon on the right flank quickly traversed the guns and laid down fire at the break. When the Krauts crossed the open break about one hundred yards away, they were perfect targets. There they lay, nineteen Krauts laid out in parade ground intervals five yards apart, dead with slugs in their chests. We had stopped them!!"]

I saw Lt. Higgins right after he was told to take command of B Company and asked him what had happened to Captain Green. He told me that when they had their first "visitors"—apparently a probe, nothing very serious—Captain Green was going down the line checking his men and just as he got close to the last of them, he heard some machine gun fire in the nearby woods. He thought it was his troops firing, so he ran to see what the problem was and ran into a platoon of Germans. He was taken prisoner.

As I was coming back from Sergeant Curtin's side, I stopped by the CP to pick up some machine gun ammunition from the half-track parked near the command post. I saw Lieutenant Colonel Fuller; he was ashen and looked really sick. He asked, "What the hell is going on up there? What is the situation?" I told him, "We are now OK. The troops have stopped the *krauts* and we have re-established our front lines." That was the last time I saw him. Soon after that he went to Division Headquarters and told General Clarke he was too sick to continue in command. His command was taken over by Major Boyer and Lieutenant Colonel Riggs, the Engineer commander.

I will not take credit for the "kills." My section sergeants were the heroes. They were the ones who kept the machine gunners firing. They encouraged the men. I was kept busy going from one side to the other. The sergeants were on the front all the time, they and their men.

[Field Marshall Model, Commander of Army Group B which had the responsibility for the offensive and breakthrough, reminded General Manteuffel that St. Vith was the exception to the orders to bypass all heavily defended towns. Even though St. Vith had been outflanked from the north and south, the town had to be taken in order for the roads and the rail lines to be used in support of the Fifth and Sixth Armies. Therefore, the Fuhrer Escort Brigade, the Fifth Panzer Army reserve, was diverted from an exploiting mission and turned against St. Vith. By the morning of 18 December, two Volksgrenadier Divisions and a combat command from the 1st SS Panzer Division began the first of a series of attacks which were to extend for six days.

At 0200, elements of the 1st SS Panzer Division struck north of St. Vith; at 0800, CCB of the 7th Armored Division (U.S.) was hit by infantry supported by tanks; at 1000, service elements west of St. Vith were engaged by elements of 1st Panzer Division which had flanked St. Vith from the north. By late afternoon, however, CCB and CCA, 7th Armored, by aggressive counterattacks, had recaptured the vital crossroads lost in the morning.

During the night of 18-19 December, two attacks against CCB were repulsed. By the end of 18 December, the German probing attacks had found St. Vith ringed on three sides by the 7th Armored Division on the north and center and by CCB of the 9th Armored Division (U.S.) to the south. The defensive perimeter, almost twenty-five miles long, was completely isolated from friendly forces. The gap to the south now stretched eighteen miles to Bastogne; to the north, the fifteen mile gap to Malmedy was filled with the Sixth Panzer Army troops.

All day on the 19th, probing attacks for soft spots were made. Attacks in turn were made against 7th Armored Division/CCB's left flank, then at the center of CCB, and then against CCB's right flank. All attacks were beaten off by combined fires and numerous individual acts of heroism. By noon Model was again pressuring Manteuffel to seize St, Vith. The traffic jam to the east of St. Vith had tied up German supply convoys and trains, not to mention the 1st Panzer Division. This time it was General Manteuffel's turn to unsnarl traffic, just as General Clarke had to do two days before, by personally directing traffic.]

Sketch showing the situation on 19 December 1944

DECEMBER 20

The morning came, finally!! We trooped the line, Major Boyer, Lieutenants Higgins, Holland, Captain Mattocks, and I. We saw where the furious action had occurred the day before. We saw many dead Jerries. Our rifles and machine guns had saved the day.

[During the check of the positions, Major Boyer found that Lieutenant Holland was completing the reorganization of his company, but on his left, Company B was licking its wounds after the savage fighting of the day before. There was a gap between the 1st platoon under 2nd Lieutenant W.A. Jamiel on the left and the 2nd platoon under 2nd Lieutenant W.C. Fradenburg in the center of the line. The 2nd platoon had suffered too many losses, so Major Boyer combined it with Lieutenant Higgins' 3rd platoon, and told Higgins to take command of Company B since Captain Green, the commander, had been missing since the previous day's early attack. Major Boyer had been told to take command since Colonel Fuller had gone to the rear. Lieutenant Holland told Major Boyer that he considered his group of Engineer troops as being under Boyer's command, and this gave Boyer a Task Force of four companies with about 450 men, including a reserve of 70 soldiers.

While the lines were being adjusted, Major Boyer and party surveyed the scene of the last attack. The only Germans they found were dead ones, most of them killed as they apparently tried to dig themselves in behind trees, logs, or any cover they could find. Those who did not have shovels had tried to scoop shallow holes with their helmets, bayonets, or even their finger nails. But the accuracy of the defenders rifles and machine gun fire had been too much for them. They counted more than 200 dead Germans within the defensive positions and did not count those in front of the lines. They also identified from the insignia on the Germans two volksgrenadier divisions, a panzer division, and a regiment of the Gross-Deutschland—the latter a unit which had always provided the guard for Hitler's headquarters when in the field.]

At that time the Germans who had been attacking us were identified. They were a Volksgrenadier Division along with a Panzer group. When I told my men who the group fighting us was, Sergeant Curtin said, "Hell, if you have seen one you've seen them all." I agreed. When someone is trying to kill you, it doesn't make much difference what kind of identifying uniform patch he is wearing.

The next attack came at mid-afternoon. An estimated enemy company supported by a tank—I think it was a heavy tank called a Panther—which was knocked out by a bazooka. The enemy was soon picked off by our rifles and machine guns. In my mind I can still hear the German non-coms directing their troops from the rear. What heavy voices they had—and how well they controlled their advancing soldiers.

Snow came again. It took a lot of individual attention to the men. All of us were uneasy. At least we didn't see our own troops fleeing from the front. All day long we were under artillery fire. Most of the shells went over us toward the rear, but we were plagued by those damned "Screaming Meemies." What a scary sound! When you hear them coming you automatically react by looking for the nearest hole. When I heard them, I would dive in the nearest fox hole, usually on top of one of my men. When I piled in on Conover, he would invariably say, "Welcome aboard, Lieutenant."

[By the morning of the 20th, the situation at St. Vith was becoming increasingly difficult for the defenders. Although bolstered by the arrival of division artillery and the addition of the 112th Infantry Regiment from the 28th Infantry Division (which had been thrust aside by the initial German penetration and out of contact with friendly forces until the 19th), the defense was greatly hampered by the lack of supply, aerial support, and aerial observation for artillery fires. Ammunition was especially critical,

since it had to be obtained by locating abandoned dumps, then running the gauntlet of the German-infested rear area with truck convoys.

However, the Germans were also having their difficulties. By this time their timetable was three days behind schedule. The St. Vith salient stuck deep into the road net to the west, impeding support of the exploiting panzers racing toward the Meuse. Traffic was jammed bumper-to-bumper for miles from the original line of departure at the Westwall. The effect of the jam was indicated by the fact that it took the Fuhrer Escort Brigade three days—until 20 December— to plow through the jammed roads to get into position to attack.

During the day on the 20th Major Boyer was ordered to the town of St. Vith to meet with General Clarke, who wanted an update on the situation. Boyer gave General Clarke his assessment of the situation and said that there had been a penetration of the Allied lines in the Engineer troop area that Boyer wanted to attend to. General Clarke stated he wanted to think about it and check other data. Boyer told him to "Go to hell" and took off for the break-through area. Years later, when Colonel Boyer was serving under General Clarke again at Fort Hood, Texas, Clarke often commented, "Colonel Boyer is the only one who has told me to 'Go to hell' and survived."]

Our troops finally got some support from our own artillery and from the 38th's Headquarters Company. Lieutenant Kinnebrew opened his forward observer position for his mortars. Lieutenant Boyd was still looking for a good observation spot for his platoon of assault guns. The 275th Artillery opened up a Forward Observer post. It seemed like we were getting stronger all the time, but our main trouble was that there were no replacements for the infantry losses. Our front lines were beginning to have too many blank spaces.

We were continually probed. The Germans would open with their burp guns and mortars. We could hear their NCOs ("Feldwebels") yelling at their men. We were using our ammunition sparingly. Many times we didn't answer their fire, because I was sure the Germans were logging every one of our positions for later artillery and mortar barrages. A fifteen man German patrol came into the draw in front of the unit next to us. Our machine guns opened up on them as the patrol came nearer. We continued to fire at them until they withdrew. Early the next morning our troops sent out a patrol to see what the results were, and when they came back they reported there was blood on the ground along with some bandages, but no enemy. Apparently they had picked up and took back their wounded.

As I recall my action, it seemed to me I was continually on the move, going from one side of the road to the other. I remember on one day when I was going from my squads on the right flank to my squads on the left side of the road, I heard a fire fight up ahead. As I proceeded toward the firing I heard someone coming through the trees toward me. I dropped and covered the noise with my weapon. From the front lines came Captain Rusty Mattocks. He had been trooping the line and had participated in a small fire fight. (That was the last time I saw Rusty until 1987 when I attended the 38th Armored Infantry Battalion, 7th Armored Division reunion in Pennsylvania.)

I was uneasy and couldn't seem to grasp the situation. Even sleep didn't come easy. I couldn't show my uneasiness as the men would have picked up on it. But just sitting and waiting was hard. Why couldn't we get more troops, more support, so we could attack? Defense is no way to win any battle, but with what we had we couldn't attack.

[During the day and the night of the 20th the defenders consolidated their positions, while the Germans jockeyed their units around for a final attack against the salient from the north, east, and south. Considerable pressure was put on CCA to the north, but the critical road leading from Becht to Poteau was held. On the 21st, two German infantry divisions and the Fuhrer Escort Brigade launched unceasing attacks along the entire front. Infantry, tank, artillery, engineer, reconnaissance, and service troops stood their ground inflicting huge losses on the attacking formations. Five major

corps attacks were hurled against CCB in the center until by 2000 the CCB line was penetrated in three places. CCB then withdrew to the high ground west of St. Vith and tied in with CCA to the north and CCB of the 9th Armored Division on the south. On that day, eleven distinct and separate attacks had been made on the entire front, in addition to the constant probing and patrolling.

The school house in St Vith had been the command post for the 106th Division, then, later, for General Clarke, and on 18 December Clarke moved his Command Post to Krombach. When the building they were in received a direct hit by artillery fire on the 20th, the 38th AIB moved its CP into the school house.

Also on the 20th, 2nd Lieutenant Bundy of the 434th Armored Field Artillery Battalion reported to Major Boyer as Forward Observer. That battalion was from VIII Corps Artillery, originally in support of the 106th Infantry Division, and had remained in position and offered their services to the 7th Armored Division. Prior to that the 275th Artillery had the job of supporting the entire 7th AD and there were not enough Forward Observers for every battalion. On 19 December, a Liaison Officer and two more Forward Observers arrived and were placed in positions where observation was the best. However, the 38th AIB had to rig up a communication system where messages could be relayed by telephone and radio to the firing batteries. Meanwhile the Assault Gun Platoon under Lieutenant Boyd and the Mortar Platoon under Lieutenant Kinnebrew performed miracles in helping to make up for the shortage of artillery. Boyd's normal three guns were augmented by a 105 mm howitzer from a tank company, and Kinnebrew's platoon manned six 81 mm mortars. Their reactions to targets were almost automatic, and they were issuing fire orders even before a rifle company could call in its mission.

At mid-morning German tanks and armored vehicles (one of which was identified as a captured American one), followed by infantrymen fanned out behind them, attacked the 38th AIB area and were met by a heavy artillery and mortar fire for over ten minutes which slaughtered the infantry, destroyed four tanks, and forced the attacking armor to turn and flee through Wallerode in the direction of Born.

At mid-afternoon, another attack came, and when the Germans had closed to within twenty-five yards of the American lines, bazookas and artillery knocked out the armored vehicles. By placing withering machine gun fire on the burning vehicles, all the German personnel were killed except two SS troopers who were seriously wounded, taken prisoners, and identified as members of the 1st SS Panzer Division.

Then a company-sized unit was seen moving through the woods to the south of the Schonburg road. Some mortar rounds came into the American positions and some automatic rifle fire, but the Germans did not close. They were apparently trying to get the American defenders to disclose their positions, but the fire discipline of the defenders must have been disappointing to the attackers, and they withdrew.

All during that night there was heavy tank and motor movement to the north, northwest, the immediate front, and the south. From map data only, some American artillery was called for, which had some success, for the defenders heard a muffled explosion, followed by a larger one and shortly thereafter a red glow was seen above the trees, which probably meant a hit on an ammunition or gas supply truck.

German losses in the 38th's sector were tallied for 20 December as five half-tracks destroyed, four tanks damaged, and forty-three killed.

All night the 38th could hear the buildup of tanks and other vehicles along its entire perimeter, but there was an especially heavy concentration of armor in the northwest which indicated a full-scale attack was imminent for the 21st of December. That proved to be true, for by 1100, a fifteen minute barrage hit the defenders and by noon the entire front was locked in combat as the Germans attacked along the Schonburg road. At 1400, the 31st Tank Battalion received a one hour barrage of heavy artillery fire and an infantry attack by a full regiment.]

DECEMBER 21

On the fifth day when dawn broke—it had snowed during the night—we knew something was going on. All night we had heard the build-up of tanks and other noises. We knew we were going to be in a fierce fight. Years later when I read the After Action reports I found out where we were, who was with us, and who was against us. But a platoon leader in an on-going operation doesn't know "doodly squat." His world is the what he can see a few yards in front of him.

The German attack started at 1100, not in my area but on our left. Company B of the 38th commanded by Lieutenant Higgins was getting the brunt of the attack. They had tried Holland's and my area before. This time they really laid it on. I was kept busy checking both areas. There were no casualties. The artillery and "screaming meemies" were away from us.

But it wasn't long before we were under the most intense artillery one can imagine. I was in a fox hole and every time enemy rounds hit the ground I would bounce. And right in the middle of the barrage the radio operator yelled at me, "Lieutenant, the headquarters wants you." So I jumped out of the foxhole and ran about twenty-five yards through the barrage to the radio. It was Sergeant Davis at headquarters, "What's going on?" My reply was, "We are receiving a heavy barrage. Enemy is attacking center and on my left." I then ran back to my foxhole with Conover. The savior of the battle was the artillery support and the guts of the riflemen and the machine gunners. The Germans had us plotted but our men had the fortitude to hang in. They were great!

The attack became fiercer all the time. There was no let up, just continuous artillery and direct fire from their tanks. About noon the Germans again started their advance on us. First, a barrage of artillery and soon the whole front was attacked by their infantry. This had to be the one attack that must be repulsed. We could see that the enemy had built up their forces and were going to make an all out effort. I was so damned busy I didn't really know what was going on anywhere else but in the immediate front of my positions. I knew the other American troops were just as fully engaged, but there was no way I could help them, or they us. Our artillery was going out and the German stuff was coming in. We had been in combat almost constantly for five days, with practically no sleep, and no food except for K rations.

The Germans kept coming all day long. Every time they got close they were stopped by our rifles and machines guns and by bringing our own artillery fire to within fifty yards of our positions. The artillery forward observer, if I remember correctly, was Lieutenant Shanahan, who did a masterful job in saving our lines time after time. He would yell to our troops, "Duck, here it comes just over your heads." The Germans had positioned their machine guns where they could fire at our lines and we were saved by our artillery knocking out them out.

In the late afternoon we had another intense barrage from the Germans. Though the regular artillery does more damage when their shells land, the "screaming meemies" did the most damage to our nerves. The sounds of their shells coming was really nerve-racking. Everyone would jump into foxholes and then, at times, you would hear the screams of the wounded. So it was screams coming in and screams going out.

The Germans had tried to break through the center of our Task Force position for most of the day. Now it seemed they were going to try the lines directly in front of us on the right. We were again successful in stopping them. Right in the middle of one of the barrages two of my men, Totoni and Marowski, were wondering about mail call. That broke us up for the moment. It did remind me of the last letter I had received from Molly which was still in my pocket—that along with my small new testament. I don't remember how many times I've said the 23rd Psalm. It was my steadying thought.

As the day was coming into darkness, their attack continued. I had trooped the line at every lull. When I saw Lieutenants Holland and Higgins, they were very much like everyone else—BEAT!!!. The continual pounding, the loss of people killed and due to wounds, and the fact we could sure use some fresh troops made us all anxious. But we were still alive. I thought of home, Molly, and the baby a lot during that day and wondered how all of them were doing. But I couldn't dwell on them too much.

I really was proud of my little troop of men. They had guts. I recall the first encounter we had here at St. Vith when one of my gunners broke and ran. I had decided at that time to leave him in his job as gunner on one of the machine guns. His name was Ryan. As I walked around the area to see how all the men were doing, I came to Ryan. He had been wounded in the arm. I said to him, "Get on back to the medics and take care of the wound." He refused saying, "I'm going to stay and do my job." I then ordered him to go back to the medics. He went but only on the condition the job would be his when he got back. I thought to myself when he departed, that's the last that I'll see of him as the Medics will probably send him to the rear. I was fooled. He was back at his gun within a couple of hours, smiling and saying, "Told you Lieutenant that I would be back!"

During the lulls, I really didn't hear many gripes. For some reason the men were quiet. No laughter. Just serious looks. We constantly had our ears open and our eyes to the front. I know each man was deep in the thoughts of home or some just were worrying what was going to be next. That's where my mind was, and still wondering where in the hell was the support that was supposed to be coming and how much longer did they expect us to hold out?

We had a couple of hours when there were no incoming artillery and mortar rounds. The men were taking stock of themselves, resting in their holes, eating anything that was available. Some of the rations were awful. In fact because of the really cold weather most of the rations were frozen. We didn't want to build any kind of fire because that would only bring in more artillery on us—God knows, we had enough of that without asking for more. I remember the cheese in the K Rations. It seemed the longer a person chewed it the larger the wad would get in his mouth. But I always kept the cigarettes, chocolate bars, and the crackers out of the K Rations. Those I kept in the lining of my overcoat.

The calm didn't last long. Again the Germans had close support from tanks. That along with assault guns plus "screaming meemies" and the yells of the German's NCOs was quite a combination of loud noises. But again our troops picked them off as they came in. Again what really saved us was the artillery fire coming from Mike Shanahan's Artillery Battalion. The Germans retreated again after leaving many dead and wounded.

The next attack was away from my troops. According to reports from Lieutenant Higgins and Major Boyer, the Germans really hit hard on our left. The Germans did break through our lines; they just kept coming until by mass of numbers caused our line to yield. I could hear the explosions of the artillery and the rattle of the small arms fire. We knew they would soon be coming our way if they were successful where they were attacking. But by valorous effort on the part of Higgins, Boyer, and my machine gun sections supporting B Company, they were able to stop the Germans again. Soon after that our line was restored.

The line had been held by the actions of some very brave men. Later, one report from B Company that I received was from Glenn Fackler of Company B: "On the 21st of December, I had dug in with my .30 caliber machine gun next to a tree. I had a good field of fire in front of me. As I surveyed the area ahead I spotted a dug-in German tank in front of my position. It was about five hundred yards ahead of me. I crawled back to a friendly tank that was near me and asked for help. The tanker commander said no. He didn't want to give away his position. His excuse was that, 'Before I could get a round off the German tank could wipe me out.' So I started back to my position. As I was going back all hell broke loose. An intense combination of German shells started to come in. I didn't get all the way back because our outfit was ordered to withdraw to a new position about a hundred yards back from the front line positions. After the barrage, which caused numerous tree bursts and much havoc, our unit was ordered to return to our the first positions. I arrived and saw that the tree that I had been under had taken a direct hit. The top half of it was gone. It had been hit about six feet above the ground and was destroyed. I knew then that the German tank I had seen must have had me in his sights."

That night the Germans attacked again. Fackler and his unit held the line. It was very dark and the men couldn't see the approaching enemy, but they heard them coming. When Fackler started firing his weapons, our machine guns and rifles along the front joined in sweeping the area in front of their positions. We fired at noises and the faint images that we could see. Many Germans were killed. All during the night we heard the moans of the wounded coming from the enemy side. The attack was finally over. The rest of the night everyone was keenly alert.

We were certainly in need of more support of any kind—air, infantry, tank destroyers, or tanks: anything would help. I knew with the enemy's continual buildup and our strength going downhill we would soon be unable to hold them back. Here we were in a small area vulnerable on our right, as the support that was supposed to be there didn't exist, and our strength just was not enough to keep the enemy from breaking through.

It was dark and dreary and cold. After the Germans to our front had pulled back, I trooped the line again. One of the men from the unit on our left was a runner for the company. He had been sent back to the Battalion CP to learn what was going on there. When he arrived there was a tank standing, with its motor idling, outside of the old building. As the runner did not see the battalion commander or any one else, he rapped on the side of the tank. The voice that came back was not speaking in English. What he heard was, "Vas is los?" He left as fast as he could and came back to advise us that there were Germans in the Battalion CP.

When I came looking for Sergeant Sicari, I was told he had been back at the company command post. Captain Mattocks had called him back for a rest from the front lines. What happened to him after that I do not know. He never returned to my platoon. Apparently he departed for the rear with the headquarters unit when they pulled out ahead of Captain Mattocks and First Sergeant Davis.

My troops on the left were OK. Sergeant Curtin's men had taken a beating but were still in good spirits. They were running low on ammunition and food but that wasn't anything new. So I went back to the right side of the road. I was about ready to get some rest when Major Boyer and Lieutenant Higgins came by with Lieutenant Holland. I had heard that they had received word of a command decision that had come over the radio: "Break up into small groups and try to get back." It was also then I finally realized the truth: we had been sacrificed. Our small group had held back the Germans long enough to let our forces regroup and build up enough to meet the Germans on more even terms. Boy, that hit me in the gut!

Major Boyer's "Personal Report, Narrative Account of Action of 38th Armored Infantry Battalion, 7th Armored Division, Battle of ST. VITH, 17-22 December 1944," which I received many years later, tells of that day and perhaps gives a larger picture of what went on than what I knew and experienced. It reads:

After 1300 [21 December] I was so heavily embroiled in the fighting within my own sector that I had no further knowledge of the general picture. Despite our standing there and tossing back attack after attack, by 2200 German tanks had blasted their way through the center of the line and were entering ST. VITH. Although I didn't know it at the time, the same thing had happened in the North and on the South, and tanks were also entering the town along the MALMEDY and PRUM roads This cut off those elements of the 38th then East of ST. VITH, and those few men who were still alive— dazed from almost 12 hours of continuous pounding by the artillery; rocked by 12 hours of ceaseless attacks by overwhelming forces of infantry, supported by heavy concentrations of *Panther* and *Tiger* tanks; and almost unnerved by 5 days of constant combat with no sleep, little food, and suffering from frost bite—were forced to break up into small groups of 5-10 men each in an attempt to regain friendly lines by infiltration. I use the phrase 'still alive,' for of an estimated 670 men who had manned the line to the right of the SCHONBURG road in the morning (my force plus B/23), there were only approximately 185 men alive at 2300. The rest were dead or severely wounded.

1150: Patrol returned with information that an esti-mated battalion of infantry was advancing against our positions, 2 companies abreast, astride the SCHON-BURG road.

1200: Heavy automatic and semiautomatic weapons fire broke out to my left along the front of Foster's and Higgins' companies (A/23 and B/38).

1200-1315: 'Jerry' kept up an unceasing series of infantry assaults against Foster and Higgins' left platoon, making strong use of *Panzerfausts*, but their efforts to break through were unsuccessful. B/87 and Higgins' right platoon were only lightly engaged.

1300: The expected attacks against B/87 and the entire B/38 were launched in force. I estimated the assault troops to consist of 2 battalions of infantry, each battalion attacking on a narrow front with 2 companies abreast.

1345-1510: The 'Krauts' kept boring in, no matter how fast we decimated their assault squads. As fast as we could kick back one assault wave, another would return. It certainly looked as if the Germans were determined that they were coming through, but their spirit alone was not enough to sustain them against the merciless hail of small arms fire which we were hurling at them.

All machine guns were employing swinging traverse and taking a deadly toll. But again and again there was a flare of flame and smoke (the explosion could not be heard because of the general din) as some 'Kraut' got in close enough to heave a grenade into a machine gun crew or to launch a dread *Panzerfaust*. (One caliber .50 squad which hitherto had been dishing out a deadly hail of fire all along the front was hit by a *Panzerfaust* which struck the barrel halfway between the breech and muzzle. The gunner fell forward on the gun with half his face torn off; the loader had his left arm torn off at the shoulder and was practically decapitated; while the gun commander was tossed about 15 feet away from the gun to lie there quite still.)

The men were magnificent, and as long as there were targets, their fire never ceased. Whenever a machine gun was silenced by having its crew killed off, other men leaped from their holes to take over the gun so that its devastating fire could be continued. Artillery: we were using it like mortars, and never before have I seen artillery do so much damage with almost no friendly casualties because of 'shorts.' As fast as Higgins, Holland, or Rogers (new CO of "B" Troop, after Stewart was wounded Tuesday night) called for fire, I relayed the request to Shanahan (FO from 275th, who had reported to me just as the noon attack started). Within 2-4 minutes we could hear the shells whistling over our heads.

Frankly, I didn't see how our men could stand up to this pounding without any cessation and no replacements. And always there were more Germans, and more Germans, and then more Germans. Where they were all coming from, I did not know but it looked as if battalion after battalion must have been massed up behind the original assault waves. That's the only way they would be able to keep on attacking, attacking, and re-attacking for better than 1 1/2 hours.

Again and again the 'Jerries' were able to emplace machine gun teams where they could rake our lines, and where it was difficult for us to get at them. Again and again I called on Mike Shanahan for fire to wipe out these guns. Whatever the fire commands, he always relayed them although he knew he was bringing fire down within 50 yards of our men. It was taking a terrific chance but never once did the gunners of the 275th AFA make an incorrect laying! How they did it so accurately while receiving missions from more than 20 different F[orward] O[bservers]'s scattered throughout the St. Vith horseshoe was beyond me.

1515: Contact had been broken all along the front, and the Germans had withdrawn. Quickly I dispatched orders to Higgins, Rogers, and Holland to readjust their lines, to redistribute ammunition, and to get their wounded out. How much time we would have I did not know, but I felt that this was only the 'lull before the storm.' Von Rundstedt apparently was making his supreme effort this day to reestablish the counter-offensive's timetable, the timetable which we had done so much to disrupt.

1520: Higgins arrived at my foxhole, and quickly we sketched what had taken place. When he asked for men from the Platoon of F/423 which had been our reserve, I had to tell him that they previously had been used to plug gaps which were torn in A/23's line during the noon attacks. *We had no reserves!*

1545: I heard the 'screaming meemie' batteries go off to our front, and for some reason I 'knew' they were coming in on us. I remember yelling 'Down,' and as we slid into our holes in came the worst hail of steel and screaming metal that I have ever seen or heard. Back and forth, right and left, then back and forth, and again right and left across our positions came the crushing, thumping, tearing scream of steel followed by steel. Huge gashes were cut in the logs over our holes, and all around us we could hear the crash and ripping of tree tops and even of trees as the merciless hail of steel swept and lashed through the forest.

Again and again we heard the anguished scream of some man somewhere who had been hit, and yet all we could do was cower in our holes with our backs against the forward walls, hoping that we would not receive a direct hit. It seemed as if our very nerves were being torn out by the roots as the screaming steel crashed around us, coming in with increasing and ever-increasing waves of hideous sounds.

1550-1620: Artillery added its din to the heavy 'screaming meemie' preparation that was being placed upon us, switching back and forth along the front and converging on the center of the line in the vicinity of the SCHON-BURG road. After 1600, the preparation definitely concentrated against the areas of B/38 and B/87. This time the main effort was to be through us—they had failed through the center; now they would try the left (Jerry's left, our right).

1619: I could see the German infantry starting to come through the woods, running a few paces, hitting the ground, then getting up to run again. This is what I expected—that they would try to charge into our positions as the barrage was lifted at the last minute and before we could recover from the stunning shock of all the steel they had poured down on us. As I called out 'Heads Up!' and the men poked their heads out of their holes with rifles and machine guns at the ready, almost simultaneously the awful hail of steel was lifted from us and into the woods to our rear.

1620-1700: This attack followed the same pattern as the two earlier ones, except that there was close support from tanks and A[ssault] G[un]s. Although we slaughtered the attacking echelons and very few 'Krauts' ever managed to cross the logging road in front of our positions, 'Jerry' kept boring in no matter how much we piled up the dead. Still he could not force a breakthrough. One AG which got within 10 yards of our lines was left a burning hulk with a beautiful deflection 'bazooka' shot through its side armor, and in front of B/38; a *Panther* was destroyed on the logging road when one soldier with a 'bazooka' climbed out of his hole, ran forward and pressing his tube against the fender-line, pulled the trigger, and as he fired, he slumped to the ground dead.

Our stubborn stand, however, was beginning to show signs of weakening; gaps were appearing which we did not have the men to fill. Had it not been for the deadly support of the 275th AFA, I feel certain that the 'Krauts' would have forced a gap somewhere. The deadly massed fire that Shanahan was bringing down was a little bit more than 'Jerry' could stand, and we could hear the screams and cries of the wounded in ever-increasing numbers. By 1705, the impetus of the German drive had been lost, and practically all small arms firing had ceased except for a few rifle shots when some 'Kraut' exposed himself while trying to withdraw.

1715: Mortar fire started clumping into woods around us, and once more we could hear the 'burp-burp-burp' of the 'Jerry' guns as they opened up with assault fire about 150-175 yards in front of us. As they moved in we could hear the guttural voices of their *Feldwebels* as they 'talked it up' among their squads. This assault apparently was to be aimed at Jamiel's Platoon (left platoon, B/38) in an attempt to open up one side of the SCHONBURG road.

1735: Heavy tank fire could be heard above the small arms fire fight to our left. At about this time Higgins called over the radio with tears in his voice asking where were the T[ank] D[estroyers]s? I tried to relay this situation to the Battalion CP, but both the radio and phone hook-ups with the Forward CP were out. I did reach Lt. Col. Riggs through Holland's phone, however, and emphasized that if we did not get TD support to break up this tank attack, I was afraid that some of the *Tigers* would get through.

1805: Jamiel reported that the Tank Section from A/31 which had been covering the SCHONBURG road had either been knocked out or had withdrawn; that 2 *Panther* tanks were shelling his foxholes systematically, 1 hole after the other, with direct fire.

1850: I called Lt. Col. Fuller through Holland's phone and reported: 'Our lines are still holding. A few Krauts got through, but we'll take care of them. I believe that we can hold through the night, but we must have relief in the morning.'

1905: Higgins and I were preparing to sweat out the night, and I was about to leave him at his CP hole while I checked the line, when 'Jerry' artillery and screaming meemies started coming in again. Once more they started a systematic raking of our entire area, and I knew that before long we would have tanks and infantry on us again. Far to the South (B/23) and to the Northwest (31st Tks and A/38) we could hear the scream of steel, as those positions also were subject to the barrage.

This looked like 'IT,' as I told Higgins, and then I directed him to go to the Fwd CP and acquaint them with the desperateness of our situation; that I didn't believe we could hold back a new assault such as this one promised to be; that we needed tank and artillery support; that we needed reinforcements and that we needed them in a hurry!

1935: Jamiel called over the SCR-300 [radio] in a voice so choked with emotion that I could hardly understand him: 'G—D—I—, they've 2 heavy tanks here on the crest, and they're blasting my men out of their holes one at a time! They're all gone, and the same thing has happened on the other side of the road. D—I—, can't you do something to stem 'em?'

Even over the radio I could hear the barking of the '88s, and Jamiel reported that one of the tanks was on the other side of the house in which he was in. Our position was desperate for we had no tanks to counter this slaughter. All we could do was use artillery, and I had little hope of this proving to be more than a nuisance value to *Panthers* or *Tigers*.

1945-1955: The initial concentration was fired by Shanahan, was corrected by an FO with A/23, and then followed by several additional concentrations but they had no affect on the tanks. (During one of the corrected concentrations, the FO with A/23 was killed when he brought the fire in on his own position in an effort to destroy the tanks.)

During one of the earlier attacks, Foster who commanded the tank company, and the other Foster who commanded A/23, were both hit by German artillery or tank fire. The tank captain was killed, and the infantry captain was badly wounded.

2000: I could hear heavy tanks clanking and creaking down the SCHONBURG road, behind the MLR (Main Line of Resistance) and toward the Fwd CP. We shifted machine gun and mortar fire to the road in an attempt to stop the infantry whom we knew would be following the tanks. By now it was quite dark, but I still hoped that if we stopped the infantry, someone would deal with the tanks in the town, and that we might be able to hold through the night. At the same time Shanahan placed all available artillery fires on the SCHONBURG road from the MLR East.

2015-2115: For an hour we kept the SCHONBURG road under heavy machine gun and bazooka fire. Although 1 Mk VI was destroyed, and 'Jerry' dead lined the ditches on both sides of the road, the 'Krauts' still kept pressing forward to follow their tanks. We were unable to stop all of them, and for the ones that we killed we were paying a terrific price! No machine guns nor bazooka team lasted more than 10-15 minutes, and each gun already had been manned by several or more teams. As soon as one team was destroyed, it was replaced by other men who crawled into position only to be killed in turn a few minutes later. Finally I refused to pay the price any longer and directed 'B' Co to hold up on replacing teams along the road.

2200-2300: Higgins and Lt. Col. Riggs came up with essentially the same information: that the Fwd CP had been wiped out; that at least 8 *Panther* or *Tiger* tanks were in town, and that infantry were pouring into St. Vith. Higgins had tried to send a patrol across the road to learn the situation in A/23 and A/38, but the patrol could not make it. He also reported that Jamiel's entire platoon had been wiped out.

Lt. Col. Riggs and I then reported to Brig. Gen. Clarke, using Shanahan's FA FDC net, and asking them to relay: 'Road cut. At least 8 heavy tanks and infantry in town. What are our orders?'

About 45 minutes later, we received the following answer: 'To Riggs or Senior Officer present: Reform; save what vehicles you can; attack to the West through St. Vith; we are forming a new line West of town.'

2355: When Gen. Clarke's orders were announced to the assembled Co Commanders (Higgins, Rogers, and Holland), they insisted that their men were not in shape to launch the attack envisaged by Gen. Clarke. I agreed with them, especially when Rogers confirmed through his Maintenance Officer (then in St. Vith) that at least 8-10 heavy tanks were in the town.

The decision was made to 'peel off' to the right, carrying all personal and crew-served weapons. A messenger was dispatched to the Mortar Platoon to destroy their vehicles, but to salvage their mortars and bipods. Holland reported that the Tk Sec originally in support of his company had taken off earlier in the evening, and it was believed that they had regained the town ahead of the German tanks. Boyd's AG Plat we hoped would have been warned by Kennebrew whom we understood had escaped from the Fwd CP before it was overrun, and had gone to the School House to warn Maj. McDaniel (Battalion Executive Officer). Higgins was to try once more to get word across the road to A/23, so as to tell them what we were doing and to direct them to 'peel off' to the left through A/38, joining the 31st Tk Bn on their Northern flank across the *Malmedy* road.

Rogers had 5 men severely wounded who could not be moved. These were to be left with an aid man who volunteered to stay with them, and in the morning he would try to surrender himself and them to a German medic. (Personally I was dubious of this arrangement, but there was nothing else we could do.)

Rogers was to order his Maintenance Officer who had 'B' Trp's vehicles in the RR yards in St. Vith to destroy such vehicles as he could not man with a crew, and to attack through the town and regain the lines being formed West of St. Vith.

Higgins and I were to move out immediately, working our way down to the right, informing each Platoon Leader along the way of what we were doing. When we reached Britton's Co, we learned that their right flank had vanished and that the PRUM road was cut. According to 1st Lt. G. A. Taylor, who was the senior officer still with the company, the 'Jerries' had been pouring tanks and infantry up the road into ST. VITH and Westward towards KROMBACH for more than 2 hours.

This was the "blackest" news of all, especially since snow had been falling for more than an hour and gave every indication of being almost knee deep by morning. When the column came down the hill, we swung out through the trees on an azimuth of 270. The progress was slow for the forests were thick, the snow was piling deeper and deeper, and the men were experiencing difficulty in keeping up. Of the estimated 150 men with me, over half were wounded in varying degrees, and all of us were suffering from the pounding we had taken all day. Twice we avoided 'Jerry' combat patrols by only a few feet, and as the gray light of dawn began to come up we still were not across the PRUM road. It was then that I issued orders to destroy all but personal weapons, to break up into small groups of 5-10 with a non-com or officer in charge of each group, and to attempt to infilter our way to our forces fighting somewhere in the West.

22 Dec 44-Fri:

By morning the full extent of the price which the 38th AIB had paid for its stand began to be realized. There were no Assault Gun, nor Mortar, nor Machine Gun Platoons—neither men, nor vehicles, nor weapons. 'A' and 'B' Cos consisted each of the Antitank Platoon plus the Co's half-tracks with their drivers. Of the attached troops, the picture was even 'blacker' if such were possible. There was no A/23, and only 1 Platoon from B/23. 'B' Trp had ceased to exist, as had the 2 Prov[isional] Eng[inee]r Co[mpanie]s. The only 'bright spot' was at 1200, when A/31 was discovered to be fighting with CCB of the 9th Armored, with whom they had joined forces after fighting their way out of St. Vith.

Throughout the morning various men worked their way back through the lines, but their numbers were pitifully few, and most of them came from A/38 and A/23. By mid-morning a composite armored infantry rifle company had been formed, consisting of approximately 110 men, and had been placed in position on the high ground Northeast of KROMBACH, where they became part of a force under the command of Lt. Col. Erlenbusch of the 31st Tk Bn.

About 90 other men filtered back through the lines, but they had to be evacuated because of wounds and almost complete exhaustion from their struggles to regain the lines. The 38th had done its job, and done it well, but it had paid a price. Those who were left had only the satisfaction that they had exacted a price far more terrific from the troops who had assaulted their positions in vain for 4 days, and who had broken through on the fifth day only after one of the most vicious attacks the 7th Armored Division had ever seen. Dead Germans actually counted totaled 604, and it was to be a rather accurate estimate if we said that they had lost in the neighborhood of 4-5 times as many killed but not counted, and 5-6 times as many wounded.

[One can imagine the physical and mental condition of the troops at this point. Five days of constantly fighting a determined enemy; fatigued men with little sleep or rest and most with wounds; the weather cold, with sleet and snow and rain; bearded men with blank stares, mouths open, drooping eyelids partly covering staring eyes, hungry, concerned with rumors, smelling the odors from the dead, the gunpowder, fuel, and burned trees and vegetation. Then, after all they had done, to get orders to quit and get back as best they could!]

It was now really snowing. The snow covered the battlefield with all its scars. It seemed so out of place: quiet, peaceful, surrealistic.

Major Boyer gave me the order to destroy our heavy machine guns. So I gave the men the word. He thought we could salvage my platoon along with Higgins' men. My platoon was to follow Higgins' troops. We, Higgins and I, were to go with Major Boyer, and to join him on the point to see if we could find our way back to our lines. That is when I found out we were many kilometers ahead of our lines. All of our support troops had pulled out and left us to hold for them while they moved to the rear.

I called Sergeants Curtin, Simeneaux, and Totoni and told them the plan. Destroy machine guns and follow us. So we leaders on the point started out going to our right. Maybe we could find that support that was supposed to be there. Where we were going, I didn't know but I supposed that Boyer knew. The snow was coming down. We kept walking through the woods. It was so dark we almost had to hold hands. We continued through the forest. At a halt I asked Conover to go back along the line of troops we were leading and see how the platoon was doing. When he didn't return I went back and searched. I couldn't yell as the Germans were nearby. After a time I gave up and returned. As I look back on the whole operation, the decision which caused me to leave my platoon gave me the worst feeling ever. But I was following orders. I should have asked permission to stay with my men, but I thought the platoon would and could keep up with the leading officers. Apparently they lost sight of the leading troops, were worn out, and were too tired to keep up.

[At 0200 on 22 December, the line between CCA and CCB was severed. The line was pulled back and by dusk, contact with CCB's of the 7th and 9th Armored Divisions had been reestablished. Contact with CCA to the north was not regained, however. On the 22nd the 9th Panzer Division from Dietrich's II Panzer Corps was hurled into the battle, and pressure continued to increase along the entire front. By this time the position of the defenders had become untenable. General Hasbrouck sent a message to the corps commander, General Ridgeway, that unless reinforcements were forthcoming immediately, "there will be no more 7th Armored Division." Later that day the following message was sent by Field Marshall Montgomery: "You have accomplished your mission—a mission well done. It is time to withdraw."
The withdrawal involved breaking contact and using a secondary road west from Vielsam. On 23 December, after continuous fighting for six days, the 7th Armored Division and its attached units broke contact and withdrew behind the 82d Airborne Division and took up positions in the defense of Manhay, which was astride the only primary road leading due north from the north flank of the German salient.]

We walked until dawn. We then rested in the forest. We could hear and see the enemy fifty yards below us. The road was filled with a

German artillery unit. Now, what to do? After a short conference, we decided to wait and see what the German action was going to be. Could we get around them? Should we try to wait until dark and see what we could do then? So we hid from the Germans to our front.

It wasn't long before a squad of Germans came into view from the rear. I was in plain view of them. I had positioned myself behind a tree that was hiding me from the Germans to our front. As I tried to move around to the other side of the tree a rock came loose. The Germans heard the noise. There, twenty yards away was a squad of Germans aiming their guns at us. Lieutenant Higgins, who was thirty yards away from me, took off but Major Boyer and I were dead ducks. The Germans had yelled to troops on the road who set up their machine guns aiming at us from below. So with great reluctance we stood.

Major Boyer and I were lucky. Our group was so far ahead of our own lines that we were captured by a German artillery unit. They were just getting their guns ready to go down the road to get into position closer to their front lines. I remembered the stories that we heard of our troops being lined up and killed after being captured. Artillery units weren't out in front like the infantry soldiers who were fighting and watching their buddies being slaughtered, so they usually didn't develop the hatred that front line troops do for the opposing forces. Emotions run pretty high when you see your buddies go down. There were many prisoners on both sides that were killed after surrendering under such circumstances. So we were probably very fortunate to be caught by that artillery unit.

We were frisked and steered to the road. I was really down in spirits. Never had a group of men fought so hard and lost. Not because of their efforts—but failed just due to unlucky circumstances.

If I could speak to the men in my platoon today: Sergeants Secari, Curtin, Simeneaux, Totoni, and Corporals and Privates, Bartz, Thompson, Marowski, Dotson and Ryan, and of course Conover, Cox, our driver, and names I have forgotten, I would say to them, "You were the bravest group of men I have ever known or read about." And the same thing to Lieutenant Holland and his engineers. What I learned about the American soldier (except for a few): He will fight. He will stand. At St Vith, and I am sure throughout the Battle of Europe, the infantry soldier was usually thrown into battle not knowing where he was or knowing anything about the enemy. But with leadership and a given purpose he fought, and fought well. And I think I know the one big reason he fights so well in combat—he will not allow himself to let his buddies down. There is a bond between the men that is difficult to describe, but it is there.

In our case at St. Vith I still wonder what happened to the men who had the responsibility of the area before we got there. Where did they go? How could a few stand so well, and a whole division could not handle the same forces that we encountered? The American soldiers who held fast in the Battle of the Bulge were real heroes, whether at Bastogne, St Vith, or any of the other great stands. And I believe if it had not been for the great effort of the men at St. Vith, there would not have been a stand at Bastogne.

I wonder, too, about the men and officers who broke and ran, so full of fear they could not even try. What do they do with their minds and consciences when they keep bringing back scenes where they broke and ran? They must be ashamed. Are they able to forgive themselves?

A letter from Captain Carl K. "Rusty" Mattocks I received long after the war ended told what had happened to him at the time we were captured:

> My first indication of a real problem was when Lt. Hugh Boyd, our forward observer of the Assault Guns, called on his radio and whispered he thought there were Germans in the house that he was in. My instructions to him were, "Do what you have to do."
> Shortly thereafter a Panther Tank crested the hill, firing high velocity shells flares destroying the four Sherman

Tanks that were located in the valley below. They did not bother any of the small houses on the right of St. Vith in which our battalion headquarters had been located. Soon thereafter they fired directly into our 81mm Mortar position and also my old CP on the east side of the town. Thankfully I had moved my people out of there when the action started and no one was injured.

The Germans were swarming over the area and I could hear the German non-coms barking out orders. Those were the busiest times of my life. I tried to call you. And it was then that I got the orders from Major McDaniels to get on the "Chattanooga Choo Choo" and head west out of St. Vith. I sent runners out to all the Platoons instructing them to head west following the railroad but I believe that all the runners were either captured or killed.

Following the orders of Major McDaniels I took my small group south of the town to a hill where the assault guns were emplaced. They had been positioned incorrectly so that we could not get them out of their present position. They had no "Route of Withdrawal." So I gave the order to "Spike them."

I then took the men from the guns and my headquarters group down the reverse slope to the railroad leading to Cromback where General Clarke had installed Battle Police to pick up stragglers. Cromback is about four kilometers southwest of St. Vith. There we were directed to set up a road block utilizing twelve stragglers of Americans and an abandoned 57mm anti-tank weapon. We did and a short time later a German tank came around the bend and in one shot wiped out the gun and all the men. One of the men killed was a man you knew, Shorty Masterson.

Next they came at us with tanks and infantry. Major McDaniels wanted to surrender but First Sergeant Davis and I said, "No thanks." With us all during the night was a woman with a baby girl. She would be safe in either way as long as she could avoid the shells. We soon had to leave her and I have wondered about her ever since. There was no way we could have helped her. As she was a native we were sure that she would be okay. We soon left that building.

About 1 p.m., two Germans came into what was left of our CP. They were looking to loot our dead soldiers. One flashed a light on Sergeant Vaughn. Vaughn killed him with his carbine. The other one ran out yelling "Americans." I shot him with a burst of my sub-machine gun. He fell on the snow covered road and for the next three hours he called on us to surrender or to get him a "Doktor."

I kept on trying to contact any one who could give me any information and/or directions. but it was a hopeless task. Finally I was able to make contact with some one from the 31st Tank Battalion. The CO recognized me by my nick-name "Rusty." He knew that I was one of "Fuller's Boys." He suggested that I go on to the north and west. Sergeant Davis and I decided to start out at the crack of dawn.

The temperature really dropped and we were bitterly cold. The engineers had left some mines outside of one of the buildings and we felt we might place then in the snow near the man who we had felled. He was still alive but it wouldn't be long as he was really getting cold and was still asking for the "Docktor." We smashed his weapon and threw the ammo into the snow. We had one more little fracas when Tomko, the mail clerk, ran into a German. The German missed and Tomko hit him so that was the end of the German.

The next morning I gathered my few men together and we traveled west using the railroad as a guide. Just as we were about to turn north to Hinderhausen I saw a dim figure running along a nearby fence. I drew down on him but at the last minute I saw that it was your driver Cox. Somehow he had made it back.

We finally made it back to Hinderhausen but not until I had a real Donnybrook with our own 87th Recon. Bn. They wondered if we were really Americans. When I cut loose with some good old American swear words they finally believed that we could come toward them.

Well, that is the story about what was happening to us while you were trying to get back. We were lucky and you were not. There was so much going on and so much confusion that I know that you people on the front lines wondered why you didn't hear from the troops at the headquarters.

Rusty

In September 1997 I received a copy of some of the Morning Reports for Headquarters Company, 38th Armored Infantry Battalion, for the period 18-28 December, 1944, while stationed at St. Vith. Morning Reports were the means the Army used to keep track of each man and the company-sized unit to which he was assigned. On 18 December the strength data showed one captain, two 1st Lts., two 2nd Lts., 127 enlisted men present and two absent. On that day two Pfcs (Girtie A. Fountain and Frank B. Murawski) were reported as going from Duty to Hospital as battle casualties. On 20 December Pvt. Paul H. Ryan was reported wounded. On 21 December, 2nd Lt. John P. Marion and Sgt.

Ralph B. Roush went from duty to 56th General Hospital with battle wounds. Entries for 28 December showed a strength of one Capt., one 1st Lt., and 67 enlisted men. The following names were entered as "From Duty to Missing in Action as of 22 Dec 44:"

Hugh K. Boyd	1st Lt.
Robert E. P. Moranda	2d Lt.
Richard K. Bates	T/Sgt
Howard L. Heacock	T/Sgt
Jay P. Moser	T/Sgt
Andrew F. Ferguson	S/Sgt
Rosco Piganell	S/Sgt
Joseph W. Russell	S/Sgt
Lionel A. Simoneaux	S/Sgt
George A. Vincent	S/Sgt
Herbert E. Brown	Sgt
Joseph M. Brzezowski	Sgt
Herbert G. Burton	Sgt
Thomas H. Cooke, Jr.	Sgt
Edward J. Curtin	Sgt
Maurice D. Galatas	Sgt
Robert Karnes	Sgt
Paul G. Mashburn	Sgt
Howard W. McCord	Sgt
Eugene A. Skillern	Sgt
James Totoni	Sgt
Eugene Adams	Tec 4
Richard J. Basner	Cpl
Woodrow I. Hudspeth	Cpl
Donald C. Lambeth	Cpl
Cletus H. Phillips	Cpl
Vergil A. Robbins	Cpl
Edward C. Wehling	Cpl

William W. Kemp	Tec 5
J. B. White	Tec 5
Joe D. Aldrich	Pfc
Earl E. Barbam	Pfc
Frank Bartz	Pfc
Maurice W. Conover	Pfc
Alfred Falter	Pfc
William Fischer	Pfc
David B. Gardner	Pfc
Paul P. Hallman	Pfc
Thomas E. Jenkins, Jr.	Pfc
Orval D. Lunsford	Pfc
John E. Masterson	Pfc
Robert F. Springer	Pfc
Ozie C. Alexander	Pvt
Ralph D. Allen	Pvt
Anthony Bavuso	Pvt
Robert E. Biddle	Pvt
Florentino Carrillo	Pvt
Lonnis C. Catoe	Pvt
Clair D. Cook	Pvt
Thomas B. Cooper	Pvt
Isaac H. Dotson	Pvt
John W. Giles	Pvt
Samuel A. Gromis	Pvt
Lewis T. Mashishneck	Pvt
Watson Petty	Pvt
Doyle J. Ross	Pvt
Paul H. Ryan	Pvt
Leo T. Sizemore	Pvt
Richard A. Walters	Pvt
Clinton G. Walker	Pvt

Wayne W. Wolfe   Pvt

Sketch showing the situation on 23 December 1944

When I read about or see the pictures of the Battle of the Bulge, it always seems to me that the reason for the losses mainly was because of very poor leadership displayed by the Field Grade Officers from the Colonels down through the Major ranks. They were the ones who broke and ran. They were the ones who surrendered whole large units without so much as a shot fired at the enemy. They were the ones I saw fleeing down the road four and five to a command car. Where were their troops? Did they leave them? Or was it just fear that broke them? I cannot say that about my immediate commanders. They were with us all the way. One got so sick that he had to leave. But he left a great Operations Officer to take his place.

And another reason was that the High Command didn't believe what they heard from the front: that there was a big build-up in front of our lines. The Intelligence people just ignored the reports. They thought the Germans were finished and all they had to do was to make points with each other through their Public Relations Departments. I am sure that if they were really honest they'd say we just goofed. I have always got a kick out of the Generals and their Public Relations. When pictures are taken showing the General in action, I can tell you for sure that the action is in a safe place.

When I hear about the great work of General Patton I smile a bit. Sure he got to the general scene in a hurry, but it took him more than four days just to get up the road ten miles from Bastogne. All the time there were thousands of GI's slogging their way back to where our troops had been. My hat is off to the men at Bastogne, for in that battle there were also heroes, especially among the Engineer troops who held long enough so that paratroopers could get to the town.

And finally we who were there wondered all through our ordeal where in the hell were our planes? It seemed to us there surely were a few hours of daylight or breaks in the cloud cover where our planes could at least drop some bombs on the enemy supply lines which must have been long and full of vehicles and personnel. But no. Not one of ours flew over. But the Germans did.

After the war ended and I was separated from the Army, I wrote to Captain Frederickson, our Battalion Intelligence Officer, and he responded telling me what had happened after my capture. His letter:

Dessau, Germany

2 June '45

Dear Bob, you ol' piano hammering bugger,

Was I glad to hear from you and more pleased you wrote to me. First, congrats in escaping from St. Vith and the rest of it. Sorry to hear of Boyer's illness, but further sorry that we have never heard since from him. You're right in Higgins, a swell unappreciated officer. Glad for Boyd's escape also.

Fuller became exhausted on the twenty-first, was evacuated by ambulance and taken to a hospital. He returned on the 24th after we had withdrawn back to Harze. On the 24th we were ordered back to stop the Jerries at Grandmenile and Manhey. We did and were relieved by the 75th Inf and Third Arm'd who came up the other way. Fuller and Gen. Clarke did not hit it off too good and Fuller was transferred on Jan 2nd to Army Hdqs. We pulled back to Verviers for refitting and reinforcements. On the 18th of January we started our comeback around Born, then took Hunningen. On the 21-22 of January retook St. Vith, on the 24th took Wallerode, where Mattocks was shot in the stomach. He was evacuated to England and the last I heard he was O.K. In February we started on the Siegfried line taking Strauch, Steckenborn and helping the 78th Inf on the Schmidt dam deal. After we pushed to the Rhine hitting it at Bad Godesburg. In March, about the 23rd or 24th we started our drive across the Rhine, spearheading the First Army's drive to Marlborough, Limburg and the Erft dams. Then we doubled back and cleaned out the Ruhr pocket. On the 16 of April four Generals and 21,000 men surrendered to the 7th Arm'd Div; in fact on the morning of the 16th our column began its push and attack. At 0645 a German car bearing a white flag met Lt. Col. Griffin our Bn Commander, and offered terms. Five hours later the surrender became effective. After that we [were] sent to the British Second Army for the push north of the Elbe with the 82nd Airborne. On May 3rd they began to surrender en mass. For two days they filled the roads, thousands of them. We are now temporarily stationed at Dessau, Halle and close to Leipzieg.

"Carmen" you old son of a gun (see how excited I am). I also heard from Capt. Emmons who is recovering in the

States. Kinnebrew is Hdq Co Commander, Corbin A
Co., Meades C Co. Lots of luck.

-'Curly' Freddy

And another letter from him dated 17 Aug '45 from Liebenstadt,
Germany, gave me additional information about some of my associates
and troops:

Hello Bob,

Glad to hear from you.

First—Nick is O.K., he's with us. All of your M G Platoon
are accounted for except Conover. All others have been
heard from. First Sgt Davis got hit on April 14th and was
evac to England.

Second, all vehicles of Hq. Co. were lost but two peeps.

Third—You said Capt Ansley, you meant Capt Anstey did-
n't you. He got most of his men out, in fact all but a couple.
He was wounded in the leg on the retake of St. Vith two
days before Carl [Mattocks] got it. I took Carl back to the
medics. He was nearly frozen and it was a long way.

Yep, I remember Overloon. Some fun eh kid. But I remember one year ago today more. It was then those kind little
fellows had me for 3 days behind their lines training on me
in the use of M. Gun grazing, point blank and tracking
fire. Gosh how I ever got out I'll never be able to say. At
night the rascals threw up flares and tried to find me. Gosh
I wasn't a chow-hound then for I didn't eat for 2 1/2 days
(prices too high, Germans asking too much).

By the way, I recommended you for the Belgium Award for
the action at St. Vith. In the course of several months you
should receive it. I didn't know of any person more wor-
thy. I spoke to Major McDaniel and he concurred.

We have but 450 men left and 14 officers. We don't know
when we shall be sent back.

Lub & Tisse
Olga and Freddie

Lt. Higgins received a letter from Don Boyer dated 3 October 1945, which he shared with me, and brought us up to that date about what happened to some of the troops:

Dear Higgins,

This is a far cry from the last time we were together in that glass factory near LIMBURG, isn't it. Certainly we are much happier and more comfortable than we were then. When I learned through a letter of Boyd's to my Mother, that you, he, Moranda, Shanahan, and the others had come through OK — well, I just cannot describe how relieved I felt.

As for myself, I seem to have spent the better part of the summer in Walter Reed General Hospital in Washington, getting over a severe attack of Yellow Jaundice. This time I believe the cure has taken, and since I came home on Friday I have felt better than at any time since we were captured. True I am listed for "temporary limited service" until February, but I am looking forward to receiving orders to a new assignment starting about the 23rd of this month. While it may not be troop duty until after a final check-up in February, I am looking forward to getting back to work—even if it will be a desk job for a few months.

Captain Anstey was a patient at Walter Reed this summer, but has been up and around most of the time. He was wounded in the leg when the battalion went back into St. Vith in January. You wouldn't know it to see him, however, for only occasionally does he limp. He does have several mortar fragments in his chest, and he probably will be retired for physical disability.

Anstey tells me that Rusty Mattocks was made CO of "B" Company after St. Vith, and that he rebuilt and reorganized it into the fighting outfit it was before it got hurt so badly. Higgins, I don't exactly know how to say it — but you and your men did a super-human job there at St. Vith, and I couldn't have asked to fight alongside finer men and better soldiers. And one of the reasons that the men did the epic job that they did was the example that you set for them. I would be proud to have you with me anytime, anywhere!

I have had some correspondence with the battalion trying to learn if certain men had received awards or not. Sgt. Revels, I feel is deserving of the *Silver Star*. Two other men whom I feel are deserving of awards are T/Sgt. George and S/Sgt. Hogan. These men are recorded as K[illed]I[n]A[ction] on Monday, 18 December 1944, and no posthumous awards. They were killed in the attack that morning when the center platoon gave way, and I seem to remember your telling me they were killed in an attempt to close the gap in the line. By the way, can you shed any light on the identification of "Frenchy." I think he was your runner whom I took over, although he may have been Captain Greene's. Along this line, do you remember the name of a radio operator from either yours or Van's platoon who took over and operated my SCR-300?…he was of medium height, wore steel framed glasses, and could not have been more than 20 or 21 years old, and was either a pvt or pfc. He was with me when my group of 5 was captured, and I would like to get in touch with him.

Rusty was wounded in January and has since been evacuated to the States. Junie East was evacuated for combat
exhaustion in January, and then later was with a rein-
forcement depot near Marseilles. Kinnebrew is a
Captain, commanding Hq Co, while Newman has been
transferred to the 1st Armored Division, 14th AIB, as
part of the Army of Occupation.

You may be interested to know that Freddie [Capt
Frederickson] also writes that Jamiel was with the battalion until about a week before he wrote me. I imagine
he went down the hill to report the situation when those
tanks started shelling his platoon's position that night,
and that is how we didn't find him when we planned to
pull out. I am glad that he was able to make it.

Here is one you may not know. When I reached Oflag
XIII-B at HAMMELBURG, GERMANY, late in
February, who should be the first one to greet me but
Captain Greene. When the first firing started that
Monday morning, 18 December, he heard a machine
gun firing in the woods on the other side of the trail
behind which the company was dug in. He thought it
was one of "B" Company's guns and ran across the trail
to stop them from firing so as not to give away the position. The rest you can guess, he ran smack into a
German squad and became a prisoner. He was taken to
the rear, and he says that Von Rundstedt had his stuff
parked almost bumper to bumper back along the road
to SCHONBURG — that the Germans were expecting
to move on that day, and that they were certainly surprised when they didn't get through. Seems that they
took a little of the exasperation out on him when he
wouldn't tell them what was holding them up. He is OK,

though, and happened to go home on the same train that Colonel Fuller did this past June.

That about exhausts the news.

With best wishes for you and your family, I am

Very sincerely,

Don Boyer

An aerial photograph of St. Vith taken after its capture by the German 5th Panzer Army and aerial bombing by Allied air forces in the last days of December 1944.

In 1975 I returned to St Vith. I was on a trip through Europe with my present wife, Verna Fay, my sister Maye, and my brother Bill and his wife Jeannette. One stop that we made was at St Vith. As we passed through the small towns before arriving at St Vith, I became very nervous and upset. I remembered the hassle we had trying to get to the front. I guess I was still upset that everyone was running away and we had to go forward to save them from themselves. To this day I do not understand why the return bothered me so much, but it did. The town was repaired and all the stores and homes were occupied. We got out and I wandered about for a short time. I went into a building that was serving drinks and looked around. But for some reason I just was not comfortable so we left. We departed via the road that took us past the small building where I met with the commanders in charge and where I met with Lieutenant Holland. I noted the road through the woods to the front lines. But I didn't take the walk. Maybe I should have, but I was too emotional.

St. Vith as it looked to Bob when he made his return visit

[*What did the heroic defense of St. Vith accomplish? Why is it considered the turning point in the Battle of the Bulge? First, the six day delay it caused in the German timetable was fatal to the entire German plan, for it gave the Allies, initially completely surprised, time to rally, regroup, and attack. Second, the defense caused the immobilization of truck and rail columns east of St. Vith, which disrupted the supply to the Fifth and Sixth Panzer Armies and slowed their movements because of the lack of gasoline and ammunition. Third, German reserves of both the Fifth and Sixth Panzer Armies were committed to the final assaults on St. Vith and thus could not proceed with the advancing troops. Fourth, the weather cleared immediately after St. Vith was taken and the supply routes were cleared, so Allied Air could decimate the supply columns by air strikes, and St. Vith itself was made impassable by massive bombardments. And lastly, it prevented General Manteuffel from going to the aid of General Dietrich's surrounded 1st Panzer Division and reopening the northern penetration, thus preventing the quick encirclement of the 2nd and 99th American Divisions holding the northern shoulder at Monshau. Dietrich had to detour his second wave around the horseshoe at St. Vith to exploit the gap created by the Fifth Panzer Army, one division of which was used at St. Vith and another bogged down in the traffic jam to the west.*

After the war, General Manteuffel stated: "I wanted to have St. Vith on December 17. Although I had expected Bastogne to be defended, I did not think that the Americans would be able to defend St. Vith. This unexpected defense was one of the outstanding achievements of the (Allied) campaign. The devotion of the American soldiers and their courageous defense of St. Vith introduced the final phase of the defeat of the German Army in Western Europe; the subsequent counter American offensive brought about the ultimate defeat of these German forces in the west. Morale factors are all-decisive, for battles are won in the hearts of men. Therefore, the dramatic weeks of December 1944 occupy an important role when the history of the U.S. Army is being written. The courage of the men and the command of the troops—especially of Combat Command B of the 7th Armored Division in action around St. Vith was, from the German viewpoint, of the highest order."

And Prime Minister Winston Churchill wrote to President Franklin Roosevelt that the 7th Armored and the 1st and 99th Divisions had performed "the highest acts of soldierly devotion at heavy personal sacrifice."]

Prisoner of War

Prisoner of War

I sat on a rock wall and waited to see what they were going to do with Major Boyer and me. Soon they took us to a nearby house where we stayed until we were joined by thirty U.S. soldiers. We were marched through the town we were defending, St. Vith. As we walked along the road I saw my half-track being driven by a German soldat. I knew then that our CP had been overrun. So I wondered what happened to Colonel Riggs and others at the Forward Command Post. I didn't have to wait long to find out, for Colonel Riggs and several others soon joined us.

I remember thinking to myself, "I have to get back. No one is going to stop me from seeing my family again. Molly and the rest of the family will be sending prayers to God to watch over me. What would happen to them if I didn't survive or return? Look for opportunities to escape. I can't let my family down. Could I ever face my brothers again if I didn't at least try? So, first to live, and next to escape—but play it cool and see what next happens and don't be foolish. I don't know where we are or the direction to go. So cool it for now."

They marched us on to Mannheim where we spent the night. That night I had the first cooked food I had had for six days. Three small cold, cooked potatoes. And those came at midnight.

The first day on our POW march, our bombers came over and seeing us they dropped bombs. We dove for ditches and any cover. But many of us asked the question, "Where in the hell have you been?" For days we requested, pleaded, begged for air support. Not one of ours came over. And yet the Germans used their aircraft. We were not very happy about the lack of air support. In fact if you ask anyone who was at the defense of St. Vith what they thought about it, they always came back, "We were really sacrificed!" A few saved many. So I guess that was worth it all to win the war—but it is tough on the men that were sent up and left to be sacrificed. No one came to our support.

On December 24th, we were marched to Prum. But the aircraft, ours, had destroyed the town so on we went to another town, Gerolstein. About forty-five kilometers was made during the day. We had to drag some of our men. They were exhausted. But by encouragement and assistance all kept going. Major Boyer was becoming weaker all the time with dysentery, but he carried on. The Germans placed us in an old building that night. We were exhausted, tired, and hungry, but we didn't receive any food. The civilians snarled at us and apparently really wanted to attack us, but our guards kept them away.

December 25th. We stumbled along for another day and ducked bombs from our planes again several times. The planes weren't after us but mainly roads and buildings and we just happened to be on roads. Surprising as it may seem we, the POWs, knew the war was soon coming to an end. The Germans had exposed most of their reserves of equipment and men on the push through the Ardennes. Now they were in the open and extended. We knew if we could survive for a time we probably would soon be freed.

That night was the first time that we were interrogated. I was called into the anteroom of a school house where they had placed us. A Captain (*Hauptman*), a lieutenant, plus a guard or two were the interrogators.

I reported, "Lieutenant Robert Moranda. Serial number 01326108." They asked, looking at the patch on my shoulder, which unit I was with. I again gave the speech, "My name is Lieutenant Robert Moranda, 01326108. According to the Geneva Convention that is all I can report to you." When the *Hauptman* saw the crossed rifles of the 2nd Lieutenant Infantry on my collar, he knew that we in the infantry never knew anything of the "Big Picture," that we only knew our assigned mission. The German *Hauptman* laughed, said to the interrogator, "A 2nd Lieutenant infantry, Ha! He could only see a few yards in any direction." He laughed and dismissed me. When I got back our men wished to know what they asked. I told them. From then on the interrogation went rapidly. Their replies were all the same, that they were in the infantry.

That night a few Psalms were recited and a few Christmas carols were mumbled, mostly as a prayer, not a celebration. "Silent Night" was sung softly and with great feeling. I heard the German guards singing along with us, vocalizing their words in German.

At dusk one of the German *soldats* came around to each one of us. He had an open can of molasses. We put out a filthy hand and he dipped a spoonful of molasses into our palm. That was our Christmas meal.

On this Christmas night one of the officers in our group told me of his capture. He was the payroll officer for his outfit. When he saw he would be soon captured, he got out of his vehicle and buried the money. He didn't have much time so he didn't get the money buried very deep. Now he wondered whether the Germans would find the money, or what would happen to the money and how long would it be there. He said when he got released he would try to find the spot again. He was quite worried about his problem. When he was released would the U.S. officers believe his story, especially if he could not find the place again? The only cheer I could give him was, "First you must survive. After that then worry. But I'm sure the Army would believe you. They certainly know of the confusion going on then."

December 26th. Major Boyer was in real bad shape. He had dysentery so bad he could barely walk. But with a lot of guts and help from others he made it to the next stop. There we were joined by another large group of American men and officers from other U.S. divisions, even two Air Corps pilots who had been shot down. We marched to a small town where we were again placed in a school building. We had covered another twenty-five kilometers. Again no food.

December 27. This was one of our worst days. It was bitter cold. We had to continually move to keep warm. We were going cross-country, plowing through snow. We had to stand for about two hours while our guards ate, rested, and asked for directions. Finally we moved along slowly for another ten kilometers to a large warehouse in Mayer, Germany. At midnight the guards woke us and handed each POW eight small boiled potatoes. It was the first food for a couple of days so we ate them slowly.

December 28. Major Boyer was taken away by the Germans. He was really sick. That was the last we saw of him, and as he left I said a silent prayer for him and all the rest of us. The troops were in really bad shape—frostbite, pneumonia, coughing. No treatment was available so all we could do was help each other along. We were exhausted, mainly because of lack of food, not much water, and no rest. Tempers became shorter all the time. We went about twenty kilometers where they placed us in another old building with no heat. But body heat from the group helped. At night we would sleep in the "spoons" position. My group was Lieutenants Boyd, Justad, Higgins, and Tate.

Boyd, who was very religious, read his Bible at every opportunity. He was from Louisiana. Justad was from South Dakota, a farm boy, who had never been out of his state before the war. A great kid. Higgins, a brave and quiet man, had assumed command of our B Company at St. Vith—forced to when, during the first battle, his commanding officer just disappeared. Tate was a youngster from Texas. That night we received a Red Cross parcel to split ten ways, and it was well-received. Boyd gave me his cigarettes, which made Tate unhappy. When people are worn out, hungry, and tired, sharing becomes a problem. At times a cigarette can start an argument, so I shared with Tate, too. I had made it a practice to stuff the cigarettes and chocolate into the lining of my overcoat. Those cigarettes and chocolate bars really came in handy for a short time. I don't know how much weight we had lost by then, but my pants were much looser.

December 29th. We were out early and crossed the Rhine north of Koblenz near Neuwied before noon, and we were all surprised at the width of the river—it was quite a barrier to cross.

On this day I was spit on as we were walking through the streets. Naturally, that many POWs was news to the German population. The civilians were on the sides of the streets as we proceeded. One man spat at me. It didn't hit me, but the hate in his eyes and his clenched fist showed me he had very little love in his heart for us.

And yet it was only a few blocks after that when a pretty lady forged out into the street and pressed a coin into my hand. Silver. I don't remember the amount, but as she pressed the coin in my hand she said, "God bless you." I wish I could have known her name or how to contact her after the war. So in one minute I was hated and the next minute blessed.

That day we had our first hot food—a hot potato soup. The warmth of the soup and the amount, a whole cup full, made a lot of men sick. I was sick for only a few minutes. Fortunately, the hall where we were placed had a toilet—with toilet paper. So after squirting out the soup I was able to clean myself. I was lucky to be sick at a place where I could relieve myself. All night we could hear the men up-chucking or rushing to the toilet. We stayed that night in that large hall. It looked like a Nazi headquarters with all the German Swastika flags draped around. I wondered if Hitler had ever been in this hall.

December 30th. A light day. We were marched about twelve kilometers to a glass factory. This was where we had to wait for a train. The building had a high ceiling. The roof either leaked or the bodies of the many POWs caused enough warmth to melt the ice on the ceiling glass.

It was very cold outside. At this place I met the first men from other countries being used as slave labor. Two Poles were assigned to keep the slit trenches (outside latrines) in order. I tried to communicate with them but was not successful. They acted like zombies. The light in their eyes was gone. They mumbled and sort of dragged themselves along.

New Year's Day we had a feast. All we needed was table cloths and candles. We each got 1/6th of a loaf of bread, one small slice of cheese, and a patty of butter. We should have dressed for dinner. We really were happy to get that much food.

Our daily routine was simple—do anything to keep warm. Many men were still very ill with dysentery and respiratory forms of sickness. It was so cold, the lion's share of the time we spent huddled together to keep warm. I did some exercising mainly to keep warm, but for most of the time we rested and waited and saved our energy.

January 3rd to 6th. We were loaded into a boxcar, forty men in each car. There was no sanitary facility. We did receive a Red Cross package, six men to a package. Again Boyd gave me his cigarettes. We didn't move for the first day but just sat in the railroad yards. I remember the fear I had: would the Allied aircraft bomb and strafe our cars? All the newsreels I saw before coming overseas to the war zone showed our planes bombing and putting the railroads out of action.

After pounding on the door and getting the Germans to understand, we got them to bring us a small barrel into our car where we could relieve ourselves. Did you ever take a crap with thirty-nine men watching and complaining? I was lucky as my position was near the door. The cars had many cracks especially near the doors so we who were near the those openings did get some relief from the odors. On the third day we were fed a soup of potatoes and oatmeal. We needed the food as the men were getting weaker by the hour. We would feel the train move for a time and then sit on the side tracks. I am sure we were not a high priority. We could hear trains passing us going in both directions.

Not much talk went on in the boxcar. Talking took energy and many of the men had very little of that left. We had some very sick people. I heard one of our men saying to another, "If so-and-so dies we won't say anything to the guards. We can then share his food." That was soon stopped as the rest of the men in the boxcar came down on the two. And I'm pleased to say the sick man did survive.

Molly wrote a letter at this time which was returned to her marked "Missing, verified by J.M. Burford." I read it when I returned:

Jan 5, 1945

My Darling,

Gee I sure hope I get a letter tomorrow cause I didn't get one today and I sure miss your chats with me.

Today we took George to the bus. He left at 11:00 and I felt so sorry for Nancy cause I know just how she felt. This darn war is always making someone feel bad.

In the afternoon we drove around the beaches and Nancy enjoyed seeing the ocean. We then went to Port Hueneme and had coffee with the gang. Clara [Barr], Bill Woodard (who has a new granddaughter), Glen Dewar, Clyde [Welch], Marie [my aunt], Nancy, Nona, Tomilyn and me. While we were there Billy Van Delinder came driving up in a huge, big, black, shining Buick convertible. He is a pilot in the Air Corps of B24's—a 2nd Lt. and he looked very nice. He sure is a big fellow. He is married now and has a two weeks old baby daughter.

Nona said to tell you that John Fitzgerald [I grew up with John during my teenage years] was commander of a submarine that went down, may still be alive as some of the men off his sub have been picked up. I don't know the fellow but Nona said you did.

You know what? We have a mouse in our pantry of all things! He runs around at nights and has a merry old time. And you know how scared I am of mice, well if I even hear a little noise I run back out the pantry door. The other night he strolled up the hall and looked at us when we were all in the living room. What a character. Today we bought three traps, we'll get him good!

Nancy is sort of expecting George to call her either tonight or tomorrow sometime. He is great on phone calls, she says.

Tomilyn was sure sleeping tonight, she runs around and plays so much when we are down at the office [my Mother's, who was Clerk for the Justice of the Peace, a job she continued after Dad died]. They all give her so much attention and does she love it.

George went out to see the Howell's [whose son-in-law was Wannie Woods, killed in Italy] last night and stayed until about 10:00 and here we had a houseful here waiting to see him. Anyway he blew out the 27 candles on his birthday cake and got to talk with them all a little bit. Ted [my uncle] & Dorothy [Newton] had to leave early as she is a policewoman at the base and works nights. And Johnny [Bott] had to drive the 11:00 bus to the beach.

I ran across some bananas today for Tomilyn and then Loraine saw them and bought some too so we have an abundant supply for a while anyway.

Marie, Nona, Nancy & Tomilyn and I are going to Ventura tomorrow. Nancy has some distant relation over there she wants to see and Nona wants to get some things that Ted needs. Scarfs, gloves, etc. Must be cold where he is too.

Bob darling, please take care of yourself for us. We love you so.

You're our precious Daddy!
We love you,
Molly and Robin

The fourth day was more of the same. We were hungry from one ration to the next. The men were weak and dehydrated from lack of water. I wondered how much more some of them could endure. But the human body, we discovered, can be abused for a long time. The mind is the key. Men who were mentally strong seemed to have more endurance than the ones who allowed themselves to lose their basic values.

We arrived at Stalag 4B. After a long wait the doors were opened and the guards told us to get down from the railroad cars. At first we had a difficult time standing as we had been confined without exercise for quite awhile. But soon we were marched to a nearby building. There each of us walked through the outside building that stood adjacent to the fences of the compound and each man was sprayed with a delousing material.

From there we were marched into a large building within the prison compound. We were greeted by a large number of POWs. The place was overcrowded. The men were standing around, gathered in groups. Most of them looked up as we passed some with a smile, some with a stare, and some would not look at us.

We were briefed by an English officer who was in charge of our barracks. We were told we should fill out a registration card the first thing, which would be sent to our homes. It didn't take any time at all for me to fill out the card. I wrote telling Molly and Mother that I was OK. I was glad to be able to do that because I knew they were worried about me and I just hoped it would get there. I knew if or when they got the news they would pass the information to the rest of the family.

The camp was run by English soldiers. Some had been there since the African Campaign, and that was a couple of years before. They had things well organized. The first thing they did was to give us a cup of tea. Then each of us was given a shave.

As we entered the compound I heard a voice calling out, "Hey, Lieutenant Moranda, over here." I looked to the direction of the voice and there I found Conover my runner. It was like finding a brother, that man who had watched over me all the time since I had joined the 38th AIB. In civilian life he was a wheat farmer in Montana, farming many hundreds of acres. Wherever our outfit went during my time in the war, he was my eyes and my provider. He watched out for me—in combat he was a Godsend to me. We had a good visit, but they soon hurried us along to our new assigned spot.

Later as I was sitting with my group talking to fellow POWs, I overheard a young Major talking to his little group telling them he was from Lancaster, California. I walked over and started to talk to him, telling him my name and that I had family in Lancaster. His name was Major Jim Burns who had been with the 28th Infantry Division. He, too, was captured during the Battle of the Bulge. He had been the S3 (operations officer) of a battalion in the 28th Infantry Division. With him were Lieutenants Duffy, Ed Kazarin, and Vince DeGort. We all became good friends, but it was Jim Burns who became very close to me. He lived near my in-laws, the Swains, in Lancaster. And after the war we continued to see each other quite often.

We soon started to recover from all the exposure. Our rations were steady. Daily we got two inches of a loaf of a black type of bread, a small hunk of cheese or sausage, and a mug of soup. A mug was issued which took the place of a mess kit. I still have the cup sitting on my dresser to remind me of the time spent as a POW.

Our daily routine was mainly to sit around and talk, as there was not enough room to really exercise and we were not allowed to go outside. Besides, it was still quite cold and we'd had enough walking for a time.

On January 12th, eighty of us officers and six enlisted men were called out, lined up, and marched to the railroad yards where we were loaded into boxcars again. The cars were the same, the count per car was the same, forty men. This time they did remember to give us a bucket to be used as a toilet.

A new leader was appointed for our group. His name was Colonel Hurley Fuller from the 28th Division. His assistant was Lieutenant Craig Campbell. Craig had been an aide to General Eisenhower in Africa and had been captured there. Also assigned to help Colonel Fuller was Major Jim Burns.

[Colonel Hurley E. Fuller commanded the 110th Infantry Regiment, 28th Division, which had been assigned a wide sector of about 9.4 miles from Kalborn south to Stolzembourg. There he positioned his main elements in a string of villages and covered the gaps only with patrols—there just wasn't enough manpower to anything more—an average of about sixty infantrymen to cover each kilometer of front. After the German forces broke through, surrounded the strongpoints held by the 110th, Colonel Fuller was captured with a group trying to escape to the west. Fuller was a Texan who had enlisted in the Army in 1916, went to Officers Training School, and served in France during World War I and had fought in the bitter campaign in the Ardennes Forest. He was embittered by that experience, but stayed in the Army and established a reputation as a tough, irascible curmudgeon. He had been assigned to command a regiment in the 2nd Infantry Division and brought the unit to Normandy on D-Day plus one. He lasted in combat just ten days, when he was relieved by the division commander, apparently because he had maneuvered his regiment into an untenable position. Fuller went to his old friend General Middleton, commander of the VIII Corps, who obtained another chance for him by assigning him to the 28th Infantry Division when a vacancy occurred in the 110th Infantry Regiment in late November. One of the first things he did was to move the regimental headquarters from a farm village to the more comfortable tourist city of Clervaux and into Hotel Claravallis.]

POLAND POW CAMP

We arrived at *Offlag* 692 in Poland around the 18th of January. The *Offlag* was occupied by fifty French and other foreign officers, and when we arrived the count went up another eighty plus.

The ride from Stalag 4B near Berlin to the *Offlag* took us six or seven days. That long in a box car with only the cracks in the sides of the box-car and a two foot square opening at each end for visibility. Our food was a very small hunk of about one inch from a loaf of a black bread and a small slice of sausage, and we were given a small amount of water daily. Our toilet was, again, a large bucket that was only emptied once in the whole trip.

Forty men in a boxcar, all weak, some with dysentery. You can't imagine the stench. One officer had a real problem. He had been constipated for a couple of weeks, and was really worried. After three more days of still being that way he decided that it was time to really try. So he got on that stinking bucket and kept trying and trying. Finally after almost an hour of grunting he was able to get some relief. The men in the box car stood around and were really rooting for him. It was the first and last time I ever rooted for a man trying to crap!

The weather outside was quite cold. To keep warm we crowded together. We had no blankets and really felt that we were quite lucky to have all of our clothes. When we first became prisoners I was with Colonel Riggs, and a couple of the German *soldats* were looking at our paratrooper boots. They had just about decided they were going to make us take off our boots and keep them for themselves. Colonel Riggs stood up and fought for our rights; he called to an officer and registered a loud complaint. That is the last we ever heard about them taking our boots.

In this boxcar I again saw the deterioration of some of the men, but others were able to control those who started to break down. Being together did make time pass more easily, but actually there was very little talking. Most of the time it seemed that our minds were far off. Toward the end of the six days things were getting bad. Men were getting weaker. There was more bickering; more heroics by the sane, more tenderness shown, more selfishness by some. Some were waiting for death, and some waiting for the rations of those who were very sick. But a few kept things going and encouraged the rest to "buck up," by promising that it would soon get better. And on January 18th it did get better. We were received at the *Offlag*. The address was Camp No. M-Stammlager 4B, Deutschland, located near Poznan, Poland.

[On the Eastern Front, by the end of 1944, the line had stabilized on its northern and central sectors along the East Prussia border extending southward along the Narew-Vistula line to the Carpathians, but was threatened on the south by the Red Army's flanking movement through the Balkans into Hungary. Hitler had placed General Guderian, a brilliant armored force commander, as Chief of General Staff, but left him with only twelve armored divisions along with fifty infantry divisions to face what intelligence sources estimated to be 225 Russian infantry divisions and twenty-two armored corps; he also shifted two Panzer divisions from Poland to Hungary without consulting Guderian. Despite Guderian's pleas for reinforcements, Hitler was committed to the Ardennes Campaign in the west and was unable to help him out.

In mid-January 1945 the Red Army started its major offensive and breached the German defenses on a 200 mile front toward East Prussia's southern border. Warsaw was captured on 17 January, Lodz on 19 January, and the Russians had advanced a hundred miles in a week. By then it was obvious to Hitler that the campaign in the west had failed, and he shifted the Sixth Panzer Army, against Guderian's advice, to Hungary rather than to Poland. The Red Army, thus, could continue its advance for two more weeks; their spearheads crossed the Oder near Breslau and cut Silesia's mineral resources off from Germany, and drove forward from Warsaw to the frontiers of Brandenburg and Pomerania; and another Red force isolated East Prussia by driving to the Gulf of Danzig. They reached within eighty miles of Berlin on 13 February.

On the Western Front, Allied Forces had, by the end of January, eliminated the Bulge and were moving eastward on a broad front.]

A person never realizes what it's like to be confined within a box car until he has to stay in one for any prolonged period of time. Debarking was done quickly as we needed to stretch our bodies. Just to be able to walk, to have some space, to breathe fresh air, to have a cup of cabbage soup even if there happened to have a couple of crickets or some other kind of animal in it. We didn't complain. One of the men said, "Goody, fresh meat." And finally a hunk of bread. That really did ease the hunger pains. That doesn't sound like much but what an improvement over the past couple of weeks, and it was so much better than what we had while in the box car.

The prisoners were kept in one large room, equipped with double bunks with straw mattresses—and I can't remember a blanket the first few nights. And as the weather was down to below zero, some of us again slept in the "spoons" position to keep warm. My bunkmate was Lieutenant Boyd.

On the third day we all received a Red Cross package. What a great gift. The box contained little tins of food, chocolate bars, cigarettes, raisins, powdered milk. Some men wolfed things down, others hoarded the things. I hoarded. What I enjoyed the most were raisins in a mixture of dried milk and water. I let the raisins soak until plump and then ate them slowly. And with a cigarette. Not bad! Not bad!

There was a courtyard where we could go out and exercise at any time. I stayed out there as much as possible. Being outside relieved me from thinking about being in prison.

As I look back, I recall some of the personal habits and character traits of the men. Some kept busy; some slept almost day and night. There really was not much talking. Some found ways to keep busy by making things out of the tins that were in the Red Cross packages. Some read the Bible. A few were like zombies, having a difficult time in adjusting to imprisonment.

Colonel Fuller from the 28th Division had been appointed our CO. Before the war he was a professor at some college in Pennsylvania. He was an older man. The trip had taken a toll on him, and he didn't join the rest of us very often. He had separate quarters and Craig Campbell and Jim Burns stayed in the room with him. They stayed pretty much to themselves, as I imagined the colonel wanted space from the rest of the prisoners.

In late January, Mother wrote to Molly:

Dear Amelia, Your letter arrived this morning, thank you for it. The enclosed also arrived this morning & I opened it thinking if it was any further good news, I'd phone you this morning. But it's just a regulation letter & not urgent so I'm just sending it on by mail & not phoning. Yesterday I had a telegram from Earle [a Lieutenant in Army Air Corps Intelligence in the Pentagon] which said "Shocked at news of Bob. Can't give up hope. Most likely prisoner. Won't get word for about 60 days. Casualty branch to advise me, in addition to telegram to Molly if any news. Will phone you when hear. Molly to receive letter confirming telegram. Writing Hugh West." The letter Earle mentioned is this one I'm enclosing. I can't remember whether Hugh West is still with Bob or not but Earle is going to write him. If you know the names of any of the men with Bob you might write them. I still believe that Bob is alright & that we'll hear good news of him.

George & Nancy came over to the house with me & yesterday they & Marie scrubbed down the walls of the kitchen. I felt awful about it but they said they wanted to do it. Yes Jeannette will be up Sat. so will have a little time with Nancy. I don't know whether Bill & Marie will feel like going to Lancaster Sunday or not. It looks & feels like rain—but may not—but I'll get word to you later.

Sure hate to see George leave again, but who knows he may be around for awhile yet.

Mary Moore had a baby son yesterday. I was surprised as I didn't think her baby was expected so soon.

Hope you are feeling alright now. You must keep up & be as cheerful as possible both for Bob & Tomilyn.

Lovingly,
Nona

The enclosed letter from Major General J.A. Ulio, the Adjutant General, was addressed to Mrs. Amelia Moranda, dated 20 January 1945, and said, in part:

This letter is to confirm my recent telegram in which you were regretfully informed that your husband, Second Lieutenant Robert E. P. Moranda, 001326108, has been reported missing in action in Belgium since 21 December 1944.

I know that added distress is caused by failure to receive more information or details. Therefore, I wish to assure you that any time additional information is received it will be transmitted to you without delay, and, if in the meantime no additional information is received, I will again communicate with you at the expiration of three months.

Experience has shown that many persons reported missing in action are subsequently reported as prisoners of war, but as this information is furnished by countries with which we are at war, the War Department is helpless to expedite such reports.

The personal effects of an individual missing overseas are held by his unit for a period of time and are then sent to the Effects Quartermaster, Kansas City, Missouri, for disposition as designated by the soldier.

Permit me to extend to you my heartfelt sympathy during this period of uncertainty.

There was an enclosure to the letter which explained the entitlements of missing persons and their dependants.

THE RUSSIANS ARE COMING

We had been at the POW camp for a short time when we noted a change in attitude of the Germans. We heard them include the names of Russkie or Bolshevik in their conversation. They seemed excited and moved at a faster pace. And they were packing things. The ones who could speak English were saying, "The Russians are coming."

It was even implied and sometimes asked of us, "Would we fight with the Germans against the Russians?" We listened and by our actions they got the message we wouldn't.

On January 21st we were told to gather up the warm items needed to protect us from the cold. They even allowed us to take things that belonged to the Germans. Apparently, they were going to save us from the Russians.

For all the time we had been at the Offlag, I had exercised and walked in the courtyard with Colonel Riggs, the engineer officer who was with us at St. Vith. We would daily walk the compound for at least an hour at a time, and doing it twice or three times a day. We would talk about escape. But the problem was and remained: where would we go, which direction, and how would we survive? But the two of us did get ourselves in pretty good shape.

So on the 21st we were lined up, counted at least twice, and with the *hauptman* leading in a horse and cart we took off. My costume was a coat, a scarf that was at least six feet long and eight inches wide, and a blanket. I gathered up food of any type I had saved and what was left of my Red Cross package, anything we had hoarded, and anything we had stolen from the *Krauts*. But the scarf and my large cup for the daily soup ration were things that I made sure I had.

The convoy was the *hauptman's* wagon plus six other horse-drawn wagons leading and carrying the Germans' supplies, and then eighty-six Americans (eighty officers and six enlisted men), plus a few French and other foreign officers walking. The foreign officers had been at the Offlag when we arrived.

By the *hauptman's* attitude we could see that he hated us all—how I disliked the manner of that arrogant bastard. He continually drove up and down the convoy urging the guards to hurry us. And when we saw there was a possibility to slow the convoy down and let the Russians catch up with us we did. We did whatever we could do to further that effort to delay the march. The *hauptman* always had his pipe in his mouth. He was a short man, stocky build, wore glasses and had a permanent frown on his face. *"Roush Mit!"* he would yell at us, which meant for us to hurry up!

According to the German guards, our destination was Berlin and that was a long, long way to go. "Why Berlin?" we asked, but we got no reply because the guards did not know either.

Our interpreter, spy, and interrogator was a German lieutenant, Paul Hegel. He had been at the Offlag and was always trying to get more information from different prisoners by being extra nice to them. He was allegedly pro-American, having been educated in America, where he had studied banking. He said he wanted to be a friend, but I did not trust him. He stayed with Colonel Fuller most of the time doing what he could for the colonel, which is well-known in the Army as "brown nosing," but in retrospect he was only trying to save his life.

"Krieges" [POWs] was what the Germans called us. Our first day we walked fifteen miles. Not many miles considering how long we were on the road. But we were not the only ones traveling. Most of the German

population in and around that part of the country was also trying to escape the Russians. Wagons pulled by horses, wheel barrows being pushed, and even one dog cart passed by us. The Germans had the right of way so we would have to wait on the side of the road and allow wagons and all to pass. Then the usual line up and the count. The people were loaded down with all of their possessions. What hate was on their faces as they passed us! They would look, snarl a word at us, and then face the road ahead. They were really trying to hurry and there was a fearful look about them.

At the end of the first day at dusk they placed us in an old barn. As always in barns there was hay and manure and that combination creates heat so we were comfortable. The German guards were able to scrounge a half-way decent ration for us. All night long we could hear artillery in the distance. Now we could really understand the nervousness of the Germans. The Russians were coming and they were getting closer.

January 22, my mother's birthday, we were lined up early in the morning. The usual counting the lines of men, the usual shifting of the men so we could disrupt the *ein, swei, drei* and so on. The Germans would have to count us at least twice. Our delaying tactics were working. The breath coming from us was white when we exhaled. It was cold, cold, bitter cold. Men kept stomping their feet and wrapping their arms around themselves.

On this day we only walked about fifteen miles. The pace was slow. Trying to keep men in line was difficult. Many men had bad feet. Even though they had a few days in Stalag 4B to try to cure the frostbite, the pain was still there. And the guards were continually trying to keep us moving. The *hauptman* would walk up and down the lines trying to get the guards to move us out. We finally reached a German youth camp where we were fed and bedded—tired but otherwise okay.

Most of the time no words were uttered, a grunt or two as most of the men were within themselves. Some I know were talking about escaping. Four men from the 28th Division—Major Burns, Lieutenants

Duffy, Kazarian, and one other young officer were planning to give it a go when the opportunity was there. But the question always came up, escape to where? The Russians? We didn't know where we were. Colonel Riggs and I discussed plans almost daily and all the possible problems, but we wanted to succeed and not have to go through this again. We agreed it took a lot of luck, but we were willing to try.

On January 23rd it was really tough. We were up early and did the usual stomping to get our blood circulating into our extremities. It was below zero the whole day. It was so cold that our skin would feel like it was burning. But as they do in cold countries, we mushed it—only without the dogs and sleds. We walked, or trudged, on, and covered about twenty miles. That night again we were put in a large barn occupied with cows, and we certainly didn't complain. The cows' body temperatures, their willingness to give us milk, and with the abundance of hay we were quite comfortable. We all took off our boots and massaged our feet back to life. Damn, it was so cold walking that day. No thought of escaping that day. We were just trying to survive.

January 24th was a short day and we covered only about twelve miles. Had to fight the snow all day. And that night we were rested in a German *bier* hall.

On January 25th we made about twenty-five miles. We crossed the border into Germany, the border town of Filchens. That night we were placed in a cold barn, still bitterly cold. By then the German civilians and others were really moving out in large numbers. It was very hard on the women and children, and I did sympathize with and feel badly for them.

After we rested, the guards would form our lines again and count us. *Ein, swei, drei*, and so on. As often as we could we would jump ranks so the count would be wrong. Delay was the order of the day. The Germans were having a hard time trying to get the count correct.

Then I learned that sometime before the day's march Colonel Riggs had escaped. When, I did not know. I had walked the courtyard with him the day before, and we were still working on plans to get away. Now he was gone. I was glad for him but wondered how he had gotten away without any of us seeing him. (Years after the war I talked to him on the telephone, after learning where he lived, and asked him how he had escaped. He said on the morning they were lining us up he was in the toilet. No one was looking for him so he waited a short time and soon saw that he could go over the fence easily so he did. He did have quite an experience before the Russians came along and took care of him.)

Our men were rapidly going downhill. By then we were spending a lot of effort helping the weak to continue. I saw one man reach down and pick up a frozen sugar beet and try to eat it. Thankfully after a trial bite he threw it away.

This reminds me of a poem written by a Lieutenant Phelan. We had been fed every night some kind of watery soup—one cup full and sometimes a slab of bread, so he dreamed of the good food at home. Phelan dedicated this poem to his wife. He knew she would understand.

I dream as only a captive can dream
of life as lived as in days before.
Of scrambled eggs and shortcake thick with cream.
And onion soup and lobster thermador.
Of roasted beef and chops and T-bone steak.
Of turkey breast and a golden leg or wing.
Of sausage, maple syrup, buckwheat cake.
And chicken broiled or fried, a la king.
I dwell on rolls or buns for days and days.
Hot corn bread biscuits, Philadelphia scrapple.
Asparagus in cream or Hollandaise.
And deep dish pies, mince, huckleberry, apple.
I long for buttered cream oyster stew.
And now and then I long for you.

On that day we were walking along with thousands of German civilians, their wagons piled high with possessions. The weather was so cold that many had their heads covered with burlap sacks with holes cut out for their eyes. They would stare at us and we would stare back. No words were spoken. It would be a bother to talk. And besides, why waste precious energy?

A bag dropped from a wagon as it passed us. As the bag was paper, it split when it hit the road. I reached and scooped a handful and tasted it. It was sugar. I slowly ate the sugar and told the men about it—and many scooped up some of it and did the same. It seemed to give us a small spark of energy inside of us.

One thing I could not understand was why so many of the slaves from Poland, Denmark, and France helped the Germans to escape from the Russians? Were they happy as slaves of the Germans? Did they know something about the coming Russians? I guessed they would rather help as slaves than face the Red Tide that was coming.

I remember one Sunday morning we had stopped to rest close to a few houses. One of the officers in our group was a French priest. Though he was ordained, it made no difference to the French, for when the men were drafted everyone in an age group was drawn into the French army. There were no exemptions. He had been with us for some time, but none of us had known he was a priest; however, we did notice he had been carrying a small case. When we were halted to rest that day, there was a wagon parked on the side of the road. The priest went to the wagon, opened his case, laid out the necessary items, put his vestments on, and started to say Mass. From houses, from wagons, from *soldats*, from guys in our group, came people to participate in the Mass. There for a few minutes they were with God, along side of a road in a cold, cold place and enemy soldiers, civilians, and we prisoners were worshiping with our heads bared. I was impressed. I remember thinking to myself, it does not matter what governments do, they cannot stamp out man's belief in God. The soldiers from Germany, the Americans, the French, the slaves from Poland, the house *fraus*, all ask God to love us and protect us. For a moment there was peace.

We stayed in another barn that night. Again it was somewhat warm, and we survived the night.

The next day, January 26th was still bitter cold. The guards were getting jumpy as hell. As one of our group said, "The guards were as nervous as a whore in church." Our antics did not help their attitude. But some of the men had toes that were frozen, which made it difficult to walk in the snow. The wind was blowing hard and the cold cut right through our clothes.

We finally reached a *bier* hall and, as the guards had had enough, we went in. The meal that night was soup and bread. We, that is most of us, ate the soup and saved the bread for morning.

We started January 27th in the usual manner, though it took longer to count that morning as it seemed someone had taken off on his own. When the guards counted we were one man short, they went up and down counting and recounting. The *hauptman* even got down and counted. The interpreter walked along the lines with the *hauptman*. They would ask, "Who is missing?" To that question he got blank looks on our faces. Actually at the first line up I didn't know who was missing, but one of the men had left for parts unknown. I don't remember the name of the man who had left. That made it two men who had departed from our group as Colonel Riggs had been the first to get away. (After the war my brother, George, met Colonel Riggs when he attended the Army War College at Carlisle Barracks in Pennsylvania. When Riggs heard the name Moranda he asked him, "Are you related to Bob?" It was then that I found out that he too got picked up by the Russians and was repatriated. He offered no apology for leaving without me. And as it turned out maybe it was for the best.)

The weather was still bad but we did make a few more miles. We actually went about twenty miles. It was one of those days that a person just puts his head down and walks on. It brought back memories of the comment of Lieutenant Babb, my first platoon leader, who said at one of our first formations, "A man can walk one hell of a lot farther, even when he is dead tired, than he thinks he can."

That night we were again placed in a barn with cows. We didn't complain about the smell. The warmth was great and we all had warm milk to drink. I was pretty good at getting next to a friendly cow and using the Swiss style of milking (that I had learned from my Uncle Walter when I had visited him on his farm near Goshen in the San Joaquin Valley) to fill my cup.

Daily the men were going further downhill physically, deteriorating badly. They all needed help—medical help. Their feet were frostbitten. We who were in the best shape would go among the men in the worst shape and get them to rub their feet. We all needed a bit of encouragement. My feet were almost okay, with just a tinge of frostbite. But I was able to walk easily.

On the next day, January 28th, the weather had not improved. But after a good night's sleep in relative warmth and plenty of milk to drink, we were rested. Even so it wasn't very long until the weather had beaten us down again. No longer did we share the road with the people who were fleeing. It seemed that we were the only ones left. We could make much better time. But then what the hell was the hurry?

Wugarten

We passed through the town of Waltenburg about 2 or 3 o'clock in the afternoon. We continued on for about five miles, and in an hour or so later we arrived at the small town of Wugarten. No matter where we were there was an air of fear. The German soldiers obviously feared the Russians. The civilians feared the Russians, their soldiers, and us. The guards were very uneasy about everything. They wanted us to speed up and we wouldn't and some couldn't. I am sure the soldiers of the Third Reich had heard of the pillaging of Russian towns, raping the women, and killing the men. That news must have been passed on to the civilians, and so they became even more fearful as the sound of artillery came closer.

Some Germans still fully expected the Americans to fight against the Russians. In fact, I recalled that in the POW camp the Germans had put out a feeler asking the British and Americans if we would help them stop the Russians. Needless to say, the offer was flatly refused.

One thing that continually had slowed our column down was dysentery. Many men had the problem. When the urge hit them they would head for a snow bank, drop their pants, and relieve themselves. Some had brought paper to wipe with but that was soon gone. Wiping was done with anything available: cloth, weeds, or just snow. And as there was no way to be hygienic, the dysentery got worse. The only paper I had with me was the last letter from Molly and I wasn't about to use that. I read it daily. It seemed to me I could hear her voice as I read it.

We halted on the road. I noticed the guards and the *hauptman* were together in a bunch and talking several yards away from us. Lieutenant Paul Hegl was with them and the discussion seemed feverish. Some of us wandered off. All at once I realized I was alone. I waited for a few minutes making certain that the guards were not coming for me. They were not. I was following at a distance. The group was coming into the town of Wugarten. Then I saw the column was going into a school, and the guards were leaving!! I thought what the hell is going on??? I soon discovered what was happening.

The Germans had decided to try to save their own necks and took off leaving us in the town. Only one German stayed with the group, the interpreter, Lieutenant Hegl. That apparently was what the heated discussion had been about with the Germans. Colonel Fuller had told Hegl that if he stayed with the Americans he would save his neck. He would dress Hegl in an American uniform, give him an insignia, and make him a Lieutenant of Infantry, U.S. Army. So when the Germans left, Hegl became Lieutenant George Mulbauer, named after an escaped American POW.

I watched from a distance. I was alone in the town, going over all my options. Could I find my way to the American line? I couldn't speak German. Would it be better to get back with the group? Good sense told me to get back with the troops as that would be the best for me. So I started up the road. Suddenly there loomed a tank. I knew it was a Russian tank. Well now, what do I do? Do I run, hide, or bluff it out? I kept walking right up the middle of the road, straight at the tank. I could see the man in the turret watching my every move. I yelled at the driver. The guns were aimed at me. I kept yelling at the tank crew, "Americanski! Americanski! Americanski!" The commander finally understood. He climbed down from the tank. He looked me over, looked at the bar on my shirt collar, the shoes on my feet, walked around me. Then he embraced me and there followed much hugging and pounding on the back. Out came the vodka. A drink was poured and I downed it. Me being emaciated, I left the group and went to the side of the road and upchucked it. Back again. Another drink poured and this time it stayed down. They called the drink "Spiritous"—a cheap vodka. I learned the Russians are given a daily ration of the stuff. I think the Russian soldiers fought half drunk—it helped their nerves and bravery. I climbed aboard the tank and we motored up the road.

Our conversation was mostly by sign language and the few words of English they knew. Stalin, Roosevelt, Studebaker trucks, Churchill, Hitler, the German *Kaput* and *Alles Kaput*. All of this time there were smiles and gestures. We did get along. They let me out and I joined my group in the school house.

So there we were. About one hundred Americans, Italians, and French. One of the French officers who had been a prisoner for some time was Alex Bertin, a tall, young, intelligent man. In fact in languages he was great. He could speak seven of them perfectly, so he became our interpreter. We also became very good friends. Later we became great partners at bridge. Earlier I had become well acquainted with the French Chaplain, so I had acquired two fine friends from France.

Soon we were visited by the German local Burgermeister. He requested that three or four of the Americans stay at his house, which was located across the street from the school. Lieutenants Higgins, Tate, and I were told to go there. We got to sleep in beds with quilts—what a great feeling. And running water! The house had two women and the father of the Burgermeister. As we were in the best shape of most of the other prisoners, we became the procurers of food.

Before leaving the German commandant gave Colonel Fuller a notice in writing that we were being abandoned. He advised the group to stay inside the school house as German soldiers were fleeing through the town. It wasn't long before I found out it was true. I took it upon myself to scout the town. As I had entered I had seen a bakery shop on a side street. I went to the shop, walked in and said, *"Haben se brod?"* (That and *"Alles Kaput"* and a couple of greetings was about the only German I knew).

The baker and his wife said they did. Now whether the word had gotten around town or not I didn't know but, without hesitation, loaves of black bread appeared. I loaded up. My arms were full of them when I departed from the bakery. No sooner than I had exited the bakery and stepped into the road I looked to my right and here came a German group of *soldats* trudging though the deep snow. Again, what do I do? Run back to the shop or try to run to the school house? Again I just continued toward the Germans. They looked at me, me at them, they with their burp guns in their right arms, me with my arms full of bread. I walked right past them, to one I said, *"Guten Morgan."* He grunted and I continued on. I did breathe with a loud exhaling sound when he didn't challenge me. As I reflect on the incident I think the Germans may have heard there were POWs in the town.

Wugarten

I was a welcome sight when I took the bread to the troops in the school house. Every man got an ample supply of it.

My next tour was to the dairy barn. I found some fresh milk and scrounged some potatoes and took them back to the school. Our men were soon able to feed themselves. Some of our enlisted men, who were our cooks at the Offlag, soon had enough items to prepare the food we had brought to the school.

Higgins and I were watching out the window of our house when we saw Russian officers talking to Lieutenant Campbell and Alex Bertin. They went in and talked with Colonel Fuller. Soon the Russians and an American group walked the town and went into the school house. We didn't know what they said, but they were out soon and came to our billet. They shook hands with us and left. As they walked back to their vehicles, they marked each place where POWs were staying, which was to be a notice to the Russian Army when they came into the town.

One thing that impressed me was the way the Russians dressed. They had real winter clothes on. They looked warm with all their parkas, wool hats, and boots.

Even though we were placed in a marked house, our presence helped only a little. One day I was in the front room of our quarters. Suddenly one of the two women came in the room and yelled at me to come quick. She was really agitated so I quickly followed her into the kitchen. There in the kitchen stood a brute of a man—a drunken Russian soldier, with his hat on, his great coat open, his pants dropped, and his penis standing at attention. He was tearing at a woman's clothes. She was screaming and saying, "*Nein! Nein! Nein!*" I shouted, "No! No! No!" shaking my head in a negative motion. I yelled at Higgins to run to get the Russian officer who was billeted nearby. The drunken soldier reeled back, swaying with his body that must have been full of vodka. I could see he was wondering what the hell was going on. As he pulled back he reached for his sidearm. Quite a sight: a drunken Russian soldier swaying back and forth, his eyes trying to focus on me and wondering what to do with his penis and at the same time wondering what to do about me. I had placed myself between him and the woman, and he gradually started backing out of the kitchen into the backyard. He slowly stuffed his penis back into his pants. His eyes were blinking trying to focus on me. He gradually raised his revolver and started to point it at me when, thankfully, a Russian officer came into the backyard. The Russian officer yelled at the drunken soldier. We were all standing near a rain barrel full of water. The soldier dropped his gun to his side. The officer stood him at attention and really berated him. The officer dipped his hands in the water and slapped the soldier. Over and over he repeated the operation and with each slap he would curse the soldier. After four or five slaps he allowed the soldier to leave. He stumbled and staggered to his horse and cart. A calm came over the backyard. Personally I had quite a fright; I had wondered what was going to be the outcome and whether or not I was about to be shot.

I thanked the Russian officer, "Thanks for coming to our rescue."

He looked at me then said, "You were lucky I was nearby. And I cannot blame the soldier. You see his women were raped when the Germans came through his village. To the soldier, he was only paying back for all the rapes that have happened in Russia." Alex Bertin, who came with the officer, said he couldn't understand why I would endanger myself by stopping the Russian. After all, he and others had suffered much at the hands of the Germans. I guess my thoughts were that even though war is a terrible, terrible thing, even in war, I didn't believe women, *hausfraus*, or children, or for that matter any noncombatant, should be abused.

Alex also couldn't understand why Colonel Fuller was trying to save Hegl, the German, especially as he had for days spent a lot of time humiliating American and French officers by his interrogations—a man who didn't provide any comfort or help to us. And now to save him from the Russians? We also knew the Russians rarely took prisoners. We saw many Germans lying dead. I even discovered our German *hauptman's* body on the outskirts of town. I did pick up his pipe. Never did I observe the Russians taking prisoners to their rear. I must admit I felt the same way about Hegl. But now looking back, I understand why none of us ever uttered a word to the Russians. It did rankle me that Hegl became a gentleman's gentleman. He served Fuller's every whim. Here he could speak the language, but the three of us, the providers who gathered food and found supplies, had to do it by sign language. Even so we, by deduction and searching, found plenty of food. Two days before we were to be trucked out of Wugarten I was called to Colonel Fuller's headquarters and found him griping about the lack of better food. At the very time he was bitching, Hegl was on his knees washing Fuller's feet. I guess I saw red because I told him that maybe if he could spare Hegl for a time to have him go with us to talk to the civilians maybe we could find even more food and supplies. Well, as they say, that remark of mine went over like a lead balloon. The truth must have hurt because the good colonel got red in the face and excused me. Later on I found out that Fuller told Major Burns and Lieutenant Campbell they should court martial me when we got into American hands. Burns said they soothed the colonel and he forgot about it. But Burns added that what I had said was the truth, and Fuller realized it—that's what made him so mad.

A few days before we left the town, an infantry unit of the Russian Army entered Wugarten. By then we had taken over the town. The first thing they did was to call out the mayor. As he walked up to the Russians, one of them pulled out his pistol and killed him. At first they didn't realize we were Americans. The situation was touch and go for a few minutes. They finally saw the signs the previous Russians had left so they eased their attitude a bit. But before that their tanks and infantry were ready to mow us down. But by yelling, "Americanski" and through Alex Bertin talking to them, they finally understood who we were. When they had been advised we were allies, we asked why they had shot the Mayor. The reply was, "We always kill the Burgermeister when we come into a town." Again the Russians wanted to celebrate with us. Again the vodka flowed. Most of our men couldn't drink much as we were too far gone physically, but they tried to celebrate. Many hugs and laughter. The Russians were happy to share in our liberation.

After that there were no more killings or rapes around us. But one rather interesting situation occurred among our group Our enlisted men bunked separately from the officers. We had six enlisted men, several of whom told me they had found billets with some young women of the town. The girls had asked the men, literally, to breed them. They said they would rather have an American baby than a Russian baby, saying they knew when we left the town they would soon be forced to have sex with the Russians. They said the affairs with our men took place away from the girls' homes.

The men were getting restless; in fact we food procurers, Higgins, Tate and I, began to get a little help. A group of our officers were well enough to find and kill and dress a couple of sheep. So we had fresh mutton, fresh eggs, chicken—the menu was great—and fresh baked black bread. Soon we started hearing gripes and grousing, which was a good sign that the men were getting stronger.

The day after the episode about my rescuing the woman from being raped, we were sitting in our room when the woman brought me a large cake with frosting. To me that was a great tribute from her to me and I was pleased. I did wonder where the sugar came from. But her attitude showed me she was really thankful.

(It was about this time that Molly in Lancaster received a letter from Mrs. C. Reedy, who had been her Practitioner in Oxnard, postmarked Feb 20, 1945:

My dearest Amelia

I am sorry I have waited so long to answer you letter. I could have dozens of excuses, but I am not. I am a very sorry letter writer, can think of a lot of things until I go to put it on paper & then I have to hunt words to write. I have been awfully busy, in fact too much so.

I was sorry to hear Bob was Missing but that doesn't mean he won't return. We must know God's Ideas are not separated from him. He lives & moves & has his Being in God. Good. Where nothing but good can touch him. You must make an effort to keep your thought above the clouds & that will not only help you, but will help him also.

When I heard it I worked all afternoon. We are not supposed to work without being asked but as I have worked for him at different times, I felt I wanted to.

If I were you I would get some good Practitioner to do some work on it if you feel the least upset about it. Some way I feel he is in God's care & all is well.

Give my love to the family & yourself & baby. Lots of love,

Your friend

According to Burns and Campbell, Colonel Fuller did keep asking when we were to be liberated to the U.S. The answer back was always the same, "When we win the war we will send you back." But Colonel Fuller continued to pressure our liaison officer.

We kept wondering how we would be handled by the Russians, but we were left alone in our town. We started doing things to keep busy— and to keep our sanity. Higgins found some cheesecloth and by experimenting learned how to make cheese. I found some baking soda and a bag of flour and, by trial and error, I learned how to make soda biscuits. My only clue was remembering how Mom did it, and especially my

Aunt Leo who used to make "soader" biscuits almost every day when I visited in Goshen. The first batch came out well so we had "soader" biscuits daily.

One morning we were told to be ready to move out. It was about 1000 in the morning when the trucks arrived and we loaded into them. Higgins, Tate, and I said goodbye to the ladies of our house. They had tears in their eyes and gave us a good hug and a handshake. I have wondered many times about the women and whether they survived.

We proceeded to Poznan, Poland. From the back of a truck a person doesn't see much of the scenery, so I can't recall much of the surroundings. My only remembrance was that it was a dark city, a commercial city, and a town with a railroad and that was what we wanted, a train to get us somewhere. As we loaded into the freight cars, we were told that we were going to Odessa on the Black Sea.

What I remember mainly about Wugarten was a cake, a cup, and a pipe. The cup I still have on my dresser to remind me of the times of hunger and to be thankful today. On the bottom of the cup is the eagle with a swastika and the date, 1940. The cake reminds me of the beautiful cake that the German lady made for me after her episode with the drunken Russian soldier. And the *hauptman's* pipe: that too I kept to remind me of being under the control of a German officer.

I learned several things during that experience as a POW, but primarily the importance of personal values: love, respect, and concern for my family and friends; doing what is right in responding to a variety of events and incidents as they occur; seeing what has to be done and then doing it without any fanfare; and a strong belief that God will take care of everything.

We were loaded into boxcars again. This was my fourth trip in a boxcar. The two in Germany were really bad, so it was with some reservations when we again began riding the rails. But this one turned out to be interesting and almost a comfortable trip. This time we only had about twenty men in each car and our rations were ample. Each car had a

Russian soldier as our guide and protector. Our train was also served by a Russian woman doctor who treated the sick. By this time most of those down with ailments had made remarkable recoveries so she didn't have too much to do.

The train wasn't fast, but we really were not unhappy as we could open the doors and watch the country go by. Most of it seemed flat. The weather was very nice so we felt we were on a tour. Once while the train was stopped, the Russian soldier jumped off and went into a field, obviously to relieve himself. I turned to Major Burns and said, "I'll bet you a package of cigarettes that he wont wipe." Burns took the bet—and paid off when we got to Odessa.

Our guide couldn't speak English. We couldn't speak Russian so we accomplished communication by sign language and teaching each other some words of our languages. I did learn quite a bit during the three days it took to go from Posen to Odessa. I was impressed by the land. I had always heard that Russians love their land, and it is understandable. Most of the laborers seen along the railroad were women—big husky women—swinging picks, using shovels, pushing brooms, toting rails, and anything else that needed to be done. Much war damage could be observed in the towns we passed through. I wondered what stories there were to tell about how the Germans treated the civilians. From all reports there had been killings of civilians, raping of women, and pillaging of the towns. By then I understood more about my encounters with the Russians.

ODESSA

We arrived in Odessa early one morning, sitting on the banks of the Black Sea—it was a great and beautiful setting for a city. As we detrained, the place was on higher ground than the harbor, so we could see ships waiting to be loaded and unloaded. I was becoming excited as I knew we were almost in American hands.

They marched us through part of the town to a large school building which was no longer occupied. There we were to be greeted by an attaché of the United States of America.

On the way to the school, as we were walking down the street, I saw an American sailor. I knew he was American by his clothes and manner. "Hey Mac!" I called out. "Got a cigarette?"

He came over and asked who we were and where we were going. As we told him our story, he took out a package of Chesterfields and gave me the package. He held his lighter for me, and I smoked the cigarette and savored every puff. On our trip through Russia we had been given Russian cigarettes. They were terrible. I passed out the rest of the package to the rest of my friends, and did save one more for me. Wish I had gotten "Mac's" name.

We arrived at the large complex. We were able to have showers, use toilets, and have a kitchen inside the building. Cots were already up, and as we had no baggage to speak of it took very little time to settle in. Soon we were greeted by a group from the U.S. Embassy. They came loaded down with goodies. Each person got a full box of Hershey bars, a carton of American cigarettes, and a few other needed items. But the best news was that we could write letters home and the embassy people would mail the messages for us. I sat down immediately and wrote to Molly and Mom.

March 31, 1945

Dearest Molly,

Well darling you have been in my mind constantly but as by this time you no doubt know it has been impossible to write. How I've wondered and wondered how you and Tomilyn were and are? How Mom and all the families are and what they're doing? Wondering if you had given me up but hoping your faith in God wouldn't let you give up hope. I know it was a shock to get a telegram stating I was M.I.A. but I always knew you would have known before you got the letter something was wrong because of the sudden stoppage of my letters.

Well to relieve your mind about my condition, I'm well as ever except for a slight case of frozen feet which are almost well. My weight is about normal again and I really do feel fine. The greatest tonic I got tho was to get started towards the hands of our own troops. By the time you see me I'll be in first class condition.

How I was captured is, I suppose, a military secret but this much I will say we fought and held until everything around us caved in. My men were the bravest of brave and really fought like demons. I still get a great feeling of comfort and satisfaction knowing they did their job so well. I cite you just one of the feats of bravery.

Making the rounds of my men after the pressure had let up, I came across one of my gun crews. Ryan, a new boy, was looking a little peaked so I asked him the trouble. "Nothing wrong Lt. except we ran out of Jerries to shoot at," was his reply. Asking him again as he did look pretty white and sickly. "Well sir, got nicked yesterday but didn't want you to send me back." He had helped stop three German counter attacks and been wounded for 24 hours and still wanted to stay. I ordered him back to the Aid Station and certainly felt bad about doing it, as he started crying. The only way he would go was for me to promise he could come back if the Doc said it was O.K. Well Molly, that boy was back in action two hours later.

Well darling I could go on and on telling you about feats of bravery but the stories will all keep until I can tell you in person. My main thought is how much I'm in love with you and how I need to see you again or at least hear from you. When I get to mail this letter I don't know but I just had to drop a line telling you how much I love you. You're my everything.

Your

Bob

Hello Pumpkin, I sure hope you still remember your Dad

Molly had written to me on Prisoner of War Post on March 18th, addressed to Lt. Robert E. P. Moranda, Prisoner of War No. 316354, Camp Name and No. M-Stammlager IV B, Deutschland. It was returned by direction of the War Department and was postmarked June 18. In it she had written:

Dearest Bob

Here it is Sunday again, we are just staying around the house and later we are going to take a walk. I saw Maye [my sister] & Forest Fuger and they were so happy about you and said to say hello. Buck and Johnny have both gone over. Tiny [her sister Rozeel] met this lady in Lancaster whose nephew is in your camp. His name is Capt. James H. Burns No. 316402. You might look him up if you can. He asked for a toothbrush on his card so I'll send you one too in case you need it. I had a letter from Lucy West. She was so happy about you and said Hugh talks about you all the time in his letters. Tiny sent me a map that the girl in the Red Cross gave her and it has all the camps on it. I know where yours is, the bulletin that came with it was very consoling and helped me a lot. You just keep up your spirits and love us lots. Just think good things and dream of the future, that's what I do! Robin and I are so proud of our Daddy and love him so very, very much. The bulletin also stated that I can send a photograph or map to you by enclosing it in an envelope without a letter and you will get it, so I'll send a colored one soon. I write you every day, darling, but they may not get thru to you consecutively so don't worry, they are on the way! You write to us often darling, as often as you can, and remember, keep that sweet chin of yours up and be patient. Love & Kisses, Molly & Robin.

The non-smokers soon had trading material and traded for Hershey bars and other items. Most of the non-smokers just gave the cigarettes to a smoker. My friend Lieutenant Boyd, my bunk buddy in the Stalag, gave me his, so I was able to share with others. One of the jokes I remember going around at that time:

First soldier: "How many Hershey Bars did you eat the first day?"

Answer: "I ate them all."

First soldier: "What did you do with the wrapper?"

Answer: "What wrapper?"

The men were fast recovering from the ordeal of being prisoners of war. They were active and even looked for games to play. That was a good sign to me; they had made it, and so had I.

One day as we were outside the building, we heard a beautiful chorus of male singers. We looked for the sound and discovered it came from a company of Russian soldiers as they were doing marching drills. As they trooped along they sang a Russian song. The blend of the voice tones was beautiful.

Since we were able to send messages home via the Embassy, I wrote quite a number of letters which was a great relief to me. While away from Molly and the baby, whenever it was possible, I would write. But for a long time I had not been able to, so I know the only communication she had possibly received was the message that I sent through the Red Cross from the prison camp.

At night as I was on my bunk I would try to visualize my family and by mental telepathy try to send word to them that I was okay. The time spent thinking about all of my family kept me sane. A man must have an anchor. I knew all of Molly's prayers that she said every day so I would say the prayer, sing or hum a song, and usually with my final prayer would say the 23rd Psalm—"The Lord in my shepherd, I shall not want." I said that prayer every time I had to do anything that was possibly dangerous. The 23rd Psalm was and remains to this day my personal prayer.

The day came when the embassy people told us to be ready to sail the next morning. We were ready! The morning came, and we were marched down to the harbor and boarded an English passenger vessel. The ship had been converted from civilian use to service by the Armed Forces. We had individual bunks, a lounge, a complete dining room, and service *par excellence*. We were on our way back. And what a great way to go!

Return to the United States

The Black Sea was very calm. We enjoyed watching the scenes from the deck. We sat and read, played cards, or just talked. Alex Bertin and I were partners in bridge. He was an excellent player and showed me the correct way to bid and play the game. We took on all challengers and did quite well. But as none of us had any money, the stakes were whatever we had: cigarettes, candy, anything, or nothing.

I think it was the second or third day that we passed by Constantinople. What a sight to behold, and we would soon be in the Mediterranean Sea. The day we passed through the Dardanelles and entered the Mediterranean every one of the passengers became sea-sick—that is everyone but me. For some reason I didn't. When I went into the dining area for lunch, not a soul was there. The motion of the ship was caused by the two sea currents coming together and the ship wrenched one way and then the other making people sick.

As we came into Naples, Italy, it was a beautiful sight. The coast line was beautiful. We could see Mount Etna from a distance as most of us stood by the rails and watched the approaching land.

From the time we left Wugarten and all during the trip, no one saw either Colonel Fuller or Hegl. On shipboard, they stayed in Colonel Fuller's cabin. We wondered what the next step would be for Hegl. We soon found out. The ship docked and we disembarked. We were back into the control of the U.S. Army. When we were in ranks for the first time, Colonel Fuller and Hegl came front and center. Both saluted and Hegl then became a prisoner of war of the Americans. Many of us could not understand the situation, but as I now look back and reflect on what happened, it took a lot of guts on Colonel Fuller's part to save Hegl. I have often wondered whatever happened to him.

We were taken to a large resort where we had hot baths, a place to replace clothes, and friendly, more familiar surroundings which increased our feeling of security. I got a new outfit from head to foot. I saved my old boots and my muffler, items that are still with me. In fact I used the same boots and shawl when I served in Korea a few years later.

On the third day I decided to take a ride into Naples and see what was there. I rode in to town in the back of an Army truck. On the way we were solicited by young boys for anything we could give them. One asked, "You want to make love to my sister? She is 14 years old. Very pretty." It made me think how bad the people were having it. I gave the kid some cigarettes. Those he could sell. And it was all I had.

We arrived at the USO and de-trucked. As I walked in I saw an old friend, Sergeant "Mac" McFarland, a former class mate at OCS. He had failed in the last week. He had been a good friend, and we had shared many Saturday nights in Columbus, Georgia. We had a great time talking about what he was doing and where he was assigned. I found out he had been there in Italy with a unit—a very safe unit—so he was pleased. He remarked during our conversation: "Glad I failed OCS. If I had made it through and had become a 2nd Lieutenant I more than likely would be dead by now." How true. Lieutenants of infantry didn't last too long, and many were the first ones killed or wounded in a battle. We said goodbye after a few minutes. I always wondered what happened to him at the OCS. I really believe that he asked to be relieved from becoming an officer, but I rather hope he was washed out.

I also met a young lady from Santa Barbara, California, who was working for the USO. We talked about home, and she said she liked Naples as it reminded her of Santa Barbara. After the war when I got home and was back working in Santa Barbara, I called her folks and learned she was still in Italy. It was nice talking to her parents, and they to find out their daughter was fine and happy. Later when the daughter did return to California she came into my service station many times.

I was in the USO in the morning for an hour or so. Then I left to see another part of the town and returned to the resort where they had us billeted. I later learned that on that same afternoon my brother Ted came into the same USO. We found out our paths almost crossed. Wouldn't that have been great! Here it was in March, and I had been missing since December. No one from home knew where I was. To have run into my youngest brother would have been the greatest thing that could have happened to me in a long time. Ted was in the Air Transport Command of the Army Air Corps and flew all over the world delivering planes, and just happened to be in Italy on that date.

On the night before we were to embark to go home, a liquor ration was given to us. I received a bottle of scotch and a bottle of gin. Our little group, Jimmy Burns et al., proceeded to drink. But first we made a pact: we promised we would help each other to board the Queen Mary the next day. Our group was Major Burns, Lieutenants Duffy, Kazarian, and one man whose name I can't remember. Snockered we got. And finally we went to bed. In my lifetime I have only been drunk twice. The first time was on my initial encounter with hard liquor when a youngster, and the second was on the occasion of our being returned to the control of our forces.

The next day the group got up, and by helping each other we packed our duffel bags and were trucked to the harbor where we boarded the Queen Mary. We were comfortable on board, but we weren't nearly so as on the ship that brought us from Odessa to Naples. I missed my friend Alex Bertin, but it was Major Jimmy Burns and his three friends that I now hung out with.

On the second day out we were sitting on the top deck sunning ourselves when all of a sudden there was a loud blast from the ships horn.

The horn was only a few feet above us. The group started to look for their foxholes. What a scare! The ship lurched and cornered sharply. We found out the ship made forty-five degree turns every so often to avoid being trapped by a U-Boat.

During the ride home I was watching a group playing poker. The stakes were high. The table had six players, and I was sitting behind one of the players. One of the hands I watched I will always remember. Across the table a man opened. The play came around to the man I was sitting behind. He raised quite heavily. The opener raised again. All players but the two dropped out of the game. The pot was very large by then.

The dealer asked, "How many cards?"

The opener said, "One."

The man I was watching picked up his hand to a position where I could see—three Jacks and a pair of Aces. Without much hesitation the man threw away the pair of Aces and said, "I'll have two cards please."

The opening bet was high and the raises were even higher. Finally the call was made. The opener had four tens.

Slowly the other man turned over his cards and exposed four jacks! Then he said to the man who opened, "You forced me to throw away my full house. No one would bet like you did with two pair or an almost flush or straight. Had I played a pat hand you would have won."

I don't remember how many days it took to get across the ocean, but I think it was six. I was disappointed we wouldn't get to see the Statue of Liberty, as we were heading for Boston. But as we sailed into Boston harbor, there on the docks waiting for us was a large crowd complete with a military band—the USO people, Red Cross representatives, and a group of young girls from a nearby college. We disembarked and went into a large warehouse where coffee and doughnuts plus other food items were served.

A few of us were singled out to be interviewed. I was introduced to a young lady who proceeded to ask me about my experiences. There really wasn't much to say. How do you tell a young lady how cruel and confining it was? How do you tell a lady you questioned your own actions? Why didn't I go out fighting and take a couple of Germans with me? But then what do you do when a machine gun is to your front aiming at your chest and a squad of German *soldats* behind you with their guns also aimed at you? I guess survival is the prime factor. At any rate I just mumbled something inconsequential.

And the question, "Do you hate the Germans?" Without a thought I said, "Yes!" At this time I hated all German soldiers but not all Germans. I remembered a couple of incidents: the *hausfrau* in Wugarten and the lady in Germany who was a part of the jeering crowd as we marched through their town, and who came forward and squeezed a silver coin into my hand. As the coin entered my hand she blessed me.

Later the reporter sent me a copy of *The Wheaton News*, Wheaton College, Norton, Mass., April 28, 1945, which contained a front page article, bylined by Eleanor Johnson, under the head, "News Interviews Ex-PWs at Standish." It went:

> "If you could get it over to your people just what it means to hear of absenteeism, sit down strikes and laxness…" Captain Donald Gilinsky spoke quietly at Camp Miles Standish, and nervously played with the bar on his cap as he talked of his experiences in a German prison camp. Lieut. Robert Moranda, who had lost 54 pounds during his internment, and Lieut. Ross Gehring, a young Oklahoma boy, silently agreed.
>
> Captured by the Germans after the Battle of the Bulge in December when Von Rundstedt had driven back the Allies, they, along with other American, British, French, Polish, Yugoslavian and Serbian prisoners of war, were marched across Germany into Poland. The Germans forced them to do an about face, however, when the Russians began to get too near in the east. Finally the

Russians surrounded the town in which they were encamped; the Germans fled and the boys marched on again this time with the Russians to Odessa on the Black Sea, and then by ship to Naples and the American Army?

"If it hadn't been for the Red Cross packages, the prisoners would have starved," blonde Lieut. Moranda from California spoke. "Many times the Germans would hold out the packages, though, and refuse to give them to the prisoners. There were at least 500 boxes stacked up that hadn't been distributed." He paused, shook his head thoughtfully in remembrance and praised the Red Cross again. "Why, I could make you a wonderful pie with potatoes and chocolate from the Red Cross packages. All the Germans gave us the 11 days we were in the camp were six potatoes, one bowl of soup, a spoonful of molasses thrown in our hands and some hard tack."

"You were lucky; we didn't even get that," the captain retorted.

"The Russians certainly are a wonderful people to have as allies," laughed Lieut. Moranda crinkling his eyes as the subject of their liberators was introduced.

"You've never been kissed until you've been kissed by a Russian officer," Lieut. Gehring added, rubbing his cheek in remembrance.

Returning to the food situation they told of being hungry and spending the night in a cow barn where a "city bred boy tried to milk an ox" as he saw his companions getting results from the cows.

Talking to Wheaton reporters they, along with many khaki clad boys, were awaiting phone calls in the small Army building. The three of them expected to be home within a week, after having been from 12 to 18 months in Europe. Lieut. Moranda unconsciously described himself and his friends when he said, "No matter what happens, the American soldier never loses his sense of humor."

Soon we were bussed to the railroad siding and boarded an old Pullman car. Each man was assigned a berth. And we even had a porter, a black man who really took marvelous care of us.

For the next few days we traveled the U.S.A. The route we took was the upper part, via Chicago, through South Dakota then swinging down southward and finally arriving at Los Angeles. At every stop where I could, I sent a telegram to Molly, telling her how much I loved her and how I was going to express that love when I arrived. I think my mother got a big kick out of the arriving telegrams. She saved them all in one of her scrap books.

HOME

We detrained in Los Angeles and I started the long walk from the train, first along side of the train saying goodbye to the fellow officers, then through the entrance to the station and finally up the long incline into the station. As I made the final curve I looked up and there stood Molly, Tomilyn, my mother, Aunt Marie and Uncle Bill Cummings. Molly was prancing and waving and calling out to me, "Hurry, hurry, please hurry." I did. I was kissed and hugged by all. What a wonderful warm feeling! To hold my baby was something, for now my family was three again. All of a sudden I heard a gasp from Molly. "You've been wounded. You have the Purple Heart. Where were you wounded? Is it bad? Does it hurt? Why didn't you tell me?" Finally I quieted her down, showed her my scars on my face, a few marks on my nose and lips, and raised my pants and showed my scars there. None of them serious, just where shell fragments had hit me while in the St. Vith forest. A tree burst got me as I was in a foxhole.

Uncle Bill had driven the family to Los Angeles from Oxnard. Uncle Bill and dear Aunt Marie were always there for the Morandas. How wonderful it was to hear the voices at home, to be embraced by my Mom, and to get the caresses and squeezes from Molly.

Mother, Molly, Loraine (Tommy Swain's wife), and brother Bill's wife, Jeannette, were all living together in Oxnard on B Street, where we soon settled in. One incident made what happened to the people at home clear to me. We who were away were memories, pictures, and letters. I was sitting in the front room the first night home and I saw, looking around the room, pictures of all the people of our families—my five brothers, my sister, and my brother-in-law—who all were in the armed forces. Nightly just before Tomi was put to bed she would go around the room saying goodnight to the pictures. "Goodnight Uncle Tom. Goodnight Uncle Earl. Goodnight Uncle Bill, Uncle George, Uncle Paul, Uncle Ted, Aunt Maye." She said to my picture, "Goodnight Daddy." Then she turned to Molly and asked, pointing at me, "Where did we get him?"

I was paraded around town by the family and saw many friends. My orders stated I was to be home for two weeks, and then Molly and I were to have a week at the Momarte Hotel in Santa Barbara. There we would be again analyzed, healed, and questioned to find out if we were able to continue in the Army.

While at the hotel the wives and families went to an "information enlightening" class conducted by the doctors. They wanted to let the women and families of the ex-POWs know that the next few months, and possibly years for some, they would have a hard time adjusting back to a peacetime life. All they told the wives to do was to love them and try to understand and soon all would return to normal.

While there I, along with a couple of others, was honored with a review of the troops. I was presented with the Silver Star for "Gallantry in Action." I wondered then if others had been rewarded. The citation read:

> Second Lt. Robert E. P. Moranda (01326108) Infantry, while serving with the Army of the United States, distinguished himself by gallantry in action in connection with military operations against the enemy from 17 December, 1944 to 21 December, 1944 in the area of St. Vith, Belgium. With the full force of the German Winter counter offensive striking our lines, 2nd Lt. Moranda's

machine gun platoon again and again repelled fierce enemy assaults. Inspired by his great courage and able leadership, the men poured devastating volleys into the ranks of the attackers, many times waiting until hostile troops were within fifty yards of our lines in order to gain maximum fire effect. Through the days and nights of bitter action, Lt. Moranda braved heavy fire to move from foxhole to foxhole checking the positions and encouraging the troops to hold their ground. When units on the flanks withdrew, Lt. Moranda remained in position, taking a heavy toll of dead and wounded even when completely surrounded and cut off. 2nd Lt. Moranda and the men he led are reported missing in action, but by their determined stand against heavy odds they helped slow the armored spearheads of the enemy, giving us time to mass our forces and halt the drive?

When The War Department sent a telegram to Molly stating that I was "Missing In Action," she screamed and fainted. Mom would not allow that. She pulled Molly to her feet and told Molly that her son was alive and she knew that he would come home. She was steadfast in her belief all through the war that her family was all going to come home safely. She must have had an inside track to God. All of her children did come home safely. She never wavered in her belief.

One humorous incident happened also. At the bottom of the telegram there were two words which said that the telegram was "Sans Origin." Mom was telling her friend Mrs. Jim Lykins about the telegram. When they compared notes, Mrs. Lykins had also received a telegram with the "Sans Origin" at the bottom of a telegram telling something about her son Gerald "Shorty" Lykins. So the two dear ladies started to look in the atlas to see if their two sons were at the same place. The ladies were looking for an island or town somewhere in the world.

Then someone soon told them that it was just the way the War Department signed their telegrams, as they did not want to give the location where the telegram was sent from.

Molly and I had left Tomilyn with her mother, so we were like honeymooners. We had great food, good friends, time to visit in Santa Barbara, and were just having fun. We spent the lion's share of the time with Jim Burns and his men from the 28th Division and their wives. Jim was single and eligible. In fact at one of the events he met "Diz," his wife-to-be.

I attended a few sessions with Army Intelligence personnel trying to piece together the war. There was not much I could tell them. Even the F.B.I. interviewed me. Later I found out they had also questioned each returning POW officer, I suppose to see if we were Americans and what we saw that could aid them in understanding Russian warfare. They seemed to be especially interested in weapons. I am sure my testimony was of little or no value.

For a few days I was lost in my memories of the past months. I wanted to forget. But at the same time I wanted to talk, but not to civilians nor to anyone in the service who was not in the infantry. My old friends were gone. The men I served with were not around, only those people who really didn't want to hear and couldn't appreciate what it was like, even though they implied that they could. How close were we who served together? I don't think I can answer that very easily except to say there was a tightly-knit bond among those of us who served together and had shared experiences. But, with regard to relationships with the men in my platoon, that closeness was tempered, because I always felt I needed to keep a distance between my men and myself. For how could I become really close and then order them into dangerous places or to perform risky jobs? Yet they were my eyes and ears, for without them I would be lost. Since I was required to read all their outgoing mail, I thought I knew their families and some of their innermost thoughts. But they didn't know mine. They didn't ask for anything but to get back home. And they were my protectors.

Soon it was time to return home and to the Army. When I got home and was visiting with one of my brothers, he saw that I had received the Silver Star. His comment was, "Who got the Gold?"

It was also a time to learn some of the things that had gone on during my absence. When the first card that I had written from the prison camp arrived advising Molly and the folks at home that I was alive and was a prisoner of war, the card came into the post office in Port Hueneme. The postmaster, Art Haycock, didn't waste any time in getting the notice to Mom. He got in his car and hand delivered the message to mother. And he also announced the news to most of the people in the township. Art and his wife Ann were good friends of the family so they had a special interest in what was going on in our family. Mom then called Molly who was in Lancaster at the time.

I had my orders assigning me to Fort Ord, California. When I had arrived in Santa Barbara I was promoted to 1st Lieutenant. The promotion was long in coming. It should have come when I was in Europe, but because I had been POW, the promotion was held up until I was liberated and returned to U.S. control.

Molly and I returned to Oxnard. I enjoyed the people there. I will admit I was quite bitter about the whole affair which caused me, at times, to react rather rudely to a few people in the town. Some did rub me the wrong way and I told them off. When an able-bodied man said to me he had done his part in the war effort by buying War Bonds, that seemed to be the fuse for an minor explosion on my part. Yes, they were patriotic and wealthy. They had been promoted to positions over the men who had gone away to serve in the Armed Forces. But it really wasn't their fault; it was just the luck of the draw. It did take some time for me to come to real grips with myself, through a lot of understanding on Molly's part and my great family. They just accepted me for what I was and treated me in the same manner as they always had.

We also went to Lancaster where Molly's folks, Henry Roe and Isabelle Swain, now lived. They were still operating the small ranch they had purchased there in conjunction with the Gabberts, Eddie and Molly's sister Rozeel, and their youngest daughter Shirley was attending high school there. When we returned to pick up the baby, she didn't remember Molly. So I teased her, reminding her of the time Tomilyn had turned to Molly when she hadn't seen me for months and asked, "Where did we get him?"

While in Lancaster, Jimmy Burns, my buddy from the prisoner of war camp, came out to the house to meet the Swains and the Gabberts. Eddie Gabbert was an Air Corps Aviation Trainer so he arranged with a friend to take the two of us on a flight, and they tried to wring us out. They were playing dog fighting and were doing all the maneuvers to make us sick. But as Eddie told Rozeel when we got home, "There we were trying to scare those nutty infantry officers. On one of my loops I looked back and there was Bob and Jimmy pretending they were firing machine guns. Here I was almost passing out and they were having fun. So I came down."

We stayed in Lancaster for a week or so and enjoyed getting re-acquainted with the families. The war was rapidly winding down in Europe. Some of us wondered whether we would be sent to the Far East to fight the Japanese.

It was soon time for me to go back to the Army. Molly and the baby stayed with her family, and I departed for Fort Ord where I was assigned to the Casual Battalion and given a job to brief the incoming soldiers on what was going to happen to them in the few days they would be in Fort Ord before getting their assignments. It was a canned speech that the commander of the battalion had composed. He sat in the audience and listened to make sure I gave it as he had written. It was easy to do.

My other job was to be the Mess Officer. I had to supervise three mess halls where they served, on an average, 5000 men every day. On my first day I went into one of the mess halls to have lunch, and as I started through the line the mess sergeant came up to me and asked me to follow him. He said I didn't have to go through the mess line and took me to the large refrigerators and opened the door of each one. There were hundreds of choice cuts of beef. The sergeant said, "This is what we in the mess eat." I asked, "Why?" I didn't like the reply he gave, so I ordered the choice cuts be served to the incoming troops as soon as possible and in the future the mess personnel would eat the same food as the troops.

Soon Molly and the baby came north and joined me. For a time we lived with my brother George and his wife Nancy who were stationed and had quarters at the Presidio of Monterey, while we looked for a house. Molly found a house in Pacific Grove. George was at that time assigned as adjutant of the Civil Affairs Staging Area. Molly and I were treated well by them, but it was not in their best interest that we overstay our welcome. And besides the Army didn't approve two service families living in one set of their quarters—another one of those silly rules. Here stood a large house that could hold two families, but rules are rules. We moved out just as soon as possible.

After we moved into the place that Molly found we were really happy. One of the things that made me even happier was the day my former runner, now Corporal, Maurice Conover saw me walking around the company area and yelled out, "Hey, Lieutenant Moranda, wait up." We both ran to each other and there on the company area we gave each other a big hug—no salute—a hug right there on the grounds at Fort Ord. We each questioned the other for a time. Then I told him where we were living and made arrangements for him and his wife to come to our house. They came that evening, Maurice and his wife Ellie, and we had a great time together. I remember when he read my Silver Star citation he commented, "Hell, if I had known how bad it really was I would have been scared." He was stationed at Fort Ord for the rest of his tour of duty, then he returned to his farm in Broadview, Montana, where they renewed their life raising wheat.

One of the great things about living in that area and being a returned veteran was the famous golf courses, and they allowed and encouraged us to golf during the week for fifty cents a round. What a challenge they were, and what a privilege. I golfed at Pebble Beach, Del Monte, Pacific Grove, Monterey Peninsula, and Cypress Point. Many afternoons, when we could, a few of us would take off and go to one of the courses and play. Brother George and I played once at Cypress. He hit his ball into one of the trees and the ball didn't come down. So he shinnied up the tree and shook one of the branches and golf balls came raining down. We picked up a dozen balls that had been up there. As golf balls were expensive and hard to get, we were happy to receive the bonanza.

[On May 2, 1945, the collapse of the German forces was complete and fighting was brought to a conclusion when a surrender document, which was signed on April 29th, came into effect.]

I was on duty on VE Day. It was quiet in the camp. I was almost alone in our area. It gave me plenty of time to wander and wonder. How many men were lost in winning that part of the war? I wondered how many more lives would it take to finally win the remaining war in the Pacific and about the inequities in the war, who serves and where. I know too that the foot sloggers, the infantrymen, know there are only a few ways to get out of the front lines: win the war, become a casualty of some kind, or come home in a bag. But there are benefits, too. With pride the infantryman could say, "I was there and where in the hell were you?"

The time spent at Fort Ord was rather uneventful and routine, just doing the same things over and over again as far as my job at the base was concerned. The weather was typical of the coastal area around Monterey Bay that summer—morning fog followed by bright sunshine. So we had plenty of outside activity.

My brother Earle and his wife Becky came from Washington, D.C., to Monterey to stay with George's family for a few days, for he was soon to ship out to the Pacific to enter the war against the Japanese. We had quite a reunion in Monterey. I brought Maye over from her nurse's station at the Army Hospital in Modesto. We had a good day catching up with the news and experiences of each other before I took her back to Modesto that night. I got lost on the way home and finally got back just in time for me to go to work at Fort Ord. But it was worth the lost sleep to have been together with at least several of the family.

[On August 10, 1945 the Japanese Government issued a statement substantially agreeing to the terms enumerated in the Potsdam Declaration and formal surrender ceremonies took place on the Battleship Missouri on September 2.]

In a couple of days Earle went to San Francisco where he boarded the ship that was to take him somewhere in the Pacific. The ship was loaded and had started to sail out of the bay of San Francisco when the orders came for the ship to come back to the harbor. The war was over, and when the point system was announced by the War Department, he found he had enough points to obtain separation from the service. So he came back, picked up Becky, and they proceeded back East to a Separation Point where he returned to civilian life as a member of the Army Reserves.

Sometime later I received a certificate, which I appreciated, from
"The Kingdom of Belgium
(SEAL)
The Ministry of National Defense
has the honour to inform
2nd Lieutenant Robert E. Moranda,
that, by Royal Decree, his Majesty Prince Regent,
from 3 Jan, 1946, N. 1578,
He was nominated

KNIGHT OF THE ORDER OF THE CROWN
WITH PALM

for the diligent and brilliant organization work and
for the courageous spirit shown in such a remarkable
way by his bravery in the battles that have led to the
complete liberation of Belgium in the hands of the
common enemy. He is happy to be addressing his sin-
cere congratulations in this nomination."

I continued to serve at Fort Ord. The war came to an end abruptly. As
I had plenty of points to get out of the Army, I took advantage of the
system and it wasn't long before we too were home again. After a week
at home in Oxnard, I went to Pasadena to the headquarters of Standard
Stations, Inc., and saw my old boss P. J. Sullivan. My old station was not
available so he asked if I would consider going to Santa Barbara. I
jumped at the chance with a quick, "Yes!" That's where Molly and I had
been the happiest. We were delighted to have the opportunity again to
work there.

The circle had been closed. We were back to home, family, and work
which I had been separated from nearly three years before. Brother
Earle went from active duty to the Officer's Reserve Corps and returned
to Washington, D.C., to take a job with the Central Intelligence Agency
when it was created. Sister Maye went back to nursing at Los Angeles
General Hospital. Bill was discharged from the Marines and went to
work for the town of Port Hueneme. George stayed in the Army for a
while then came back to Port Hueneme to try civilian life for a while.
Paul left the Navy and Ted the Army Air Corps and both went back to
college under the GI Bill. Things were never the same as before the war,
but we were still a loving and caring family. And Mom took the ribbon
with seven blue stars down from the window.

The Old Man

The Old man stopped atop the hill
Not to rest but to stare
Across the horizon searching each rill
For the life he passed with care.

Now it was time to stop and think
What went good and what was bad
Some that happened did but stink
All told, things made him glad.

So many wrongs and so many rights
So many bads and so many goods
Deeds of good give value to heights
The bads are lost in the woods

What is there when you are born
That happens from birth, if you believe
That to the end with your tools you perform
What you gather or achieve.

EPILOGUE

I had elected to join the Army Reserve Corps upon my separation from active service, but after a couple of years transferred to the California National Guard and joined the 981st Field Artillery Battalion, 40th Infantry Division, where I became the commander of Headquarters Company. We built a house in the northern part of Santa Barbara, and I was enjoying work running the Standard Station. Our life was running smoothly again until September 1, 1950, when the 40th Division was one of the four National Guard Divisions called into active duty for the Korean War. Brother George, then commander of Battery A of the same battalion, was also recalled at the same time. We were sent to Camp Cooke, California, for training, then to Fort Sill to learned how to become artillerymen. Upon completion, I became an assistant G3 (operations) at division headquarters just in time to join the advanced party for the division move to Japan. After several months in a training mode there, the division was sent to Korea where we replaced the 24th Infantry Division on the front line in December 1951. What a difference a war makes! Here I was on a division staff, well behind the infantrymen who still had to do the dirty, rotten job of facing an enemy a few yards away. By the summer of 1952 I had enough points to return home but stayed in the National Guard (and eventually retired as a lieutenant colonel when I had reached the twenty year service criterion). When I checked back in with Standard Stations they gave me a regional super-intendent's position in the Imperial Valley where again I renewed my family life.

Molly had developed cancer and fought it for years with will and faith, determined to raise Tomilyn to maturity. And she did, but finally lost the battle in December 1956.

The company, now Chevron, transferred me to the Los Angeles area for a few years, then to run the retail operations in Hawaii, and finally to head up the Los Angeles office as Retail Manager. Just before the Hawaii assignment in 1963, I met and married another great woman, my present wife Verna Faye. Tomilyn passed away eleven years ago and left two sons and a daughter who are all raising families of their own. Faye and I are spending our remaining years on a hillside in Granada Hills over-looking the San Fernando Valley.

I think I am entitled to make a few observations in the twilight of my years, based upon my experiences. We have the greatest country in the world by God's will, and we can keep it so only if we follow what He has told us to do in His book—the Bible. We still have the chance to continue to lead all the nations today in the struggle for liberty, equality, and justice. But that chance will be gone if we continue to condone the immorality, inequity of treatment, and unethical conduct by leaders in our business, social, and political life. I say we have the chance to correct the ills of society because those who created our system provided the devices that allow us to do so—basically the power of the vote. To exercise that power properly requires an intelligent citizenry, and I'm not so sure we have that today—but we could have.

Those of us who were the "kids that saved the world for democracy" and who are still around may be unable to do it again. But we can pass on our devotion to country and family by example and by helping the following generations to understand their importance and what this country is all about.

Maj. George, Lt. Bob, and Ens. Paul, 1945

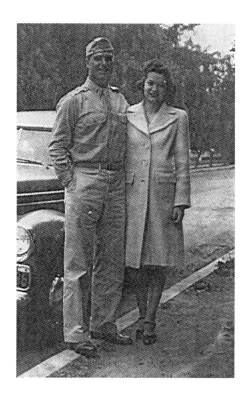

Lt. Wannie and Jean Wood, 1943

Lt. Bob being awarded Silver Star after his return to California, 1945

Donald P. Boyer, Jr.
This picture was taken in the spring of 1964 when Colonel Boyer com-
manded the 11th Armored Cavalry regiment. Colonel Boyer is now
retired and resides in Carmel, California.

Capt. Bob when recalled to active service during the Korean War in 1950 as Headquarters Company Commander, 981st Field Artillery Battalion, 40th Infantry Division.

Bob and Sgt. Totoni at the 1997 Reunion of the 7th Armored Division.

CONCLUSIONS

On the day before Christmas in 1944, while General Patton's Third Army was slowly approaching Bastogne to relieve the surrounded 101st Airborne Division and its attached units, four war correspondents, Joseph Driscoll of the New York Herald Tribune, Norman Clark of the London News Chronicle, Walter Cronkite of the United Press, and Cornelius Ryan of the London Daily Telegraph were following along on the road from Arlon to Bastogne, the route Patton's forces were using in their drive north. While freezing in the bitter cold and waiting for the route to open wider, because of the fighting that was going on in the area, they had run into Major General Maxwell D. Taylor en route to rejoin his command, the 101st Airborne Division, after his return from the States, and soon followed his route when the road was less dangerous to travel. When they reached the 101st Airborne Division's encircled troops, their reports amplified the Bastogne story—which by then had captured the public's imagination. Public Relations Officers at all levels from the Pentagon down had a great story and the media played and expanded it so that the public perception of the 101st Division's stand became almost the entire story about the Battle of the Bulge.

It is small wonder that veterans who served with the 1st, 2nd, 28th, and 99th Infantry Divisions, the 7th and 9th Armored Divisions, the 14th Cavalry Group, and many other units during that battle have feelings of resentment for not having been recognized for their vitally important services, some heroic, especially the 7th Armored. It was these units and smaller groups who made the Germans stumble, delaying them long enough for the Allied High Command to finally recognize what was going on, their errors of judgment, and the need to provide forces to counter the Nazi drive. After the war, General Manteuffel, Fifth Panzer Army commander, in an interview stated that he needed, wanted, and intended to take the vital communications center of St. Vith by December 17 in order to have a means to logistically support the main German effort, his Fifth Panzer Army, and the Sixth Panzer Army to his north. Prevented from doing so by stubborn defenders, his plans were disrupted which caused much shifting of troops intended for other missions, some that were to assist and support the major thrust to the Meuse River along the avenues opened both north and south of St. Vith and clogged routes for their supply trains. And Bastogne, which was not a first priority target in the German attack and was ordered by Hitler to be bypassed if defended, became important to the German effort only after St. Vith could not be captured and that essential communications hub was destroyed by artillery and, later, by Allied air attacks after the withdrawal of the 7th Armored units to a more cohesive line immediately west of St. Vith. Hitler didn't order Bastogne to be taken until St. Vith was unusable to provide the logistical support to the two Panzer Armies. This by no means diminishes their valiant performance, but there is more to the story of this campaign than what is now generally known in the public's knowledge.

During World War II, there were four critical events that significantly altered the course of that war, and they all involved the element of surprise: the German invasion of Russia in 1941; the Japanese attack at Pearl Harbor on December 7, 1941; the Ardennes Campaign, popularly known as the Battle of the Bulge, in December and January, 1944-5; and the atomic bombing of Hiroshima and Nagasaki. The first event split the German-Russian alliance and brought the USSR, with its tremendous source of manpower, into the Allied camp. The second event brought the United States, with its industrial and military and naval might, into the war. The third marked the demise of the German war machine and the collapse of the Nazi regime. And, of course, the last caused the sudden end to the Japanese conflict.

By the Fall of 1944, the Germans were beset on all fronts. The Allied Forces were pressing on all of them, shrinking the German lines. On the Eastern Front the Russian army had pushed through a major offensive that overran most of Eastern Poland. In Italy the American Fifth and British Eighth armies had shoved the Germans northward beyond the Po River. And on the Western Front, two German armies had been destroyed by British, Canadian, French, and American forces after their breakout from the Normandy beaches. There was pressure on the Germans along the entire western front, and to many of the Allied leaders there was a sense that the German collapse was not only inevitable but also imminent. After all, the German homeland had been reached and the Allied generals were talking about their troops being home for Christmas—and even betting that they would.

Complacency or false anticipation was beginning to creep in. On the home front, plans were being discussed about when to implement programs to convert the industrial might back to civilian products. Consideration was being given to the matter of which units to transfer to the Pacific to bring that part of the war to a conclusion. The Allied Command was continuing its efforts of constant pressure throughout the entire western front and preparing to maintain it. The military leadership was quite well-developed and the top leaders winnowed into an effective command structure. Their fighting forces were "blooded" and had reached the level of a seasoned fighting machine. Logistics seemed well organized and supply lines were humming with activity. Air was under the control of Allied Air Forces and had almost driven the *Luftwaffe* from the skies. The personnel replacement system was sending streams of new soldiers to fill the ranks of those units with losses. All seemed to be going smoothly. Major plans were being made for schedules to attack the Roer River dams in the north and, in the southern sector, to reduce the Colmar Pocket. The only threat to the Allied positions was considered to be a counterattack to delay or prevent an attack on the Roer River dams and the approach to the Ruhr. So with such a positive and rosy outlook, why not put a newly arrived Infantry Division (106th), which had just come from the States on December 10, with a Cavalry Group attached, and a badly mauled, under-strength, veteran infantry division (28th) just pulled back after a bitter fight in the Hurtgen Forest to recuperate and receive replacements, to cover the Ardennes forest area—about sixty air miles across, several more in ground miles. And not worry or be too concerned over the fact that it was a route used by the Germans twice before: to implement the Schlieffen Plan at the start of World War I which brought the Germans to within sight of Paris, and in 1940 for the invasion of Belgium and France which resulted in the conquest of those countries.

About the same time that General Eisenhower was holding his conference with Allied leaders on December 7 at Maastricht to discuss and settle some difficulties concerning the top command structure and differences in strategic plans, Hitler's armies were assembling for the execution of what he called *WACHT AM RHEIN*—the Ardennes Campaign. General Eisenhower felt it was necessary to get his top field commanders together to arrive at a meeting of the minds about which strategy to follow. So there were many presentations in which individual opinions were expressed about whether the Ruhr or Saar basins, or both, should be the main effort. Mentioned, but not seriously, was the thinly spread defenses in the Ardennes area. The Ardennes and the Eifel were not considered as avenues of approach in their consideration of objectives, rather they were deemed to be obstacles for the enemy. General Eisenhower in his command post had remarked about the thinness of American forces there, and General Bradley even made a visit to consult with his VIII Corps commander, General Troy Middleton, who had also expressed concern about the frontage he had to cover. General Bradley calmed him by telling Middleton not to worry, "They won't come through here."

General Bradley's Intelligence Officer (G-2), Brigadier General Edwin Sibert, wrote his analysis of the situation in Bradley's 12th Army Group's area in his weekly summary of December 12: "It is now certain that attrition is steadily sapping the strength of German forces on the Western Front and that the crust of defenses is thinner, more brittle, and more vulnerable than it appears on our G-2 maps, or to the troops in the line.The enemy divisions have been cut by at least fifty percent...The German breaking point may develop suddenly and without warning." General Bradley backed his G-2 over the intelligence estimate of Major General Kenneth Strong, SHAEF's Intelligence Officer, who suggested the increasing German reserve buildup, which had been detected, might be used to disrupt the overstretched American VIII Corps. (But Strong in November had made note of the German losses and that they were shifting their meager resources to meet various threats, like a "dwindling fire brigade.") Bradley's rather flippant retort was, "Let them come." And Field Marshall Montgomery's Intelligence Officer, Brigadier E. T. Williams, at that time declared the Germans were in a bad way and could not mount a major offensive.

Some did recognize the possibility of a German offensive. First Army's G-2, Colonel Benjamin "Monk" Dickson, and his Third Army counterpart, Colonel Oscar Koch, both identified the Ardennes front as being vulnerable and likely to be attacked. Colonel Dickson must not have felt too strongly about it, or he became piqued at General Sibert's conclusions, and went on a long delayed four-day leave to Paris on December 12. On the other hand, Colonel Koch's estimate fell on more receptive ears with General Patton, who put his staff to work to develop three alternate plans for such a contingency. After the German attack started, and General Eisenhower hurriedly called his Army Group and Army commanders to a war council in Verdun on December 19 to deal with what had finally been recognized as a major effort by the Germans, he asked General Patton how soon he could shift his forces to counter the German breakthrough. General Patton replied that he could do it immediately, which was met with considerable skepticism and laughter, for no one believed he could swing his army around on a ninety degree angle over snowbound roads after disengaging from his ongoing battle. He was confident about doing so because he had accepted the Koch estimate and ordered his staff to develop plans for just such a contingency. He left the conference with orders to move, made a phone call to his Command Post to execute the plan, and was able to begin attacking by the 22d and not later than the 23d, as General Eisenhower had directed.

The intelligence system in the U.S. Army was one which had too many road blocks in it. Reports from the front line troops of sightings, patrol activities, interrogations of enemy prisoners, and other bits and pieces of information had to be funneled through inexperienced, untrained battalion and regimental S2 or brigade G2s, divisional G2s, corps G2s, Army G2s and Army Group G2s (S2 and G2 are designations for the staff intelligence officer) before they reached the top command structure. And at each level they were given interpretations or otherwise influenced by officers who did not have the training or experience to adequately evaluate the material. It is small wonder that patrols reporting tank movements at the front would have some S2 or G2 down-play the information to "trucks with chains" in their analyses sent up the chain of command, if it was passed on at all.

On December 15, General Eisenhower received his promotion to General of the Army, with five stars, putting him equal in grade to that of Field Marshal in other armies. That same day Field Marshal Montgomery requested and received permission from General Eisenhower to "hop over to England" to celebrate the approaching Christmas holiday with his son. At the same time he asked Ike to pay him the five pounds they had bet that the war would end by Christmas, which Ike refused to pay until that date arrived. At dawn the next day the German attack commenced in General Bradley's area of responsibility, and Field Marshall Montgomery was called off the golf course at Eindhoven.

The fact is there was a terrible breakdown of the American intelligence system in their failure to recognize the threat, their disregard of historical data, and their disregard of reports from the front line troops of enemy activities, as well as the signal intercepts by army signal intelligence groups that reported significant enemy movement. And it was costly in the number of casualties, for in this battle, the largest of the war, there were heavy American losses of about 100,000 soldiers, of which 15,000 were captured and over 19,000 killed—the equivalent of approximately six infantry divisions. The losses of equipment and weapons were monumental.

When Patton's Third Army commenced its attack against the southern shoulder to relieve the surrounded troops at Bastogne, the 7th Armored Division had delayed the German advance through St. Vith by six days. That bitter, magnificent defense, along with other delaying actions, gave the Allied Command the time to shift forces to contain the German drive, disrupt their timetable, cause them to shift the attack's center of gravity from that of General Dietrich's 6th Panzer Army to General Manteuffel's 5th Panzer Army, and put some starch back into the retreating American forces.

When the three German panzer armies began their attack on the morning of December 16th and reports came in during the day to the VIII Corps, First Army, and 12th Army Group headquarters, it became apparent that something had to be done. That evening General Bradley made a decision to shift the 7th Armored Division, then in Ninth Army reserve, to the VIII Corps, an order that proved to be one of the most important ones given during the battle. But what the 7th Armored ran into on the forced march from their positions in Holland to St. Vith was almost impossible to describe. Bitter cold, icy roads, snow, uncertainty, and rumors about enemy forces (spearheaded by Lt. Col. Jochen Peiper's leading troops of the Sixth Panzer Army) passing through the 7th's eastern march route, and obstacles created by displacing artillery units and supply and support units, as well as fleeing soldiers of all ranks causing almost impenetrable traffic jams, were conditions they faced. Communications were all fouled up, orders were late in reaching intended commanders—if they were received at all. Information was anything but timely or accurate.

Brigadier General Bruce C. Clarke, CCB commander, upon arrival in St. Vith, found the 106th Infantry Division's Commanding General and staff in a state of shock and bewilderment. Told to take charge, General Clarke, even though junior in rank to the 106th Infantry Division commander Major General Jones, began to funnel units piecemeal as they arrived to build a line east of St. Vith using a small engineer aggregation under Lt. Colonel Riggs as a base. Elements of the 38th Armored Infantry Battalion, including its Headquarters Company commanded by Captain Rusty Mattocks, were among the first to report and were sent into the line. They were gradually supplemented with a few additional units of the 38th Armored Infantry Battalion, parts of the 87th Cavalry Squadron, 23d Armored Infantry Battalion, and 31st Tank Battalion when they arrived in the area. All this done while heavy fighting was in progress. Gradually the entire 7th Armored Division was deployed to defend northward, eastward, and southeastward in what has come to be called the "Fortified Goose-egg"—actually a horseshoe shaped defense with a large gap to the south. But the only reason that build-up could occur was the group of units under Lt. Col. Tom Riggs, and later Major Don Boyer, defending bitterly and gallantly about a mile east of St. Vith across the Prumerberg road.

But on December 17 everything was fluid and vague. The German 6th Panzer Army was moving west rapidly after it was unable to break through the American 1st, 2nd, and 99th Infantry Divisions at Elsenborn, and was heading for Stavelot beyond Malmedy. On their southern flank the German 5th Panzer Army was making progress westward north of St. Vith and was pushing westward toward Andler and Recht. The latter was also through Bleialf heading for Winterspelt to the southeast of St. Vith, after having completed the encirclement and the surrender of two regiments of the 106th Infantry Division and badly mauling the veteran 28th Infantry Division. As they progressed westward during the next four days, the two Panzer Armies moved both north and south of St. Vith and created what appeared to be a long finger, pointed toward Germany, with the nail of the finger being just east of St. Vith. Within that finger was the 7th Armored Division with a miscellaneous group of attached units under the command of Brigadier General Robert W. Hasbrouck who had established his headquarters in Vielsam. The tip of the nail was Major Boyer's Task Force just a mile east of St. Vith across the Plummerville road.

The chains of command had been disrupted throughout the entire battle area. Corps, divisions, regiments, and battalions were being shifted around in an attempt to provide some cohesiveness, with some success and some failure. On December 20th, Montgomery's 21st British Army Group was given responsibility for the northern sector and the U.S. First Army (less the VIII Corps which was to become part of Third Army) and Ninth Armies were assigned to him from General Bradley's 12th Army Group, leaving Bradley with just the Third Army and that part of First Army south of the German penetration. Corps were reassigned as indicated above with the VIIIth transferred from the First to the Third Army. The XVIII Airborne Corps under Major General Matthew Ridgeway, which had been in reserve in France, was moved in and assigned the area from Malmedy to Houffalize, linking up with the VIIth Corps at Malmedy and with the VIIIth Corps to the south and southeast and the Third Army when they got there. This resulted in the 106th Infantry Division and the 7th Armored Division being placed under the XVIIIth Airborne Corps along with the 82d Airborne Division, 3rd Armored Division, and the 30th Infantry Division. The latter three were en route to the Werbomont-Stavelot area from the west and north. While all this was going on, neither Hasbrouck in the 7th Armored nor Jones in the 106th Infantry were aware of the changes because they were out of communication with VIIIth Corps. By that time, the 112th Infantry Regiment of the 28th Infantry Division, which had fought a brilliant delaying action, about half of the 424th Infantry Regiment—all that remained of the 106th Infantry Division after its other two regiments had earlier surrendered—and CCB of the 9th Armored Division were all under the control of General Hasbrouck of the 7th Armored—a Brigadier General (Major General Jones was little more than a spectator). Dropping down to the fighting troops, Lt. Col. Riggs who had established the original line east of St. Vith with elements of his 81st Engineer Battalion of the 106th Division, relinquished command to Lt. Col. Fuller when the 38th Armored Infantry arrived on the scene. Then when Fuller decided to leave, his Operations Officer Major Don Boyer became the *de facto* commander of the troops. So there was a great deal of shifting of responsibilities, and command lines were anything but clear—but they were, in most part, worked out on the ground.

Another example of the disruption of command occurred in the 14th Cavalry Group which had been decimated during the breakthrough at Losheim Gap and had lost over half of the group on December 17th. Colonel Devine had issued orders to his northern unit, the 32d Squadron which was under heavy attack, to withdraw to a line from Born to Wallerode, when he received orders from the 106th Infantry Division headquarters to hold his present line. That was impossible, and the 14th Cavalry Group continued its withdrawal through St. Vith to Poteau and Vielsam running into the tremendous traffic jam on the Vielsam road. Colonel Devine met some Germans near Recht and his party was shot up but escaped on foot. When he got to Poteau, Colonel Devine was so shaken he turned over command to Lt. Col. William F. Damon, commander of the 18th Squadron. Damon was ordered shortly afterwards to VIIIth Corps headquarters and Lt. Col. Ridge of the 32d Squadron took over. Then Lt. Col. Augustine Dugan, the Group's executive officer, arrived and he assumed command as senior officer present. So in a period of four hours the Group had four different commanders.

Most of the command relationships were amicably and cooperatively settled, although some with great reluctance. But it became a little touchy when General Ridgeway arrived on the scene at Werbomont to set up the XVIIIth Airborne Corps headquarters. On December 21st Ridgeway sent a message to General Hasbrouck telling him that the 106th was no longer attached to the 7th Armored and that the two divisions henceforth were to cooperate in carrying out XVIII Corps orders. At the same time General Hoge, Commander of CCB of the 9th Armored Division who had worked out an informal but effective working relationship with General Hasbrouck, was told that his Combat Command was no longer attached to the 7th Armored. These orders destroyed a clear, if unorthodox, relationship. Later General Ridgeway sent a plan calling for the perimeter defense of the St. Vith-Vielsam area and had sent a message to the 7th Armored to hold their present positions. When Generals Clarke and Hasbrouck decided to shorten the lines and withdraw to a more tenable position west of St. Vith on December 21, anticipating a strong assault by the Germans the next day, apparently General Ridgeway got his nose out of joint. Generals Clarke and Hasbrouck wanted no part of General Ridgeway's scheme and probably recognized it as something typical for airborne units and not for armored forces which depend on ground supply lines rather than airborne droppings. Ridgeway's orders were very confusing; at one point he placed General Jones (being senior to Hasbrouck) in command of the 7th Armored Division and then told General Hasbrouck to make the decision and inform General Jones. Talk about double-speak!! What words were passed is not known, but it has been reported that neither Bruce Clarke nor Matthew Ridgeway ever spoke to each other again for the remainder of their careers— both of whom wound up with four stars before retiring from the

Army. It's probably a good thing that the front line troops didn't know of such confusion and rancor. They just continued to slog it out with the attacking enemy.

Field Marshall Montgomery, then in command of that sector, on December 22, after being briefed on the situation at St. Vith, overruled General Ridgeway by concluding that there was nothing more to be gained by holding the St. Vith salient and directed that the troops in it be withdrawn behind the 82d Airborne Division. Both he and General Eisenhower then sent congratulatory messages to General Hasbrouck for the magnificent stand of the 7th Armored Division and the units attached to it during the critical time they held off the German assaulting forces.

On December 22, General Clarke withdrew CCB west of St. Vith, and General Jones alerted General Hoge of CCB, 9th Armored Division, and Colonel Reid, commander of the 424th Infantry Regiment, to shorten their lines for the contraction of the salient. What happened then to the Task Force under Major Boyer? Were they forgotten? Did the division plan to leave them as a covering force? Did communications again fail? Whatever the situation, it is small wonder that Don Boyer, Bob Moranda, and the others up there would feel that they were "sacrificed."

There were many, many heroic and daring deeds during this battle in the Ardennes during that bitter winter, such as: the two Lt. Cols. William F. Slayden and Earle Williams who delayed the German advance three hours (every minute causing the Germans to fall behind their schedule was extremely important) around Schonberg by successively establishing positions with small groups of various soldiers they could find and then calling for artillery fire on advancing enemy troop and tanks which caused the attackers to deploy their troops; the tough, begrudging withdrawals, fighting as they withdrew, all the way back to the St. Vith horseshoe, by the 112th Infantry Regiment of the 28th Infantry Division and the remnants of the 424th Regiment of the 106th Division; the great defense by the divisions holding the northern shoulder at Elsenborn, especially the 2d and 99th Infantry Divisions; the tree cutting, sawmill-operating 51st Engineer Battalion which had been producing lumber each day for the First Army winterization program about ten miles west of Trois Point, who were ordered to blow up the three bridges at the confluence of the Ambleve and Salm Rivers, got there, prepared the bridges for demolition, then with a 57-mm anti-tank gun and crew they found wandering around, stopped the leading tanks of Jochen Peiper's assault troops with rifle and machine gun fire, bazookas (firing to give the impression of artillery), and by wrapping chains around the tires of a truck, running it up and down the road west of the bridges to simulate the sound of tanks, which convinced Peiper that he had to find an alternate route and caused him to turn north where he was stopped; and yes, the surrounded troops at Bastogne. These are just a small representation of the many exemplary deeds done by those fighting men of the American army.

And there were many, many failures and poor performances. Accurate and timely communications was a large problem which was only overcome by the initiative, training, and experience of the troops. The intelligence function belied its name: there was extremely poor traffic control and inadequate provision by planners for road conditions, weather, numbers of military police, and possible withdrawals. Individuals, officers, and enlisted men who were unable to withstand the pressures of combat and "bugged out" complicated command lines and added to the horrendous traffic problems.

The German attack was contained, but it was a costly operation to squeeze the Bulge as the Allied forces did, for it permitted a good portion of the German army to escape. Both Generals George Patton and J. Lawton Collins had recommended the counterattacks should be at both of the shoulders of the bulge to pinch off the invaders, but they were overruled at the Verdun War Council by General Eisenhower. Such a strategy would have cut off any escape by the Germans and undoubtedly would have shortened the war and prevented many casualties.

How many lives were lost in the Ardennes Campaign? A 1953 statistic reported 19,246 American soldiers were killed in action, 62,489 received non-fatal wounds, and 23,554 were taken prisoner—making it the heaviest battle toll in U.S. history. That report did not count the British, Canadian, or Germans. It has been estimated that the German losses were one-third greater. Prime Minister Winston Churchill told the House of Commons that there were sixty to eighty Americans killed for every British casualty—which he felt justified in calling it the greatest American battle of the war and a total American victory.

There is no question that the Germans had already lost the war by the time the Ardennes campaign occurred. Had the Germans not squandered their manpower and supplies and used them more sparingly in slowing the Allied advances, they could have extended the war until late Summer or early Fall of 1945. By conducting the campaign as they did, the war was considerably shortened.

The men of the 7th Armored Division can stand tall in the company of those throughout history who have performed magnificently, gallantly, and heroically in our country's service. The Germans called the 7th Armored Division "the Ghost Division" for they never knew where it would show up against their armies. After the war, recommendations for the Presidential Unit Citation were submitted, approved by both the Commanding Generals of the First U.S. Army and the European Theater, but rejected by the Department of the Army on November 26, 1947, saying that there would be no more awards to divisions, but only for smaller units. It seems reasonable to question the War Department's decision upon investigating the valorous stand of the entire division under some of the most difficult conditions that existed during the entire war. They had met an entire German Army corps, encouraged with an easy victorious breakthrough, and they halted it in its tracks for several critical days. They had choked the main enemy line of communication and supply and forced a crucial delay on the enemy's westward movement of troops, guns, tanks, and supplies needed by two German armies. They had given the XVIII Airborne Corps badly needed time to gather and get itself organized and acquainted with the situation to conduct an effective defense. And they had carried out a successful withdrawal under most difficult conditions. They, along with others, bought the time needed for Eisenhower to get forces into action to foil Hitler's plan. If the Germans had been more successful at St. Vith, they almost certainly would have reached the Meuse River and perhaps farther, American casualties would have been much greater, and recovery by Allied Forces would have been greatly delayed. Field Marshal Keitel and Colonel-General Jodl of the German High Command both ascribed the main reason for the failure of their offensive was, "Tougher resistance then expected of, in themselves, weak U. S. troops especially at St. Vith." In his Biennial Report to the Secretary of the Army covering the period July 1, 1943 to June 30, 1945, General George C. Marshall wrote: "The Ardennes battle deserves a prominent place in the history of the U. S. Army. The splendid stand of the 7th Armored Division at St. Vith, the tenacity of the 101st Airborne Division and elements of the 10th Armored at Bastogne, . . .were in the finest American tradition."

The units of the 7th Armored that were cited and did receive the award were: the 17th and 31st Tank Battalions; 23d and 38th Armored Infantry Battalions; 434th Armored Field Artillery Battalion; 87th Cavalry Reconnaissance Squadron; Company B, 33d Armored Engineer Battalion; Company A, 814th Tank Destroyer Battalion; and Headquarters Company, Combat Command B.

The critical remarks I have made, of course, are hindsight and are based on the many studies and writings about this historic campaign. We must never forget that the American Army was victorious. It won the battle. It was a tremendous victory, and it was the American Army that did it as no other elements of the Allied Forces were involved in the actual fighting. All who served honorably in that fray deserve our undying gratitude.

Furthermore, I became greatly impressed with the tremendous accomplishments of the 7th Armored Division during that battle and am convinced that they were not adequately recognized, for whatever reasons. My research led me to discover the many mistakes, some of which I have enumerated, that were made before, during, and after that battle. If you disagree with these comments, your argument is with me—not Bob.

George E. Moranda
Colonel, U.S. Army, Retired

ABOUT THE AUTHORS

Robert E. P. "Bob" Moranda spent most of his work life with Chevron Oil Company, starting as a service station attendant and retired from the company as Retail Manager of the Los Angeles Area. His work with Chevron was interrupted twice: first when he was drafted into the U. S. Army during World War II and served until the war ended, after which he joined the California National Guard's 40th Infantry Division; and second, when that division was ordered to active service and sent into combat during the Korean War. He and his wife Verna Faye are enjoying their retirement years in Granada Hills, California.

George E. Moranda was drafted into the U. S. Army in July 1941and assigned to the Corps of Engineers. He was commissioned at the Engineer Officer Candidate School and served in administrative and training positions during World War II. Following the war, he was in the Army Reserve and the California National Guard in an artillery battalion and served with his brother Bob with the 40th Infantry Division in Korea. He remained on active service and was integrated into the Armor Branch of the Regular Army. George is a graduate of the Command and General Staff College and the Army War College, and holds Masters Degrees in Political Science from the University of Hawaii and the University of Wisconsin in

Journalism. He retired from the Army in 1970 and now lives with his wife Nancy in Dinuba, California.

BIBLIOGRAPHY

Books

Ambrose, Stephen E., *Citizen Soldiers*. New York, Simon & Schuster, 1997.

_____, *The Victors: Eisenhower and His Boys: The Men of World War II*. New York, Simon & Schuster, 1998.

Astor, Gerald, *A Blood-Dimmed Tide: The Battle of the Bulge By the Men Who Fought It*. New York, Dell Publishing, 1992, reprinted 1994.

Baldwin, Hanson W., ed., *Command Decisions*. New York, Harcourt, Brace and Co., 1959.

Bradley, Omar N., *A Soldier's Story*. New York, Henry Holt & Co., 1951.

Chapin, Neil (Ed), *The Seventh Armored Division: A Historical Overview, 1942-1945*. Dallas, Taylor Publishing Co., 1982

Churchill, Winston S., *Triumph and Tragedy*. Boston, Houghton Mifflin Co., 1955.

Cole, Hugh M., *The Ardennes: The Battle of the Bulge*. Washington, Historical Division, Department of the Army, 1965.

Dupuy, Colonel R. Ernest, *St. Vith, Lion in the Way*. Washington, The Infantry Journal Press, 1949.

Dupuy, Trevor N., Bongard, David L., and Anderson, Richard C., Hitler's Last Gamble; The Battle of the Bulge December 1944-January 1945. Harper Perennial, Division of Harper Collins Publishers, 1994.

Eisenhower, John S.D., The Bitter Woods: The Battle of the Bulge. New York, Da Capo Press, 1995. Reprint of G. P. Putnam's Sons, 1969 edition, with a new introduction by Stephen E. Ambrose.

_____Encyclopedia Britannica.15th Edition, Encyclopedia Britannica, Inc.

Esposito, Colonel Vincent J., The West Point Atlas of American Wars. New York, Frederick A. Praeger, 1959.

Farago, Ladislas, Patton: Ordeal and Triumph. New York, Dell Publishing Co., 1965.

Gantter, Raymond, Roll Me Over: An Infantryman's World War II. New York, Ivy Books, 1997.

MacDonald, Charles B., A Time For Trumpets: The Untold Story of the Battle of the Bulge. New York, William Morrow and Co., 1985

Merriam, Robert E., Dark December: The Full Account of the Battle of the Bulge. New York-Chicago, Ziff-Davis Publishing, 1947.

Parker, Danny S., ed., Hitler's Ardennes Offensive: The German View of the Battle of the Bulge. London, Greenhill Books, 1997. (From interviews with SS-Oberstgruppenfuhrer Josef 'Sepp' Dietrich, General der Panzertruppen Hasso von Manteuffel, General der Panzertruppen Erich Brandenberger, and others.)

Toland, John, Battle: The Story of the Bulge. Lincoln, Neb. Bison Books, 1959 reprinted 1999.

Whiting, Charles, Patton. New York, Ballantine Books Inc., 1970.

Wilson, George, If You Survive. New York, Ivy Books, 1987.

Magazines

MacDonald Charles, "The Neglected Ardennes," Military Review, (April, 1963).

Raymond, Captain Allen D. III, "The Battle of St. Vith," Armor (Nov.-Dec., 1964.

GLOSSARY

Explanatory Notes

Recognizing that many readers might not be familiar with military terms used during World War II, the following might assist in understanding the organization, maps, and text used.

World War II was fought by the U.S. Army with what was called the Triangular Division. It was organized from the bottom up with squads (9-12 men), commanded by a sergeant. Three squads made up a platoon, commanded by a lieutenant. Companies or troops (a cavalry or armored designation) were commanded by a captain and consisted of three platoons. Battalions or squadrons (a cavalry term) were commanded by a lieutenant colonel with three companies. Regiments were commanded by a colonel and had three battalions. The infantry divisions, commanded by a major general with two assistant brigadier generals (one commanded the artillery), usually functioned with RCT's, or regimental combat teams. The RCT's were made up of a regiment, an artillery battalion, and combat support units such as signal, engineer, cavalry, and supply and maintenance units. (A brigade was a separate, non-divisional, large tactical unit usually formed of one or two infantry regiments with supporting artillery, armor, signal, and logistical units, and might have attached to it combat elements such as tank destroyers.) The size of an infantry division was approximately 14,500 personnel. As for equipment, these divisions contained 5 halftracks, 13 armored cars, 18 assault guns (105mm), 36 of 105mm and 12 of 155mm field artillery howitzers, 1371 motor vehicles, and 10 light aircraft.

Armored divisions had considerably more organizational flexibility. The divisions were triangular and generally formed into combat commands, which were constructed of units for specific missions. The armored divisions were either light (about 10,500 men with 168 medium and 77 light tanks, 450 halftracks, 54 self-propelled 105mm howitzers, 35 assault guns (105mm), 54 armored cars, 1031 motor vehicles and 8 light aircraft), or heavy (14,400 men, 232 medium and 158 light tanks, 54 self-propelled 105mm howitzers, 18 of 105mm and 14 of 75mm assault guns, 54 armored cars and 1242 motor vehicles). The legend below might assist the reader in understanding the maps:

A Task Force was any size grouping of units organized for a specific mission.

A Corps was a tactical organization made up of two or more divisions.

Armies were both administrative and tactical with two or more corps plus attached combat, administrative, supply and maintenance units.

Army Groups were essentially tactical headquarters, having two or more armies.

At the time of the Ardennes Campaign, the Allied Forces were organized under the Supreme Commander, General Dwight D. Eisenhower. His headquarters was called SHAEF (Supreme Headquarters, Allied Expeditionary Forces). He commanded three Army Groups: the 12th U.S. Army Group, commanded by Lieutenant General Omar N. Bradley; the 21st British Army Group, commanded by Field Marshal Bernard Law Montgomery; and the 6th U.S. Army Group, commanded by Lieutenant General Jacob L. Devers.

12th U.S. Army Group elements, on December 16, 1944:

Ninth U.S. Army under Lieutenant General William H. Simpson

First U.S. Army under Lieutenant General Courtney H. Hodges

Third U.S. Army under Lieutenant General George S. Patton

21st British Army Group elements, on December 16, 1944:
  Second British Army under Lieutenant General Miles
  C. Dempsey
  First Canadian Army under Lieutenant General
  H.D.H. Crerar
  6th U.S. Army Group elements on December 16, 1944: Seventh
  U.S. Army under Lieutenant General Alexander M. Patch
  First French Army under General J. de Lattre de Tassigny
Within the First U.S. Army were corps:
  V Corps under Major General Leonard T. Gerow
  VII Corps under Major General J. Lawton Collins
  XVIII Airborne Corps under Major General Matthew
  B. Ridgeway
Within the Third U.S. Army were corps:
  VIII Corps under Major General Troy H. Middleton
  III Corps under Major General John Millikin
  XX Corps under Major General Walton H. Walker
  XII Corps under Major General Manton S. Eddy
Within the Ninth U.S.Army were corps:
  XIII Corps under Major General Alvan C. Gillem
  XIX Corps under Major General Raymond S. McLain
  During the Ardennes Campaign, corps, divisions, regiments
  battalions and companies were shifted around considerably to
  meet the requirements and conditions of battle, as described in
  the story.
Some commonly used abbreviations and acronyms are:
  AWOL–Absent Without Leave
  CP–Command Post
  CO–Commanding Officer
  ETO–European Theater of Operations
  FEBA–Forward Edge of the Battle Area

Type of Army Unit:

LEGEND

Military Unit Size:

x x x x x Army Group
x x x x Army
x x x Corps
x x Division
x Brigade
ı ı ı Regiment
ı ı Battalion
ı Company

Examples:

Allied unit *

German unit

infantry

airborne
infantry

armor,
'Panzer' if
German

artillery

self-propelled
artillery

Non-standard unit configuration.
'size' symbol beneath bracket
suggests equivalent strength.

Second British Army

Second German Corps

82nd Airborne Infantry Division (US)

Combat Command B,
4th Armored Division (US)

Panzer Lehr Division (German)

130th Assault Gun Battalion (German)

7th Armored Division (US)

9th SS Panzer Division (German)

unit size   parent unit

unit numeric
designation
may include
nationality *

112th Infantry Regiment
of the US
28 Division.

unit function (role)
or "arms" branch"

6th UK Airborne Infantry Brigade

125 Panzergrenadier Regiment (German)

* Allied units are U.S. unless another country is specified.

** (+) unit reinforced, or
(-) unit less some components

Printed in the United States
91518LV00006B/15/A